M000315952

To, Sylvia,

Dia Dú,

(Howdy in Irish)

Patrick Foley

APRIL 2013

Missionary Bishop

Number 118
Centennial Series of the Association of Former Students
Texas A&M University

MISSIONARY BISHOP

Jean-Marie Odin in Galveston and New Orleans

PATRICK FOLEY

Foreword by Gilbert R. Cruz

TEXAS A&M UNIVERSITY PRESS
COLLEGE STATION, TEXAS

Copyright © 2013 by Patrick Foley
Manufactured in the United States of America
All rights reserved
First edition

This paper meets the requirements of ANSI/NISO z39.48–1992 (Permanence of Paper).

Binding materials have been chosen for durability.

LIBRARY OF CONGRESS CATALOGING-IN-PUBLICATION DATA

Foley, Patrick, 1933–
  Missionary bishop : Jean-Marie Odin in Galveston and New Orleans / Patrick Foley ;
with a foreword by Gilbert R. Cruz. — 1st ed.
      p. cm. — (Centennial series of the Association of Former Students ; no. 118)
  Includes bibliographical references and index.
  ISBN-13: 978-1-60344-824-6 (cloth : alk. paper)
  ISBN-10: 1-60344-824-1 (cloth : alk. paper)
  ISBN-13: 978-1-60344-994-6 (e-book)
  ISBN-10: 1-60344-994-9 (e-book)
  1. Odin, Jean Marie, 1801–1870.   2. Catholic Church—Texas—Bishops—Biography.
3. Bishops—Texas—Biography.   4. Texas—Church history.   5. Catholic Church—
Texas—History.   I. Title.   II. Series: Centennial series of the Association
of Former Students, Texas A&M University ; no. 118.
  BX4705.03385F65   2013
  282.092—dc23
  [B]
  2012044072

To Linda, My Wife
Our Daughter, Elizabeth Maureen, Our Son, Sean Patrick
And Our Grandchildren, Edmund "Ned," Grace, Philip, Fred, and Gabriel

Go gentlemen, in the name of Our Lord. It is He who is sending you; it is for His service and His glory that you are undertaking this voyage and this mission. It will also be He who will lead you, and who will assist and protect you. We hope for this from His Infinite Goodness. Always hold fast with faithful guidance. We have recourse to Him in all places and on all occasions. Throw yourselves into His arms, as the one whom you should recognize as your very good Father, with firm confidence that He will assist you and bless all your works.

SAINT VINCENT DE PAUL
Advice Given on the Departure of
Missionaries for Distant Countries
Abelly, bk. III, 12

Contents

Foreword

O<small>N</small> C<small>HRISTMAS</small> D<small>AY</small> 499, King Clovis of the Franks professed his belief in Christianity, and Saint Remigius, bishop of Rheims, baptized him. The Catholic monarch's fervent act of faith permeated the subjects of his kingdom. France came to be known as the "Eldest Daughter of the Church," a prestigious title among the emerging nations of Christendom. This title was not entirely without merit. Over the centuries, the Eldest Daughter served in the Crusades, a notable feat for those times. France hosted the Successor of Peter during the papal residence at Avignon (1304–78). France and her colonial empire flourished during the reign of the Catholic monarchs. In the age of Cardinal Richelieu (1585–1642) the church enjoyed unprecedented prestige, while during the French Revolution (1789–95) the church experienced the ravages of civil war. But French Catholicism is far more the "Deposit of Faith," and Catholic traditions are deeply rooted in the people of the small hamlets, rural villages, and town centers across France. As late as the nineteenth century, French folk of the countryside halted their daily routines at the sound of the steeple bell and with devotion recited the "Angelus Domini nunciavit Mariae" at dawn, noon, and in the evening.

This was the France from which the United States was to draw the religious fervor needed to reinforce the Christian faith of frontier settlers in the Ohio Valley, the Lower Mississippi Valley, the emerging state of Texas, and westward to New Mexico. The call went forth to several of the finest religious communities of men in the land, notably the Congregation of the Mission, the Vincentians of Saint Vincent de Paul; the Oblates of Mary Immaculate, which Saint Eugene de Mazenod, bishop of Marseilles, founded; and the Society of Mary, which Blessed Joseph Chaminade established. The teaching Brothers of the Society of Mary went on to found St. Mary's University in San Antonio, Texas, in 1853. Nor were the daughters of Catholic France to be outdone. The Ursulines; the Sisters of the Incarnate Word; those of the Order of Divine Providence; and the Vincentians (Daughters of Charity) also joined in the edifying endeavor to bring faith, charitable work, and education to the United States beyond the Appalachian Highlands.

Patrick Foley's volume *Missionary Bishop* has capsulated this splendid history of the missionary undertaking in the life and times of Jean-Marie Odin. In Hauteville, a rural community of sturdy family homes west of the city of Lyon, France, was the farmhouse in which Jean-Marie was born February 25, 1800. The author's pen vividly outlines the early life of Odin, including his studies at the Sulpician grande seminaire in Lyon, leading him onward to the order of subdeacon and ultimately his decision to follow in the footsteps of French missionaries trailblazing frontiers west of the Mississippi River in the United States. At St. Mary of the Barrens Seminary in Perryville, Missouri, he completed his priestly studies and was ordained in 1823, served as seminary instructor, and was received into the Congregation of the Mission. His first assignments as a frontier missionary in Missouri and Arkansas prepared him for his later service in Texas. In 1839, Vincentian Father John Timon, a veteran missionary assigned to Texas, requested that Odin accompany him. Timon returned to Missouri and Odin ventured to Texas as vice-prefect in 1840. Laboring as vicar apostolic of Texas from 1841 to 1847, he was then named first bishop of Galveston. Odin held that hierarchical office until 1861, when he succeeded Antoine Blanc as second archbishop of New Orleans. For more than twenty years Odin worked among the frontier settlers in Texas and then spent another decade doing the same in Louisiana as archbishop during the American Civil War and Reconstruction eras. Catholics of diverse cultures as well as Protestants were drawn to him by his learning and his extraordinary generosity in laboring for so many.

Foley's skillful narration of Odin's life provides new insights, especially into the history of nineteenth-century Texas, by enabling the reader to observe French missionaries and their collaborators treading the almost limitless Texas landscape to serve encampments of settlers and to preach the Gospel in English, French, Spanish, and German. The Gallic missionaries enkindled anew the dormant cinders and ancient roots of Catholicism planted by the Franciscans almost two centuries earlier, again giving the Catholic Church an important role in the state's history. Significantly, they gave the immigrant tradition to Texas a new dimension. Most voyagers arrived from afar to obtain land. The French missionaries came to embellish the new land with a lasting faith in an eternal land that was to follow.

Impressed by the rare virtue of these missionaries who believed more in giving than in receiving, the Texas legislature, in 1841, conveyed to them title to ancient Spanish missions so that they could continue the work of promulgating the values of religion, learning, and good works. Today, many of the oldest private institutions of higher learning in Texas can trace their origins to the brave men and women who embarked from Catholic France to Texas during the nineteenth century.

Foley has engaged in research of the highest order. His disarming narrative provides smooth reading, and his scholarship renders substantive accuracy. His Irish Catholic heritage permeates with vigor the construction of his manuscript. His loyalties to Texas history are equally evident. This biography of Jean-Marie Odin is a refreshing journey through pristine Texas that transforms the reader, and for others it may well be breathtaking.

GILBERT R. CRUZ

Preface

IN THE NARRATIVE OF THE GROWTH of the Roman Catholic religion in the United States many personages who played unique roles through their inspiration in building the faith among the people have emerged as heroes or heroines. Nowhere is this more true than in Texas and Louisiana. In these two lands that matured from the colonial era to become states of the United States, no name stands out more honored and respected than that of the French-born Vincentian missionary priest, bishop, and archbishop, Jean-Marie Odin. Born in Hauteville in the western reaches of the ancient Archdiocese of Lyon, France, just at the turn of the nineteenth century, when that nation was experiencing the post-revolutionary, early Napoleonic eras that had devastated the land's centuries-old Catholic heritage, Odin as a young man entered the seminary system of the archdiocese. Eventually matriculating to the grand seminaire of St. Irenaeus located in the city of Lyon, he ventured from there in 1822 to the US mission field to commence his life's work as a Catholic missionary. Having absorbed the spirit of the Sulpicians at the grand seminaire, upon his arrival on the American continent he joined the Congregation of the Mission while at their seminary of St. Mary's the Barrens in Perryville, Missouri. Thus, it would be the formation of Saint Vincent de Paul that was to guide him for the remainder of his life. After almost a half century of missioning in areas that grew as parts of the United States, Jean-Marie Odin returned to France and died in the same farmhouse in Hauteville where he was born more than seventy years earlier, in 1870. His story must now be told.

Historians who attempt to narrate the life story of a personage in history must confess that the time spent with that life is like a journey. One gets to know well the figure of his or her study. That person, in a sense, becomes part of the author carrying out the research and writing. In such a project, especially one that consumed more than twenty years as this one did, many people are due credit for their help to the author of the biography.

The original suggestion to me to write a biography of the life of Jean-Marie Odin came from the dedicated Sister Dolores Kasner, who in the early 1980s was archivist of the Catholic Archives of Texas. Her encouragement and support were inspirational. My wife, Linda Sandoval Foley, who had to put up with me spending years laboring on the project, must also be lovingly thanked. The patience that our daughter, Elizabeth Maureen, and son, Sean Patrick, offered needs also to be mentioned.

Several members of the Texas Catholic Historical Society offered their continued help. Among these scholars were Félix D. Almaráz Jr.; Gilbert Ralph Cruz; Thomas W. Jodziewicz (and his wife, Janet); Timothy Matovina; Jesús F. de la Teja; Rev. James Talmadge Moore; L. Tuffly Ellis; Roy R. Barkley; Hubert Miller; Rev. Robert E. Wright, O.M.I.; Gilberto Miguel Hinojosa; Robert M. Senkewicz (and his wife, Rose Marie); José Roberto Juarez; the late Susan Anderson Kerr; and Anne Butler. Among others of the Texas Catholic Historical Society, special thank yous should go out to the former president of that group, Susan Eason, archivist of the Catholic Archives of Texas, and the late Kinga Perzynska, former archivist of the Catholic Archives of Texas. Brother Richard Daly, for years with the Texas Catholic Conference, consistently offered his support.

Other historians, professors, archivists, staff members, and more who steadily encouraged this project and need to be mentioned would be Marina Ochoa of the Archdiocese of Santa Fe, New Mexico; Rev. Thomas J. Steele, S.J., of the Jesuit Fathers, Albuquerque, New Mexico; Gerard Wegemer of the University of Dallas; Frank Nickell of Southeast Missouri State University; Michal Glazier and his wife, Joan, noted Catholic editor and publisher; the late Donald J. D'Elia, former emeritus professor of the State University of New York, New Paltz; and Andy and Fran Kozusko. Finally, my sincere appreciation also must be extended to Becky and Chris Wade as well as Brendan Loughran, all of Azle, Texas, for their great help in getting the manuscript into the computer software as needed for publication. To all of these people, and any others who should have been mentioned, I offer my sincere gratitude.

Missionary Bishop

I

❧

From France He Came

THE NINETEENTH CENTURY dawned over France recoiling from the recent upheavals associated with the French Revolution that had devastated the country and the 1799 coup d'état of Napoleon Bonaparte. Among the regions of the land known for having remained faithful to the realm's centuries-old Roman Catholic heritage during those difficult years was the ancient Archdiocese of Lyon. The historical narrative of this metropolitan see had its origins dating back to the early days of Christianity, to even before the inspiring episcopacy of Saint Irenaeus spanning the years A.D. 177–202. Over the course of its long history, the Archdiocese of Lyon had emerged as one of the Catholic Church's most important ecclesiastical strongholds.

A few weeks into the 1800s, the tiny hamlet of Hauteville, situated in the far western reaches of the archdiocese, celebrated the birth of a baby boy who was destined to go down in history as a renowned Catholic missionary on the American continent. His name was Jean-Marie Odin. The story of that Frenchman's life serves as a testimony to the faith that numerous churchmen and women brought to the Americas as they labored to build a Catholic presence in their adopted lands.

Hauteville existed as a rustic rural community nestled into a wooded area amidst surrounding farmlands, lying a few miles west of the city of Roanne. At the time of Jean-Marie's birth the historic priory church of St. Martin d'Ambierle served as the Catholic community of that locale, a church that could trace its origins back to the waning days of Roman Gaul.[1] Prominent among the residences of Hauteville stood the sturdy but unpretentious home of Jean Odin and his wife, Claudine-Marie (Serol). Typical of the region, the Odin house was a squared multifloored building erected on a family-owned plot of land set in close to a clump of trees for shade. Abundantly planted in crops of the season for that particular region of France, the Odin property blended in well with the verdant, tilled, low-rolling hills and flatland acreage that dominated the area's landscape. Neighbors held the Odins in high regard, viewing them as one of the locale's best-liked and most-respected Catholic clans. That proved to be significant for a family living in an archdiocese where the church had been targeted for attack from revolutionaries from the very outbreak of the French Revolution in 1789.[2]

In that house about noontime on a cold twenty-fifth day of February in the year 1800, Jean and Claudine-Marie welcomed into their family their seventh child, a son. As often occurred throughout much of Catholic Europe in those days, this newest addition to the Odin family received the sacrament of baptism within just a few hours following his birth. He was given the Christian name Jean-Marie. The devout Jean and Claudine-Marie elected not to have their newborn baptized in the local church, because the cure of St. Martin d'Ambierle at the time, Pere (Father) Francois Loche, pastor in residence there since 1785, had earlier pledged fealty to the infamous 1790 Civil Constitution of the Clergy, which the revolutionaries had forced upon Catholic France. Instead of Pere Loche, a nonjuring priest—that is, one who had refused to swear by the despised document—Pere Didier from the nearby town of Boisset, administered the sacrament. However, Jean-Marie's baptism was recorded in the sacramental records of St. Martin d'Ambierle. Just exactly where the baptism occurred remains shrouded in uncertainty. Likely, though, Pere Didier officiated at the sacrament in the Odin home, given that it was the place of birth. According to Jean-Marie's baptismal certificate, an aunt on Claudine-Marie's side of the family, Virginia Serol, served as the baby's godmother (marraine). A cousin, Jean-Perrichon, acted as godfather (parrain).[3]

Ultimately Jean and Claudine-Marie were blessed with three more children, bringing the total number of Odin offspring to ten. Young Jean-Marie grew into his adolescence in a home atmosphere that early on nurtured his natural inclination toward a life of Catholic piety. His attraction to religious matters unquestionably received encouragement from such a strongly Catholic household environment. A circle of immediate family, relatives, and friends who were themselves devoted Roman Catholics surrounded Jean-Marie throughout his youth. As a result, the future missionary's early years were steeped in the life of the church, its sacramental and sacerdotal character, and embellished through national and local Catholic devotions, customs, and traditions.

During those days also, Jean-Marie began to show a sensitivity to the needs of other people, a characteristic that would deepen in him as he grew to maturity. Of this aspect of him Odin's nineteenth-century biographer, the Abbe Bony, described the youth: "He delights in helping the poor. He brings food to needy neighbors; his mother greatly encourages him; he becomes bold. . . . The impetuosity of charity [sometimes] had carried away young Odin, who was by nature timid and reserved.[4]

Jean-Marie, in addition, endeavored to share without complaint the household chores that his mere (mother) and pere assigned him and his siblings.

Jean-Marie Odin's home in Hauteville, where Odin was born, lived as a youth, and died in 1870. Courtesy Catholic Archives of Texas, Austin.

He enjoyed especially tending the sheep that his parents owned. As an aging Archbishop of New Orleans many decades later, Odin reminisced that among his happiest experiences at home back in Hauteville as a youngster were those times he spent as a shepherd in the countryside. A half-century beyond those pleasant days at Hauteville, and thousands of miles removed from his native land, the missionary from France looked back to that period in his life with nostalgia.[5]

As Jean-Marie reached his seventh birthday, his parents began to seek out ways to get him started along the path to a formal education. A distant relative of the family, a cousin who prior to the outbreak of the French Revolution had been a seminarian and now lived in the nearby village of Tremieres, proved to be the answer. That unnamed cousin had gathered around him a group of children for the purpose of teaching them to read and to write. Jean-Marie joined those pupils. Two years later, in 1809, Jean and Claudine-Marie sent their son to stay with another relative, an Uncle Serol, quite possibly—though not for certain—Claudine-Marie's brother. Uncle Serol was a priest who served as cure of the parish church in the nearby town of Nouilly. Jean-Marie experienced firsthand at Nouilly, under the watchful eye of Cure Serol, life in a rural French Catholic rectory. Odin's residence there brought with it another first—his introduction to Latin. Pere Serol, perhaps sensing that his nephew might have a vocation to the priesthood, labored enthusiastically to instruct the boy in the rudiments of the language of the church.

Painfully for Jean-Marie, Claudine-Marie, and the rest of the Odin and Serol families, in 1811 his uncle died. Only eleven years old at the time, Jean-Marie was returned to his parents' home at Hauteville, his happiness over his being back home with his family tempered somewhat his sadness at the death of his priest uncle.[6] Quite likely, by that time Jean and Claudine Marie suspected that their son might have a vocation to the religious state in life. Thus, they deemed it time for him to embark upon his seminary training.

The Seminaries of Lyon and Cardinal Fesch

From the days of the conversion of King Clovis of the Franks under the influence of his Catholic wife, Clotilda, at the end of the fifth century, to the outbreak of the French Revolution more than thirteen hundred years later, France had ripened to maturity thoroughly Roman Catholic. The noted French historian Gillaume Bertier de Sauvigny described the realm's Catholic legacy as one in which "every Frenchman, from the king to the lowest 'villain,' considered himself to be first and foremost a Christian, a member of the vast society of the Church."[7]

The late eighteenth and early nineteenth centuries, however, witnessed France being wracked with a destructive assault on that Catholic heritage from, first, the revolutionaries of 1789–95 and then by the presumptuous reign of Emperor Napoleon Bonaparte. As the revolution that had begun with the fall of the Bastille on July 14, 1789, intensified into a de-Christianization movement, the church took the brunt of the attack.

The Catholic Church became a target because it was viewed as an integral part of the ancient regime. Thus, one of the earliest decisions of the revolutionaries was to nationalize ecclesiastical properties. Such was to include not only arable lands and forests but real estate as well.[8] Concomitantly there developed among the Enlightenment-influenced leaders of the revolution an intellectual opposition to the teachings and traditions of Christianity, especially as the Catholic Church represented them.

From the perspective of the revolutionaries, the attitudes and ideals of the Enlightenment must replace the nation's traditional Catholic ideology. Fundamental to such a development would be a need to energize an onslaught against France's seminaries. In tandem with this, the French clergy's interaction with the state had to be redefined. No document of that period more clearly mirrored this antireligious feeling of the revolutionaries than the aforementioned 1790 Civil Constitution of the Clergy. Through that law—which much of the population detested—a reluctant French Catholic nation and its clergy and religious were pressured to render to Caesar not only that which was Caesar's, but to Caesar also that which was God's.

Bertier de Sauvigny wrote of this constitution:

> Inasmuch as the state undertook to support the clergy, the Assembly [a revolutionary establishment] held that it could reorganize the Church of France as it might any other public service. It began by abolishing religious vows as contrary to fundamental human liberties (February 1790). The diocesan clergy was given a new organization called the "Civil Constitution," based on that of the general administration. There was one diocese to a department [France had been divided into separate civil departments], one parish to a commune. Bishops and priests were elected like other civil officials. In a Gallican spirit the Assembly also decreed that the elected bishops would receive spiritual investiture from one of their colleagues, called the metropolitan bishop, and no longer from Rome, as the Concordat of 1516 [France's current concordat with the Holy See] had ordained. The Holy See would only be "informed" of the elections.[9]

The revolutionary assembly pushed matters even further by requiring by law that "all paid churchmen must take an oath to support the Civil Constitution of the Clergy under penalty of losing their posts."[10] The lower clergy's reaction to that demand varied both geographically and demographically. Approximately two-thirds of them either refused to take the pledge or swore fealty under pressure but with reservations (with Pere Didier an example of the former and St. Martin d'Ambierle's Cure Loche the latter). The French historian Andre Latreille wrote about the power clergy had that "on the one side were those who took the oath, and on the other those who did not: those who in disdain, were called 'juring,' or 'refactory,' or who in admiration were styled 'civic,' or 'good' priests." Of the country's 160 prelates, active or retired, only seven gave their assent. On March 10, 1791, Pope Pius VI condemned the Civil Constitution of the Clergy as having "as its aim and effect the destruction of the Catholic Religion."[11]

Within a short period of time (as early as 1793) the revolutionary leaders initiated a de-Christianization program. France's centuries-old Catholic legacy came under an even more intense assault, with radical secularism emerging as the aim of the defiant rebels. The September 17, 1793, Law of Suspects allowed the arrest of all persons presumed enemies of the revolution. The revolutionary tribunals in Paris and in the provinces multiplied the number of death sentences until the guillotine became the symbol of the new regime. Between thirty-five and forty thousand victims were executed and more than three hundred thousand were imprisoned.[12] As the revolution took shape, its anti-religious tone intensified. Seminaries were closed, religious communities—both male and female—were aggressively expelled from France, and ecclesiastical holdings were further nationalized.

Some respite was eventually to come for the church with the 1799 recognition at Paris of the ascendancy of Napoleon Bonaparte. He signed the Concordat of 1801 with the Holy See. That agreement superseded the former Concordat of 1516 and eliminated, or moderated, many of the atrocities against the Catholic Church that the revolution represented. The grandiose Corsican, however, proved to be no special friend of the church. In his vision for learning, the Imperial University that he established oversaw an educational system aimed at training military officers and civil officials, while marginalizing the system. Furthermore, during the initial decade of the nineteenth century, a period contemporary with Jean-Marie Odin's early years, Catholic seminaries continued to suffer from lack of support in several regions of the country, and several religious orders remained suppressed. In addition, Napoleon's well-recorded brusque treatment of Pope Pius VII resulted in the emperor's eventual alienation of the Catholic clergy and masses of the laity. In 1809, Pius VII excommunicated Napoleon because of the French ruler's earlier expropriation of Rome and the Papal States. Finally, when Napoleon divorced his legitimate wife, Josephine, and married Archduchess Marie Louise of Hapsburg, daughter of the Austrian emperor, the pope refused to recognize the marriage.[13]

Unknowingly, Bonaparte did act in a beneficial way for the seminaries of the Archdiocese of Lyon when he nominated his priest-uncle, Joseph Fesch, to be the new archbishop of that metropolitan see in 1802. Soon named a cardinal, Fesch served as Archbishop of Lyon for thirty-seven years, from 1802 to 1839. When he nominated his uncle for the Lyon post, Napoleon most probably assumed that he was rewarding a family member who had been loyal to him during the recent past. Surprisingly, however, the emperor had named a man who was to emerge as the great rebuilder of the seminaries of the archdiocese, a system of priestly formation that the revolution had decimated. In his later years Cardinal Fesch became a dedicated supporter of missionaries to foreign lands, including noticeable support given to Jean-Marie Odin.

Almost immediately after he was named archbishop, Fesch turned his attention to seminaries. Cardinal Fesch steadily matured as the leader of a religious renewal throughout the Archdiocese of Lyon, inspiring clergy, religious (male as well as female), and laypeople alike. Dom Jean-Baptiste Chautard, a Cistercian abbot of Notre Dame de Sept-Fons, writing a century after Fesch ascended to the episcopal chair of the archdiocese, exclaimed that "the fact that France got back on her feet after the revolution must be accredited to a priesthood [of which Cardinal Fesch was a leading member] that learned the interior life the hard way, by persecution."[14]

The late Father J. Edgar Bruns of New Orleans, a Catholic historian, offered his estimation of Cardinal Fesch: "The cardinal archbishop of Lyon at this time was Joseph Fesch, Napoleon's uncle, a man not easy to characterize. Most would see him as a grasping opportunist, but it is a known fact that in his diocese he gave shelter to every kind of prelate, vagrant, or displaced monk and humblest lay brother, while he surrounded himself with dedicated young priests who were to lead the Catholic revival of France for the next generation. Fesch's seminary [St. Irenaeus] was outstanding for the quality and caliber of its students."[15]

In 1816, *L'Ami*, an influential French church newspaper, reported that regarding the renovation of Catholicism in France following the French Revolution, the faithful of the city of Lyon "are not limiting themselves to momentary succor, they are taking steps to perpetuate it."[16] As the years passed the French church was steadily restored, although it was not exempt from constant pressure from Napoleon's government until the Archdiocese of Lyon was reborn under the guidance of Cardinal Fesch. Back at Hauteville, Jean-Marie Odin seemed drawn unhesitatingly along the path of an apparent vocation to the priesthood while the restoration was underway.

Jean-Marie—Seminarian Attracted to the American Continent

Not long after he returned to his family following his Uncle Serol's death in 1811, young Jean-Marie received the sacrament of First Holy Communion. Then, in 1813, Cardinal Fesch journeyed westward from Lyon to St. Martin d'Ambierle Church and administered the sacrament of confirmation to young Odin and several other youths of the parish. It could be speculated that the cardinal archbishop's visit offered Jean-Marie and his family their first ever opportunity to meet the ordinary of Lyon who would later in his life prove to be such a great aid to Jean-Marie as a missionary to America.

In his rebuilding of the seminary system of Lyon, Cardinal Fesch resurrected or founded anew several such centers of formation and training. Among these were the petit seminaries (small though not necessarily minor) of Saint Jodard, Maximeux dans L'Ain, Alix dans Le Rhone, and L'Argentiere. Fesch also reopened the former seminary of Roche et Verrieres dans La Loire as a preparatory seminary. Jean-Marie Odin was to study at and receive religious instruction at the latter three.[17] Lodged in the mountains near the city of Montbrison, lying due south of Roanne, was situated Roche et Verrieres dans La Loire. That one-time major seminary, with its difficult physical environment and demanding academic and likewise spiritual climate, was well designed to challenge, and thus prepare, beginning seminarians. Jean-Marie Odin entered Roche et Verrieres dans La Loire slightly more than two weeks after the Grand Alliance of Austria, Russia, and Prussia—having defeated Napoleon—exiled the emperor to the island of Elba April 20, 1814). At that seminary Jean-Marie Odin stayed for two, or possibly even three, years (the exact dates are unclear).

While spending his summer vacation of 1816 back home at Hauteville, the young seminarian met for the first time Father Antoine Blanc, a newly ordained priest who in the future was to play an influential role in Odin's life as a fellow missionary, close friend, and confidant. Blanc had been elevated to the priesthood only a few days when he received his first assignment as an assistant pastor, to St. Martin d'Ambierle Church. This station, however, was for Father Blanc only a temporary one. His eventual destination was to America as a missionary, to serve with another French cleric, Sulpician Bishop Louis William DuBourg, head of the Diocese of Louisiana and the Floridas. Upon the death of Blanc decades later, in 1860, who at the time was the first archbishop of New Orleans, Odin, then first bishop of Galveston, Texas, would succeed his longtime co-laborer in the mission field as the episcopal leader of that Louisiana metropolitan see (1861).

Antoine Blanc was almost eight years older than Jean-Marie Odin, having been born on October 11, 1792, at Sury-le-Comtal, a small town of about 3,000 souls situated in the department of the Loire. He was the fourth child in a family of nine offspring. In 1813, Blanc enrolled in the grand seminaire of St. Irenaeus at Lyon, a major archdiocesan seminary conducted by the Sulpicians and an institution that Odin himself would attend a few years later. On July 22, 1816, Bishop DuBourg, who was traveling throughout much of Europe recruiting clergy and religious (both male and female) for his diocese, ordained Blanc to the priesthood. The new priest from Sury-le-Comtal departed for Louisiana on June 2, 1817, aboard the French ship *Caravane*.[18] In the meantime, Jean-Marie's seminary training continued along a steady pace.

Following his time spent at Roche et Verrieres dans La Loire, Jean-Marie matriculated on to the seminary L'Argentiere to pursue the study of philosophy. That was a period in young Odin's life during which he was maturing spiritually, intellectually, and physically. In 1818, he was admitted to the seminary college of Alix dans la Rhone near Villefranche, located between the cities of Roanne and Lyon. Two years later, in the fall of 1820, twenty-year-old Jean-Marie Odin entered the grand seminaire of St. Irenaeus at Lyon, where for more than a year-and-a-half he prepared for the priestly life under the religious formation and academic training of the Sulpicians. This spiritual and scholarly experience would leave its mark on him for the remainder of his earthly life. While at St. Irenaeus, in 1821, Odin became a subdeacon in the Catholic Church.[19]

Back in 1642, the Abbe Jean-Jacques Olier, one of France's most intense seventeenth-century Catholic religious reformers, founded the society of secular priests known as the Compagnie des Pretres des Saint-Sulpice, or the

Society of the Priests of Saint Sulpice. The noted American Catholic Church historian Christopher J. Kauffman has described the Sulpician spirituality that Olier established and developed during the first few decades of the Sulpicians' existence thus:

> The spirit of Saint Sulpice, derived from the charisma of Olier, was manifested in a specific method of prayer, the *haute culture* [high culture] of an aristocratic concept of the priesthood, and in the Sulpician drive to model the interior and the exterior ideals of the priesthood for those aspiring to the sacerdotal life. Institutionalized during the age of Louis XIV, this spirit became identified with the revival of religious idealism, the restoration of the nonregular clergy (diocesan priests), and the reform of parish life. The Sulpician was a diocesan priest dedicated to the spiritual direction of those called to sacred orders. A community of diocesan priests with a superior general is a juridical anomaly, but in practice the directors of each house formed a collegial body authorized to make all policy decisions.[20]

As the decades passed by in France, from the mid-to-latter 1700s, after the reign of King Louis XIV (1661–1715) the French witnessed a general period of religious, cultural, political, and social decline. The growing strength of Gallicanism, a continuing struggle for French Catholics with Jansenism, the ever-present destruction and cost of wars, and a noticeable decline in French everyday moral life—the latter mirrored in the Sulpician community with a relaxation of the original high ecclesiastical spirit of Olier—became evident. However, Olier's dedication was revived under the leadership of a much-admired Sulpician superior general, Jacques-Andre Emery, head of the Sulpicians from 1782 through 1808.

The Sulpicians were one of the religious societies that Napoleon Bonaparte's government had insisted remain suppressed in France. But they reappeared in 1814 with the Bourbon Restoration, and they soon regained strong influence in the administration of and teaching in seminaries. In their ranks the memory of Emery was much alive. The influence of Emery was still felt heavy in the halls of St. Irenaeus when Jean-Marie Odin was there.

A number of influences had an impact upon Odin's religious character: his personal piety, so deeply intensified through the seeds sown and cultivated by his devout parents and siblings; the experience of having lived with his Uncle Serol, a priest in the rectory at Nouilly; his studies in the archdiocesan seminary system; his acquaintance with young Father Antoine Blanc; the example of the Sulpicians at St. Irenaeus; reminders constantly placed before him of the devastation done to the church from the revolutionary and Bonaparte eras. All were significant.

When exactly Jean-Marie Odin began to think about becoming a foreign missionary will likely forever remain a mystery. Perhaps not until the last weeks of his studies at St. Irenaeus did he finalize his decision. It seems possible, though, that he started entertaining such thoughts back home at Hauteville during that summer of 1816 when he first met Pere Blanc. Regardless of when the hope of carrying the Good News to distant lands first germinated in his heart and mind, Jean-Marie's opportunity to volunteer for the foreign mission field came in the spring of 1822 while he was a seminarian at St. Irenaeus.

Bishop DuBourg, the recruiter of Father Blanc earlier, had dispatched a priest representative of his Diocese of Louisiana and the Floridas, Father Angelo Inglesi, to Europe in that year seeking out priests, seminarians, sisters, and novices to serve the Catholics in his see.[21] At St. Irenaeus Father Inglesi found Jean-Marie Odin to be an enthusiastic responder to Bishop DuBourg's appeal for missioning laborers.

As had countless missioners to regions remote from their homelands before him, and still more to come after him, Jean-Marie Odin for a time suffered through a period of struggle with his conscience regarding his family. He wondered how he might tell his parents, siblings, grandparents, cousins, aunts, uncles, and other members of his clan, as well as lifelong neighbors in his small village of Hauteville, about his decision to leave them and his native France forever to venture across the seas to serve as a Catholic missionary. The young Frenchman hesitated, ever so briefly as it came to be, also because he felt uncertain about how his superiors at St. Irenaeus might react. After all, he argued with himself, he was a twenty-two-year-old subdeacon not yet ordained to the priesthood. Odin's concerns about his superiors possibly objecting to his call proved to be unfounded. The Sulpicians at St. Irenaeus enthusiastically approved of his decision.[22]

Communicating his plans to his family and friends, especially to his *pere* and *mere,* Jean and Claudine-Marie Odin, was for him another matter indeed. The son ultimately decided to inform his parents by letter, fearing that a personal farewell at home in Hauteville would prove too wrenching for all. Writing to them from St. Irenaeus on April 22, shortly after the Sulpicians at the seminary had granted him permission to depart for the Americas, Jean-Marie poured out his heart:

> My superiors announced to me that the Bishop of Louisiana wanted someone to establish some seminaries in his diocese. They were of the opinion that I should accept this post; it is a very great honor that heaven grants me and which my unworthiness would never have permitted me to hope for. However, the joy that this news should have caused me was very troubled by the apprehension that it would not at all be pleasing to you. Your attachment for me is so great that a

separation of several years is going to sadden you perhaps, and cause you chagrin and anxiety. But no, the will of God was always precious, and you always loved to follow it. This thought cheers me up, for my dear father and mother, in having accepted this post it is only after most serious deliberation.[23]

No record is extant as to how Jean and Claudine-Marie reacted to their son's news and the prospect of his imminent departure for the American continent. But son and parents kept in close contact through the mails, until his father passed away several years later, preceding his wife in death and having never again seen in person his missionary son. The strength that Jean-Marie received from the love and affection that his parents and other family members showered upon him—even from beyond the seas—and the deep memories of that after both *pere* and *mere* had both passed on, buoyed the missionary from France throughout his long life on the American frontier. That closeness within the Odin family, strengthened by their common devotion to the church, was reflected over the years in their exchange of correspondence across the ocean.

As just one example of this, a letter penned to his sister Benoite on May 3, 1822, revealed more about how he lamented leaving all of them. He showed great trust in her as a consoler to the family. To Benoite Jean-Marie pleaded:

Providence, my dear sister, designs to associate me with the zealous missionaries of America, and that in spite of my unworthiness. It [Providence] is willing to select me to go to the aid of the miserable savages of these unfortunate lands. Through the love that you have for your God and the affections that you always show me, permit your poor brother to solicit various services of your goodness. I again count on that tenderness that will always persuade you to oblige me. My departure will be, I hope, for you a new reason for praising God, if you look at it through the eyes of faith. But, my poor father and mother, my brothers and sisters and the entire family, will find in my departure a great cause for sadness and chagrin. Ah! My dear sister, it is upon you that all my hope rests; you will console them; you will make them face and understand the obligations under which I find myself, to support the design of Providence for me.[24]

Le Havre, an historic port city located about 180 kilometers northwest of Paris on the French coast of the English Channel, served as a major point of departure for countless emigrants—including missionaries—from continental Europe making passage across the Atlantic Ocean to the American continent throughout much of the nineteenth century. To Le Havre Jean-Marie Odin set out immediately following the posting of his letter to Benoite. Traveling by stagecoach except for the final few kilometers of his trip, which he hurriedly covered on foot since he missed his last stagecoach connection, Odin reached Le Havre on May 8. He arrived at the dockage of the ship *Highlander,* which Capt. August Welch commanded, a mere half hour before the vessel was scheduled to weigh anchor. There Jean-Marie Odin bid farewell to his native country, not to return for as much as even a brief visit for a dozen years.[25]

❧❀❧

At the Barrens

THE VOYAGE ACROSS THE ATLANTIC OCEAN to New Orleans on the ship *Highlander* was long and arduous for Jean-Marie Odin and his fellow passengers and took more than two months to complete. Jean-Marie described the passage in a letter written to his *mere* and *pere* shortly following his arrival at that southern port city: "On July 11, after a voyage of two months and three days, we entered the port of New Orleans. The first thirty days of our sailing were rather pleasant; then for an entire week we were buffeted by unfavorable winds. The periods of calm delayed our progress and four or five storms that we experienced made our arrival somewhat less prompt than one had cause to hope for. There were five clergymen on board with us." The five churchmen to whom Jean-Marie referred were Jean-Baptiste Blanc, Father Antoine Blanc's younger brother destined also to serve in DuBourg's diocese; a French deacon named Eugene Michaud; and three Italian clerics: Lorenzo Peyretti of Turpin, as well as Giovanni Audizio and Giovanni Carretti of Piedmont.[1]

Upon disembarking the *Highlander* on that summer morning in 1822, Odin seemed already to sense that he had ventured into a new world vastly different from that one which he had known back in his homeland. This American West and Southwest was a land, however, that embodied the frontier character of a country that the Frenchman would come to find endearing. Enthusiastically drawn to those persons he knew best in that initially foreign environment, Jean-Marie happily knew that his priest-friend of several years earlier at Hauteville, Father Antoine Blanc, was somewhat nearby. At that time Blanc was laboring as pastor of the Catholic parish at Pointe-Coupee located approximately one hundred miles north of New Orleans, just beyond the west bank of the Mississippi River. There Odin went immediately after stepping ashore in the bayou city, accompanied by Jean-Baptiste Blanc.

The brief visit with Father Antoine at Pointe-Coupee proved to be inspiring for both Jean-Marie and Jean-Baptiste. The latter was able to embrace his older brother after several years of separation. What a delight that must have been for both Blancs! And beyond any doubt Father Antoine was overjoyed at seeing once again his former teenage parishioner and altar boy from St. Martin d'Ambierle. How pleased must Father Blanc have been that the Hauteville youth had become a missionary to the very diocese in which he himself served. The three Frenchmen reminisced about their families and friends back home, St. Irenaeus grand seminaire, and beloved France. *Ah La Belle* France!

Jean-Marie Odin and Antoine and Jean-Baptiste Blanc shared reflections on the realities of missionary life on the trans-Mississippi American frontier. Jean-Marie and Jean-Baptiste eagerly sought the advice and views of Father Antoine, whose own experience in Louisiana by that time had totaled more than five years. The two new arrivals understood that they were now to serve in a region of the American continent that formed the confluence of three former colonial empires: those of New Spain, New France, and the English colonies. Both French churchmen also were aware that they had been called to evangelize souls in a territory situated at the frontal edge of a growing population moving westward from the Atlantic coastal and inland areas. This migration included Americans long settled upon the land as well as immigrant peoples from Europe.

A hint about the substance of the conversations that Jean-Marie, Jean-Baptiste, and Father Antoine Blanc enjoyed at Pointe Coupee can be found in a letter that Odin composed to his sister Benoite following this visit. Jean-Marie recounted, "M. Blanc was very pleased to see me[,] and he immediately inquired about the whole family. He did not forget anyone. He does a lot of good in the missions, but the congregation of which he is in charge is so large and scattered that he has not been able to attend to the savage tribes."[2]

It was well known among Odin's fellow missionaries that before he began his work along the Mississippi River frontier, in fact while still a seminarian back in France, he had longed to work among the American indigenous peoples. As it was to develop, he would enjoy several opportunities to catechize among those earliest of Americans as the years passed, especially in Missouri, Arkansas, and Texas. But New Orleans society introduced Odin to a human condition with which he had no previous experience, and toward which he exhibited an immediate abhorrence—slavery.

Odin Reacts to Slavery

At that period of history, while Louisiana itself existed as a slave state in which many French Catholics of Louisiana owned slaves, some French immigrants to the United States viewed slavery with suspicion and considered the institution depressing. The latter saw in the "peculiar institution" a serious contradiction to the values enunciated in the US Declaration of Independence—"We hold these truths to be self-evident, that all men are created equal." Moreover, racial prejudice, which acted ideologically as a major justification for slavery in the United States, was not nearly as visible in France.[3]

Most French priests, brothers, and nuns who labored in the US mission field looked upon slaves with sympathy. Jean-Marie Odin too mirrored great empathy for slaves, in particular those he first encountered upon his arrival in Louisiana. He recoiled against the institution of slavery as repugnant. Ironically, any number of Catholic religious communities in the United States, including the Congregation of the Mission (Vincentians) in Perryville, Missouri, which Jean-Marie would soon join, themselves owned slaves.[4]

More will be said later about Odin's viewing slavery as a shameful time in the narrative of US history, but his initial distaste for that form of human degradation is well recorded. Writing once again to his sister Benoite not long after having penned his first letter to her from New Orleans, Jean-Marie bared his soul about his grief over slavery: "There is one spectacle very deserving of pity; it is that of the Negroes, who are in great number in this country. They are almost all slaves. They are treated as one would treat a beast of burden in France. In the fields they are almost always naked. I have found some who do not even know there is a God. One should not be amazed if they are corrupted; they live, alas, rather like beasts than men."[5]

In another letter to Benoite, composed several months after he had departed New Orleans and settled in at the Congregation of the Mission Barrens Seminary upriver at Perryville in Missouri, where he found that the Vincentians there owned slaves, he protested, "The greatest cause of sadness is the slavery of the Negroes. In lower Louisiana the masters, for the most part, do not want to hear people talking about having their slaves educated or married. Often they do not permit them to go to church. You easily comprehend what degradation results from this. How grieved I was in the beginning in the face of this situation.[6]

For Odin slavery would continue to survive in the United States as a contradiction to basic Christianity regarding the treatment of humankind.[7]

The Barrens

Meanwhile, it was to be only a few weeks after his landing at New Orleans that Jean-Marie Odin would commence his religious formation and training as a missionary under the guidance of the Vincentians (known better in Europe as Lazarists). More than seven hundred miles upriver from New Orleans on the Mississippi River, a short distance inland from the west bank of that great river, located in the eastern reaches of the newly created state of Missouri, was situated the small immigrant settlement known as the Barrens Colony.

Catholics of English heritage from Maryland, some of whose ancestry could be traced back to the days of the Calverts in seventeenth-century Maryland, had migrated westward at the turn of the nineteenth century. Settling initially in Kentucky, those pioneers soon crossed the Mississippi River into Missouri, a region at the time not even part of the United States. There they established a site that was to grow as the Barrens Colony.[8] A seminary was founded at the Barrens in 1818, where Jean-Marie Odin lived for more than seventeen years, from 1822 to 1840. The Barrens Seminary matured as an institution that was to prepare Odin well for his future labors as a missionary and bishop in Texas as well as an archbishop at New Orleans.

The first permanent settlers in the region of the Barrens Colony, an area that would later boast such names as Perry County and Perryville—in honor of the naval war hero of the War of 1812, Oliver Hazard Perry—had arrived back in 1787. Two Frenchmen who in all likelihood were Catholics, Jean Baptiste Barsaloux and his unnamed father, in that year moved onto a tract of land that they had attained from the royal government of Spain. Such information bolsters the belief that they were Catholics, because Spain gave land only to Catholics in those days. The Barsalouxs had in mind to build a home there and to settle into a life of farming.[9]

By 1804, between eighty and ninety more pilgrims, mainly Protestants, had located themselves in the vicinity. In the meantime, the transmigration of the aforementioned Maryland Catholics had been underway for more than seven years, with a hearty migrant named Joseph Fenwick in its vanguard. As a part of that historical movement, Isidore Moore, on February 9, 1801, had settled "with his wife, two children and an orphan girl," as the first Catholic settlers in that area that would ultimately come to be known as the Barrens Colony.[10]

In June of 1801, Joseph Tucker and his sons visited the Moore family at their new home. Within a few months the Tuckers had planted roots in the same vicinity. Joseph Tucker occupied his acreage based upon a US government grant even though the United States did not own the territory until the 1803 Louisiana Purchase. Nonetheless, Joseph Tucker succeeded in building his 640-acre plot into a prosperous farm; it was not long until other families were attracted to the locale, and the site became known locally as the Tucker Settlement.

Within a few years Tucker Settlement grew with the addition of the Catholics from Maryland, and the settlement came to be known as Barrens Colony. The designation Barrens Colony may have come from the Marylanders' experience in Kentucky prior to their venturing on to Missouri. During their trek westward the Marylanders lived for a time in a part of Kentucky which featured terrain that was unproductive and under a dominating influence of barren tracts of scrubby growths of trees and other foliage. Another account of the possible origin of the name "Barrens" emerges from the pages of one of the Vincentians' own histories of the parish of Saint Mary's of the Barrens: "Since

Missouri was once the home of various Indian tribes, it is not surprising that part of Perry County was called *Bois Brule*. It was the Indians' custom to burn the trees and underbrush to provide thicker pastures for the buffalo and other large game."[11]

According to one recent assessment, those Marylander Catholics who settled the Barrens Colony had "a firm grasp of their faith and endeavored to practice religion in a serious way." They erected a church—or at least a chapel—at the settlement in 1812 and dedicated it to the Virgin Mary. Father Maxwell blessed that house of worship and from it served the Catholics of the colony until his accidental death the following year. At different times two other priests from that church or chapel also served the Catholics of the Barrens Colony—Fathers Charles de la Croix and Secundo Valenzano. Both of them were laboring out of the Diocese of Bardstown, Kentucky.[12]

In the spring of 1814, the French Trappist pastor at Florissant, Missouri, Father Joseph Dunand, began visiting the Barrens Colony to minister to the Catholics there. Dunand continued to serve the Barrens Colony off and on until Bishop DuBourg was able to turn to the priests of the Congregation of the Mission in 1818.[13] The Barrens Colony Catholics had longed for a permanent pastor for years. Thus, they were elated in late 1817 to hear that their bishop, DuBourg, planned to move his episcopal seat from New Orleans to St. Louis, just eighty miles north of their settlement. When the Barrens Catholic community also learned that DuBourg planned to establish a seminary somewhere in the vicinity, they laid plans to convince him to build it at their colony. Father Dunand urged on the Barrens Catholics in their quest, and Bishop Benedict Joseph Flaget of Bardstown, Kentucky, the former diocesan ordinary for those migrants who had earlier resided in Kentucky, gave them his support as well. On October 17, 1817, as Bishop Flaget was visiting in St. Louis at the request of DuBourg and laying the groundwork for the latter's appearance among his people, a representative from the Barrens participated in a meeting with Flaget in which Flaget was asked that he "intercede with Bishop DuBourg to accept their offer of a church and land in order to have his seminary located in their midst."[14] The Barrens group seemed to have impressed Bishop DuBourg with their sincerity. The Barrens Catholics dispatched a delegation of parish trustees—Aquila Hagan, Wilfred Layton, and Joseph Layton—to St. Louis in January 1818 to meet with their newly arrived bishop and to offer him 640 acres of land at the Barrens for his seminary.

Three months later, as the month of March gave way to April, DuBourg traveled the eighty miles south from St. Louis to the Barrens for his first get-together with his flock at that location. At that time, he promised that a seminary, as well as priests to minister among the Catholics there, were in the immediate future for the settlement.[15] Jean-Marie Odin would be one of those priests.

The heart of the agreement between the bishop and the Barrens Catholics was a document dated April 10, 1818, whereby "Ignatius Layton and his wife placed themselves under a bond of $1,800 to Bishop DuBourg . . . guaranteeing the delivery to Bishop DuBourg of a deed of 640 [acres]."[16] After acquiring the property for his seminary DuBourg returned to St. Louis. From there he wrote to Father Joseph Rosati, a Vincentian priest who, along with Father Felix De Andreis, in 1816 had ventured to the Mississippi River frontier from Italy to establish the Congregation of the Mission in America.

Rosati at the time was in residence at Bardstown with Bishop Flaget and most of the Vincentians then laboring in the United States. Bishop DuBourg explained to Father Rosati that he had asked Flaget to assign "his Flemish band of cultivating Brothers to depart immediately [for the Barrens] under the guidance of their saintly Father Delacroix [de la Croix]."[17] In his letter DuBourg requested that Rosati send along with the group four members of Rosati's Congregation of the Mission.

The Seminary Erected

When Father de la Croix arrived at the Barrens with the Flemish Brothers and the four Vincentians, the foundation for the future seminary was ready to be laid. With the help of several of the parishioners, de la Croix and his contingent were able to start showing progress quickly in the initial stages of the construction of the seminary buildings. Bishop DuBourg, in his letter to Father Rosati back at Bardstown, had described the planned edifice as a vast undertaking in which: "The house will measure sixty by thirty-six feet, 2 1/2 stories high, with a cellar underneath—much like the brick house at St. Thomas in Kentucky. There will be two halls, 25 by 17 feet, both on the first floor and in the cellar."[18]

DuBourg visited the Barrens again in July 1818. He then returned to St. Louis, where on August 2 he mailed another letter to Father Rosati at Bardstown, expressing his satisfaction with the headway being made at the Barrens. In addition DuBourg informed Rosati that even though the seminary would not at the time be ready for them, he wanted all of his missionaries, including the seminarians, with him by early fall.[19]

To be sure, the seminary was not ready for occupancy when Father Rosati and his clerics appeared on the scene. So the "first home of the seminary" proved to be a moderate-sized house measuring some twenty by thirty feet, which one of the pillars of the parish, the wealthy widow Sarah Haydon, donated for the seminarians' use. Not long thereafter, Bishop DuBourg withdrew Father de la Croix and his workers from the building site, needing them for assignment elsewhere. That left Father Rosati to oversee the completion of the seminary.[20]

Before the end of the next year, 1819, Rosati also was named pastor of the new St. Mary's of the Barrens parish.

Within a few weeks of the Vincentians' arrival, log cabins were being constructed on the seminary grounds to serve as lodging for those sons of St. Vincent. By the end of the spring of 1819, enough of those structures were in place to allow the young clerics to settle on the premises. By the early 1820s, the seminary building was completed, a lay college connected to the seminary was built, and enrollments for both institutions had begun and were on the increase. All of this had taken place at the Barrens before Jean-Marie Odin appeared on the scene. .

Odin, Priest and Vincentian

According to Father John Rybolt, "In 1823 the Congregation of the Mission received some of its most important recruits. John Mary [Jean-Marie] Odin, a native of France, and John Timon, a native of Pennsylvania, both entered the community and would eventually be numbered among its greatest men." Actually Jean-Marie Odin entered the Congregation of the Mission shortly after his arrival at the Barrens, on November 8, 1822. Odin confirmed this in a March 30, 1823, letter to Sulpician Father Jean Cholleton back at Lyon. Cholleton had held the position of rector of St. Irenaeus grand seminaire when Odin was a seminarian there, and at the time of Odin's missive he served as vicar of the Archdiocese of Lyon. Cholleton knew the Frenchman well. On October 12, 1822, Odin had been ordained a deacon in the church. Bishop DuBourg had traveled to the Barrens Seminary from St. Louis, arriving on the tenth of the month. Two days later the prelate elevated Odin to the deaconate.[21]

A mere seven months later, in a letter to his mother and father dated May 22, 1823, Jean-Marie joyously announced that he had reached the pinnacle of his religious vocation: ordination to the priesthood. He wrote, "What favors the Lord has bestowed on me. Here I am a priest! Oh, what a dignity, what an honor!" Bishop DuBourg had once again trekked south from St. Louis the eighty miles to the Barrens Seminary, where on May 4 he ordained the twenty-three-year-old deacon from Hauteville a Roman Catholic priest. The new Father Odin confirmed the date of his ordination in another epistle to Father Cholleton back at Lyon. To the vicar of Lyon Odin confided, "on May 4, I had the good fortune of being elevated to the saintly, consoling and redoubtable priesthood."[22]

Another milestone awaited the missionary from France, that of becoming a fully professed Vincentian. Six weeks before his twenty-fifth birthday that goal was reached. In the dead of winter at the Barrens Seminary, on January 12, 1825, Jean-Marie Odin took his final vows as a priest of the Congregation of the Mission. He was answering the same call that St. Vincent de Paul, founder of the Vincentians, had urged on some of his priests and brothers who were preparing to depart France for the mission field of Asia more than a century and a half earlier: "Go gentlemen, in the name of the Lord. It is He who is sending you; it is For His services and His glory that you are undertaking this voyage and this mission. It will also be He who will lead you and who will assist and protect you."[23]

There is no way of knowing whether the new Father Odin had these words of St. Vincent de Paul on his mind and in his heart as he professed his final vows as a Vincentian, but most assuredly he embraced the spirit of them. Odin would come to rely heavily on such profound expressions of inspiration from the founder of the Congregation of the Mission as his life as a Vincentian missionary unfolded.

During his almost eighteen years stationed at the Barrens Seminary Odin immersed himself in virtually every aspect of Vincentian apostolic life. Writing to one of his sisters, likely Josephine, on July 24, 1825, he described his ongoing responsibilities as those of being a professor of theology at the seminary, pastor of the Barrens Colony parish church (St. Mary's of the Barrens), and spiritual director for a community of nuns recently established in the vicinity of the Barrens.[24] They would have been Sisters of Loreto who only recently had begun the foundation of their Bethlehem Convent in the area.

In the years following his ordination, Odin encountered new experiences in his life and career. He was named a professor of theology at the seminary right after he was ordained a priest. Thirteen months later, on June 5, 1824, he was tabbed as secretary to Father Rosati, rector of the seminary. Before the end of 1820s, Odin himself would assume the duties of heading up the seminary. Meanwhile, on March 25, 1824, Rosati was consecrated coadjutor bishop of New Orleans (formerly the Diocese of Louisiana and the Floridas), intensifying the demands on Odin in terms of time and effort once he was appointed Rosati's secretary at the Barrens Seminary in June.

The situation regarding Rosati's being named coadjutor bishop of New Orleans was complicated. The Vatican planned to divide the former Diocese of Louisiana and the Floridas, carving from it the new bishoprics of New Orleans and St. Louis. Bishop DuBourg was to be given first choice as to whether he would assume episcopal authority over New Orleans or St. Louis. Rosati agreed to accept the second proffered miter. DuBourg, as expected, chose New Orleans with Rosati his coadjutor. But Rosati knew that he would be named the first bishop of St. Louis as soon as that diocese was erected. This arrangement involved Jean-Marie Odin because for a while Rosati continued as rector of the Barrens Seminary and resided there, while at the same time he held the episcopal office of coadjutor bishop of New Orleans under Bishop DuBourg. And while Rosati did not succeed Bishop DuBourg at New Orleans after the latter's sudden and unexpected resignation on June 26, 1826, just a few months later, on March 20, 1827, he was named the first bishop of St. Louis. After his consecration as bishop of St. Louis, Rosati moved his residence to his episcopal see city, leaving Odin in effect to act as the administrator of the Barrens Seminary.

In the very year of his ordination to the priesthood Odin began in earnest his labors as a frontier missionary. His enthusiasm for catechizing and bringing the sacraments to Catholic populations scattered throughout Missouri, Arkansas, and Louisiana—as well as much of Texas later—became legendary and can be better appreciated in the context of coming to some understanding about his immersion in Vincentian priestly formation.

The religious revival in France that matured under the watchful and prayerful guidance of St. Vincent de Paul and his Congregation of the Mission developed as integral to the lifeblood of a post-Reformation Roman Catholic renewal that spread throughout much of western and central Europe during the sixteenth and seventeenth centuries. This rebirth was sustained by several generations of Catholic reform that included the efforts of the Spanish mystics St. Teresa of Avila; St. John of the Cross; Francisco de Osuna; Luis of Granada; the founder of the Society of Jesus, St. Ignatius of Loyola; as well as the labors St. Philip Neri and his Congregation of the Oratory; Pierre Cardinal Berulle and his French Oratorians; St. Jean Eudes and his order of Jesus and Mary; and Jean-Jacques Olier and his Sulpicians. More than is popularly realized, the writings of the Spanish mystics and Luis of Granada immeasurably influenced the Catholic religious revival beyond the territorial boundaries of Spain. This was especially true regarding their impact on the spiritual formation of the Vincentians. Luis of Granada helped to sow the seeds of religious enthusiasm in the heart and soul of St. Vincent de Paul. So also did that Spaniard, two centuries after St. Vincent had founded the Congregation of the Mission in 1625, make an impression on the spiritual growth of Jean-Marie Odin.

Luis of Sarria, who was a contemporary of St. Teresa of Avila, living from 1504 to 1588, commonly used the name Luis of Granada in his writings. He entered the Dominican Order of Preachers at the age of twenty-two, and by the time he had reached his mid-fifties he had earned a reputation for being one of Spain's most spiritually profound authors. Luis of Granada focused on mental prayer as the base for the interior life. Widely sought as a preacher of missions, he also was a popular director of retreats.

Just before he departed Spain for Portugal, where he would spend the final three decades of his life, Luis of Granada published in 1554 his most profound and lasting work, *Libro de oracóin y meditación (Book on Prayer and Meditation)*. His almost equally famous *Guia de pecadores (Guide for Sinners)* appeared in 1556–57.[25] As Vincentian formation and spirituality matured, it reflected a strong inheritance from Granada's concentration on mental prayer and the interior life, the preaching of missions, and the directing of retreats. Jean-Marie

Odin, who had discovered the works of Luis of Granada at St. Irenaeus grand seminaire even before he became a Vincentian in America, found Granada to be such a major influence on his own religious life that he recommended the Spanish Dominican's books to one of his sisters who was anticipating becoming a nun.

Like the Sulpicians, the Vincentians are secular priests and brothers forming a society of common life. Vincentians, however, do take four simple vows: those of poverty, chastity, obedience, and stability. "We know that our works are worthless if they are not living and animated by God's will," Vincent de Paul had argued.[26] This insistence on adherence to God's will, which compelled the priest or brother to seek the divine will for himself by cooperating with divine grace and developing a strong internal life built on mental prayer, emerged as the central focus of Vincentian spirituality and formation.

Recently Father Rybolt analyzed Vincentian and Sulpician spirituality and formation, as Jean-Marie Odin would have absorbed them at St. Irenaeus grand seminaire and the Barrens Seminary, in this manner:

> Despite many similarities the Vincentian and the Sulpician approaches to priestly formation had noticeable differences. The Sulpicians had seminary work as their sole apostolate, while the Vincentians were also involved in missions and to a higher degree in the United States in parishes. In the earlier period, as they had in France, the Vincentians tended to conduct seminaries jointly with mission houses. In some of these the students would go on missions with the faculty. The Sulpicians, on the other hand, rarely had apostolic experiences for their students but tended to have a stronger intellectual tradition. Sulpician formation also called for the directors and faculty to live together with the seminarians in a one-to-one approach. It has been said, with a great deal of exaggeration, that the Vincentian formation produced pastors, while Sulpician formation produced bishops. Also, in contrast with the Sulpicians, the European Vincentians in the United States Americanized more rapidly, and their personnel became native much earlier.[27]

As he immersed himself in his labors as a frontier missionary, a vocation which eventually took the French "Son of St. Vincent" from the Mississippi River Valley to the lower Rio Grande Valley of Texas, Father Jean-Marie Odin, was steadily to mature in his Vincentian formation and spirituality.

A Lifelong Friendship Established

In the late spring of 1823, the new Father Odin commenced his missionary rounds in the vicinity of the Barrens Seminary with another bright light of the Congregation of the Mission, John Timon. That Irish American, along with Odin, was to take his place in the story of Roman Catholicism in the United States as one of the church's outstanding personages. In the process of their laboring together, Odin and Timon grew to become steadfast friends and confreres.

James and Eleanor Leddy Timon, John's parents, emigrated from County Craven, Ireland, to the United States in 1796, where they first settled at Conewego Settlement near York, Pennsylvania. John was born there on February 12, 1797. Not long thereafter, in 1800, James Timon resettled his family at Baltimore, Maryland, the heart of Catholic life in early English America. For the next decade and a half the Timons lived a comfortable existence, enjoying the material fruits of James's success as a mercantile businessman. At the same time the Timons came to be viewed as a devout Catholic family. Eventually, though, the devastating economic depression that developed in the United States on the heels of the War of 1812, recorded in history as the "Panic of 1819," stagnated James Timon's merchandising enterprise. As a result, the Timons were forced to depart Baltimore in search of a more stable business environment elsewhere. As with so many others, they ventured westward.[28]

Following a brief stay in Pittsburgh, James, Eleanor, and their family traveled beyond the Ohio River finally to St. Louis on the Mississippi River. Even at that increasingly significant town situated on the west bank of the Great River, the Timons found themselves unable to outdistance the depression. While James and Eleanor labored determinedly to adjust to their altered financial and social circumstances, John seems to have concluded that he had a religious vocation. On his twenty-fifth birthday, February 12, 1822, and with his parents' blessing, he moved into the episcopal residence of Bishop DuBourg. Under the watchful eye of DuBourg John began his study and training for the priesthood.[29]

Father Ralph Bayard, a preeminent historian of the Vincentians in the 1940s, described John Timon's sojourn from his family home at St. Louis to the bishop's quarters and Timon's connection with DuBourg's nearby St. Louis academy with these words: "Three or four months before he wrote to Rosati [John Timon would correspond with Father Rosati about his possible priestly vocation in midsummer], John had left the family hearth with the blessings of James and Eleanor, February 12, his twenty-fifth birthday. Quartered in the *eveche,* the episcopal "mansion," he had become associated with the small college under DuBourg's auspices nearby. Such a term of postulancy, spent in study and teaching, the prelate had wisely decided, would ensure Timon's adjustment to life in the seminary. From the St. Louis academy Timon transferred on 19 July 1822 to St. Mary of the Barrens Seminary."[30]

John Timon had arrived at the Barrens Seminary a month and a half before Jean-Marie Odin. However, even though Timon was three years older than Odin and predated the Frenchman at the seminary, Jean-Marie was further along in his studies for the priesthood than was John. From their initial meeting at the seminary in the late summer of 1822, Odin and Timon struck up a strong comradeship, one that endured until Timon passed away forty-five years later while serving as the first bishop of Buffalo, New York.

Decades after their first meeting, while Timon was the ordinary of Buffalo in the 1860s, he was to write of his confrere as a priest in those early years at the Barrens Seminary:

> The few priests at the seminary were gradually dispersed. The bishop was forced often to be absent. For a considerable time Odin was left as the sole priest in the seminary. He had to attend to the duties of the provisional superior, parish priest, confessor of the brothers, students, collegians, and Loretto nuns, and at the same time direct the general course of teaching. Often, on Saturdays, he would be out until ten at night on sick calls; and when he came home would find students and brothers waiting to go to confession and occupying him a great part of what remained of the night. He went through these excessive labors with a peace and joy of holy zeal which alone can account for not having entirely lost his health. He suffered, however, much, and his headaches, migraines, would often for days be the penalty for having taxed his body and mind so much.[31]

Notwithstanding the dedication and holy zeal that he exhibited in carrying out those many duties assigned to him in his capacity as a priest at the Barrens, it was as a frontier missionary that Father Jean-Marie Odin would most visibly live out his clerical vocation. For almost four decades following his ordination, the French churchman was to cover thousands of miles in all kinds of weather, via horseback, on foot, riding in wagons, or using any other mode of transportation available. In the course of his journeys he forged rivers, creeks, lakes, and other bodies of water by whatever means he might (Odin could barely swim) to labor among Catholics. Sometimes he even helped Protestants and nonbelievers. That quest carried him from Missouri and its surrounding regions to Texas. In his final years, he would maintain his missionary spirit while serving as the second archbishop of New Orleans.

3

Missouri and Arkansas

A Prelude to Texas

ODIN'S YEARNING FOR MISSIONARY ADVENTURES was soon to be fulfilled after his ordination. With Timon accompanying him whenever possible, Odin plunged into a regular schedule of visiting the Catholics living in and around the vicinity of the Barrens Seminary. His earliest rounds were made to the small settlements of Apple Creek—situated south of the Barrens Colony—Silverlake, and Crosstown.[1] Foremost on Odin's agenda was to bring to those Catholics, many of whom had not seen a priest for years, the sacraments and religious instruction. As the young cleric's missioning horizons broadened, he began to labor within a wider boundary, to encompass not only towns and other settlements, but to include any locale where a respectable site could be found for setting up a temporary altar to celebrate Holy Mass.

On occasion, a home, a store, or some other building was used. Through this effort Odin was able to bring to the people the life of the Catholic Church, reinforcing or sometimes introducing Catholic teaching and the universal sacramental system as well as Catholic traditions and customs. In so laboring, the young French priest regularized marriages for some of the Catholics he encountered, baptized, and brought all of the comforts of the faith. Odin made his rounds every Thursday; when possible Timon joined him. Together they ventured outward from the seminary in a circle "to a distance of fifteen or twenty miles."[2] At Apple Creek the two Vincentians first erected a station for Mass. Soon, however, they transferred that Mass station to a site upon which St. Joseph's Church would be built. In his 1861 *Barrens Memoir* Timon remembered that church: "A pretty hog pen was the first church: the missionaries dug out the dung, cleaned as well as possible the wretched cabin, adorned it with green branches, built a rustic altar, which was for its beauty the wonder of the neighborhood, celebrated Mass, heard confessions, etc."[3]

Another significant aspect of Odin's and Timon's early life as missionaries appeared in Timon's *Barrens Memoir*. Timon wrote that oftentimes their evangelizing jaunts proved to be more challenging than might have been expected, because regions were overwhelmingly Protestant and "prejudices were very strong against Catholics."[4] As Catholic immigration from Europe into the United States swelled following the War of 1812, nativism, a crusade to reinforce a Caucasian Protestant ideological base throughout all aspects of American life—religious, social, educational, cultural, political, and so forth—began to flourish. Nativism had matured with its origins set deep in English American colonial history. At the same time it came to exist as central to certain preconceived Protestant notions of the American Revolution and the forming of the US republic, a patriotic story which excluded Catholics. Visible throughout US history, a strongly anti-Catholic nativism reached its apex in the mid-nineteenth century.

From the Atlantic coastal region inland, nativism had advanced westward as characteristic of the non-Catholic migration of people that moved beyond the Trans-Appalachian West and crossed the Mississippi River into territories such as Missouri. Timon observed that many of the nativists "were far less Protestants than haters of the Pope and Papists."[5] During his first month at the Barrens Seminary Odin—confronting nativism head on—developed a great interest in laboring among Protestants and non-believers in order to bring them to a more friendly understanding of Catholics if not the Catholic religion itself.

At the same time Odin grew increasingly appreciative of Timon's ability to counter attacks against Catholicism, especially those by Protestant ministers. In early 1824, Odin wrote to Father Cholleton back at Lyon, exclaiming that: "A Methodist minister wished to profit from the absence of monsignor [he was referring to Rosati who was away from the seminary at the time] by entering into controversy. However, he attacked only one member of our congregation, but the letters were made known to us. One of our theologians, a young American [Timon], a novice in our congregation, full of zeal and knowledge, began a public series of controversial lectures; he has already preached several times with success. Protestants, non-believers, Methodist ministers, etc. . . . All attend assiduously, listen to him with pleasure, and what is the best, do not retort anything. On all sides one speaks of these instructions; we hope they will not be fruitless."[6]

Into Arkansas

The year 1824 marked the beginning of the new Father Odin's more extended missioning ventures, featuring longer and more demanding excursions away from the Barrens Seminary. The most exacting of those adventures, again taken with Timon, was launched during the vacation period at the seminary toward the end of summer. It sent the two evangelizers south past New Madrid, Missouri, deep into Arkansas, to Arkansas Post. It was a trip of several hundred miles that Timon later in his *Barrens Memoir* described as "a continual mission among a population that had never seen a priest."[7]

The journey unfolded in an environment of complicated historical circumstances. The year 1824 was a time when historical complexities had come together to focus the Catholic Church on that region where just a few decades earlier there existed a territorial confluence of the empires of Spain, France, and England. On February 22, 1819, the American government and the court of King Fernando VII of Spain (1814–33) finalized the Adams-Onis Treaty. That pact, often referred to as the Transcontinental Treaty, defined the boundaries of the two nations from Louisiana to the Pacific Coast. The agreement recognized that the vast areas existing south of the pact's line of demarcation had historically evolved as a part of New Spain and that Spain made no territorial demands north of those agreed-upon confines from the Gulf of Mexico along the Sabine River to the Red River and then veering due west to the one-hundredth meridian. The initial leg of the treaty line outlined the western extension of the present-day state of Louisiana and the southern perimeter of the area that would emerge as Oklahoma. Cutting a path north once again along the meridian to the forty-second parallel, the boundary line then turned westward and extended all the way to the Pacific Coast. According to the Transcontinental Treaty, in that same year of 1819, Arkansas was made a territory of the United States.[8] Later, setting aside the agreement, the United States would forcibly take lands from Mexico that were located south of the Adams-Onis line of demarcation in the Mexican-American War (1846–48), eventually carving out Texas and the future states of New Mexico, Arizona, Colorado, Utah, Nevada, and California.

That whole western region was important to the Catholic Church essentially because it was an expansive area where Catholicism needed to be strengthened among a small and scattered Hispanic population that had long been residing on the land south of the line, as well as Irish, German, French, Polish, Wend, Czech, and other nationalities who were nineteenth-century immigrants. As we have seen, Odin had begun to experience firsthand the impact of European immigration on the Protestant character of various sections of the Trans-Mississippi West. A visible number of those newcomers were, like Odin himself, Roman Catholics and non-Anglo, and they were increasingly in need of priests.

Odin's and Timon's 1824 tour south from the Barrens Seminary came as a response by Bishop Rosati, whom it will be remembered had recently been consecrated coadjutor bishop to DuBourg, to a group of Catholics in Arkansas Post who in the early summer of that year had asked him to send them priests. Arkansas Post survived as the oldest settlement in Arkansas Territory. The explorer Henri de Tonti, a Sicilian officer who had been second in command to the French entrepreneur Rene Robert Cavalier, Sieur de La Salle during La Salle's 1682 explorations down the Mississippi River to its mouth, established a colony at Arkansas Post in 1686.[9] Under de Tonti and the French, Arkansas Post grew as a settlement among the Quapaw people a few miles up the Arkansas River to the west beyond the Mississippi. As the years passed, de Tonti's colony matured as a center of Roman Catholic missionary efforts in the lower Arkansas vicinity. The Odin-Timon jaunt into Arkansas, however, was the first serious attempt at Catholic missioning in lower Arkansas since that land had come into the possession of United States with the Louisiana Purchase in 1803.[10] Although he had no way of realizing it at the time, for Odin in particular, the Arkansas expedition would prove to be a kind of training ground for his later labors in Texas as a missionary and bishop from 1840 through early 1861.

They made their way on horseback south to Apple Creek, Cape Girardeau, and on to New Madrid where they offered a mission "which was long remembered." Striking out from New Madrid on a direct but extremely hazardous path to Little Rock in the heart of central Arkansas Territory, the two missionaries were forced to negotiate their way over a dangerous swampy terrain without the guide they had hired. He had determined that the venture appeared too menacing and left the priest and seminarian to return to his home. Following the desertion of their guide, Odin and Timon crossed the swamp, where a dry spot to lie down could not be found and potable water could not be obtained.[11]

Little Rock had been founded in 1821 as the second capital of Arkansas Territory a mere three years prior to the visit of Odin and Timon. That frontier village, where violence, drunkenness, and lawlessness abounded as a normal way of life, in 1824 contained approximately forty families. Odin and Timon were surprised but pleased to find a number of Catholics among the inhabitants of the settlement.[12]

After spending a while serving the Catholics of Little Rock, it was downriver on the Arkansas to Arkansas Post for the two evangelizers. But several stops along the way proved to be in order. One of the most impressive receptions given to the two sons of St. Vincent was that of Quapaw Chief Saracen. He received the two "blackrobes" in a kindly manner and allowed them to erect a temporary altar in front of his wigwam, where Father Odin celebrated Mass. Saracen enthusiastically urged his people to attend the Mass. Timon preached, explaining Catholic doctrine in his usual profound way. The two Vincentians left the village of the Quapaw having made many friends there and having established a potential base for future Catholic missioning.

With their journey completed a few days later at Arkansas Post, Odin and Timon made their way back to Missouri and the Barrens Seminary, where they resumed the duties that had occupied them prior to their vacation time. Timon, in his *Barrens Memoir* decades later, simply recorded that "after this laborious mission the two Lazarists returned to teach at the college of the Barrens, but continuing on vacation days their excursions for twenty miles around." To the present day, that trip of Odin and Timon is recalled vividly in the annals of the Vincentian narrative in America.[13]

The Maturing of a Missionary

As he immersed himself in his priestly life following the Arkansas venture, Jean-Marie Odin turned his focus increasingly to his labors at the seminary and missioning in the surrounding vicinity. So beloved was Odin to become on the frontier by those among whom he worked that one biographer of the Catholic bishops in the America in the nineteenth century wrote the following about him in 1872, two years after Odin's death: "The name of Odin is destined to fill an honored place in the Catholic history of the United States; a name worthy of being inscribed in our annals with Marquette and Jogues; a name ever to be associated with the recital of heroic deeds of missionary life and labor.[14]

By the latter 1820s, Odin had already established the practice of writing frequent and detailed letters to persons and organizations close to him and his work. From that correspondence can be gleaned a wealth of information not only about Odin and his legacy to the church in the United States but developments and Odin's interpretations of them that offer his readers a clearer picture of the story of the Congregation of the Mission and their presence in the United States during the decades of the mid-nineteenth century.

Some indications as to how he had been living and what his experiences had been since his ordination as a priest are contained in a lengthy letter that he wrote to his parents on January 14, 1828. After complaining to them that he was concerned because "it has been a long time since I have received a letter from you," he described his situation: "The seminary of the Barrens is still my place of residence. At this moment I find myself entirely in charge of the direction of this house. Bishop Rosati almost always is on a trip visiting the immense diocese confined to his care. The burden that his absence imposes upon me is very heavy for my weak shoulders." Jean-Marie emphasized to his *mere* and *pere* the good that Bishop Rosati accomplished. He also stressed the need for all of the missionaries to evangelize and proselytize to not only the area's Catholics but also non-Catholics, the unbaptized, and the indigenous. "The difficulties and obstacles that must be surmounted are, no doubt, very great, but the small successes for God deign to reward us," Odin exclaimed to his parents. And then the French priest revealed to his parents his own feeling that "our holy religion is respected and loved by those who are fortunate enough to encounter it."[15]

In that letter Odin went on to describe much about the make-up of the personnel at the Barrens. There were, he explained, three newly ordained young priests who helped in teaching and in the ministry. The seminary enjoyed an enrollment of twenty, and twenty-seven "scholars" had matriculated to the lay college attached to the seminary. In addition, eight lay brothers and eighteen "people of color" (slaves) worked the property. Jean-Marie finished his letter to his parents with a few private remarks about the growth of the Catholic Church on the American frontier. He directed his comments particularly to the dedicated labors of the Jesuits among the Osage families, bands, and tribes. But he also reflected about the endeavors of other religious communities such as the Redemptorists; the building of a new convent at St. Louis; and the steady support that the Propagation de la Foi provided to the missionaries.[16]

The evangelizing jaunts on Thursdays and during vacation periods at the seminary continued well into the 1830s, with Odin by then—as he had said he wanted to—regularly catechizing among not only the Catholics in the vicinity but also reaching out to Protestants and the indigenous peoples. Meanwhile, on September 23, 1826, John Timon had been ordained a priest.[17]

During those years of the latter 1820s and early 1830s, Jean-Marie Odin was maturing in his priestly character. His spiritual and intellectual development would serve him well in his future years as a missionary from Missouri to Texas. Earlier, as a seminarian, he had established a reputation for being a serious student of philosophy. Odin even assumed responsibility for instructing his Irish American friend John Timon in that discipline as the latter progressed through his studies at the Barrens Seminary. With the passage of time, Odin intellectually advanced in his ability to teach philosophy and theology and surfaced as the most prominent young theologian at the Barrens Seminary.[18]

In those early years Odin also was already earning a reputation as a disciplined priest, one who appreciated the importance of discipline in life, both on the spiritual-intellectual level as well as from a practical perspective. That distinction for being well ordered in his thinking, faithful to his spiritual exercises, and focused in his personal behavior, was to follow Odin for the remainder of his life. Recently it was remembered that during his tenure as archbishop of New Orleans in the 1860s, "Odin was remarkable as a disciplinarian."[19] He demanded much from himself as a priest, sensitive and careful always to follow church teaching and tradition.

Odin expected no less a fervid commitment from the clerics laboring with him on the frontier. Most often, however, his dealings with his *confreres* were marked by heartfelt encouragement. For example, just two months after Timon had been ordained a priest and subsequently stationed at St. Louis, Odin responded to his colleague's fears that he was unworthy to be an apostle by writing to his friend and urging him to "Banish entirely this spirit of anxiety that is always disquieting you. It seems to me that you are too apprehensive in the exercise of your ministry; confidence in God is the great consolation of Christianity."[20] In that instance Odin's Vincentian spirituality shone forth brightly. Such advice was exactly the kind that Saint Vincent de Paul had offered his priests and brothers of the Congregation of the Mission back in the seventeenth century.

But Odin's service as a priest-missionary on the frontier aggravated some of the personal challenges that consistently plagued him in his evangelizing. Most noticeable was his suffering from devastating migraine headaches that would incapacitate him for days at a time. He also struggled to learn the English language. At the same time, Odin was forced to confront the reality of slavery existing throughout many parts of the United States. That institution and the human suppression that it represented remained repugnant to Odin throughout his decades of labors in Missouri, Arkansas, Texas, and Louisiana. This was a period of time that extended five years beyond the abolition of slavery in America and its territories by the thirteenth amendment to the US Constitution, ratified in December 1865.

Regarding his migraine headaches, they continued with apparent increasing intensity. Odin began to keep a daily diary of his travels as he departed Perryville for Texas in early May of the year 1840, a journal in which he made entries for several years. Therein he carefully recorded the facts of those migraine headaches, their frequency and intensity as well as in what manner and for how long they incapacitated him. It might be, thus, that a reader of Odin's diary would simply be more aware of the migraines than would be anyone looking at his life before the journal appeared, before Odin's venture to Texas.

Like most missionaries from Europe to the Americas, especially areas that formed or were to form parts of the United States, Jean-Marie Odin had to learn the language, or languages, of the dominant culture, or cultures, of his area of missioning.[21] He knew well, even before he departed his native France, that at the Barrens Seminary he would be required to learn English. Fluent in his native French and proficient in Latin, Odin found developing a command of English to be an enduring struggle. In his first year as a priest at the seminary, on August 2, 1823, he had written to Father Cholleton back at Lyon regarding his learning English, "I am scarcely able to stutter phrases, and that hurts me in attending the dying, hearing confessions, and preaching. It confuses and frightens me as well."[22]

Odin's inability to speak English in his missioning trips with Timon doubtless acted as one of the reasons why he celebrated the Masses while Timon, even after his ordination, usually preached. As Odin helped Timon with his study of philosophy, Timon coached his French confrere in learning the English language. Odin clearly made steady progress in gaining familiarity with English. Referring to his advance in understanding the language, Odin commented to Timon in his November 20, 1826, letter that "the bishop [Rosati] often has me preach [in English], and I am glad to learn the language."[23] Through his years of labor on the American frontier Odin grew able—though never eloquent—in English.

And finally, it is obvious that Odin remained saddened by the plight of the slaves in America long after his initial encounter with the "peculiar institution" upon his arrival at New Orleans in July 1822. In his very same November 20, 1826, letter to Father Timon at St. Louis, Odin reiterated his relentless support for improving the condition of the slaves, and free Negroes as well, lamenting: "I plan to speak to Monsignor [Bishop Rosati] on behalf of the Negroes whom you mentioned. You know the extreme circumstances in which they find themselves; they are unable prudently to improve their condition of increasing obligations [this referred likely to free Negroes], and I hope that Madame Duchesne [Odin probably here was referring to Blessed Philippine Duchesne of the religious order of the Sacred Heart at St. Louis] might be able to help them. If she is unable to relieve their poverty, then they might speak with Madame Eugenie, who appears able to help."[24] Jean-Marie Odin's view of slavery as a loathsome and dark aspect of US history likely influenced Father John Timon's perceptions regarding that subject. Timon, as first bishop of Buffalo, New York, two decades later, emerged as one of the US episcopacy's most outspoken critics of slavery.

Those years of the latter 1820s and early 1830s featuring his maturation as a Catholic missionary in Missouri and Arkansas, with occasional treks into Illinois, were ones that not only prepared Father Odin for his later heroic labors in Texas, but they covered a period in which his vocation as a Vincentian in America noticeably broadened and intensified.

4

Odin and the Emerging American Vincentian Presence

T HE 1830s IN THE NARRATIVE OF THE VINCENTIANS in America are seen
as a memorable decade. Along with the growth of the Vincentian presence in the United States and the maturation of the Congregation of the
Mission to the status of becoming a notable Catholic religious community
in the nation during that ten-year period, Jean-Marie Odin was becoming
more prominent among Catholic churchmen of the country. He was also being
immersed in frontier evangelistic life in a manner that was to prove invaluable
to him a decade later when he was destined to play his greatest role as a Catholic missionary in Texas.

Before that period had passed from the scene, the American Vincentians
had witnessed their seminary at the Barrens, by then renamed St. Mary of the
Barrens, developing into the foremost such institution west of the Appalachian
Mountains. Each new year brought with it a wider variety—in terms of ethnicity, family background, and socio-economic status—of young men arriving at
the seminary and the lay college attached to it. At the same time additional
parishes were being established and a greater number of missions preached up
and down the Mississippi Valley. The Vincentian apostolate along the frontier
was growing rapidly. By the end of the 1830s the vast territory of Texas, situated hundreds of miles to the south of Perryville and the seminary, would be
given to the Sons of St. Vincent as a part of their mission. Odin would be
destined to head up that venture. Ultimately devoting more than twenty years
of his life to Texas, he was to lay the foundation for the future building of the
Catholic Church in that vast land following the secularization of the Franciscan missions.

In the meantime, changes in the international ecclesiastical leadership of
the Congregation of the Mission, commencing in 1829, significantly impacted
Vincentian operations in America. A recent study of the Congregation of the
Mission in the United States described those modifications thusly:

When France finally ended its suppression of the Congregation of the Mission, or the Vincentians, the community held a General Assembly in 1829 and elected Father [Dominique] Salhorgne as Superior General. Though the parishioners as such were generally unaffected by this, the Vincentians in America were no longer ultimately subject to the Vicar General in Rome, Father [Francesco Antonio] Baccari, but to the Superior General, Father Salhorgne, in Paris. Once again, Bishop Rosati repeated his plea for an older and experienced priest to succeed him as superior at the Barrens in order to give him [Rosati] more time and freedom to exercise his duties as bishop. Father Salhorgne fulfilled this long-desired wish of the bishop in 1830 when he sent Father [John Baptiste] Tornatore to be the superior at the Barrens.[1]

Odin, having barely reached his thirtieth birthday and at the time serving as president of the lay college attached to the seminary, found himself in a difficult position after Tornatore's arrival. Tornatore, though a scholarly and deeply spiritual priest, proved to be an extremely rigid disciplinarian. As a result, many of the Vincentians at the seminary came to resent him.[2]

The problems that grew concomitantly with this situation were exacerbated, because, as with other communities throughout the United States, men of varying temperaments made up the population of St. Mary of the Barrens. A few of them complained about the relatively primitive living conditions at the seminary and college, grumbling especially about the extremes in weather that Missouri frequently experienced. Some of those Vincentians, especially the Americans, voiced strong opposition to laboring alongside slaves. Finally, a few questioned the nature of the Vincentian mission in the United States as carried out under Father Tornatore.[3]

Through all of that, Jean-Marie Odin attempted to foster peace and tranquility where possible among the Vincentians, seminarians, and students at the lay college. During his tenure as president of the college Odin himself seems to have gotten along well with Father Tornatore. This may have been in part due to Odin's characteristic desire to show enthusiasm for his brother Vincentians' spiritual growth—to elevate personal views and attitudes to a more supernatural level among all of them.

A Vincentian Bishop at New Orleans and Odin's Reaction

The decade of the thirties opened happily for Odin when he traveled south from Perryville to New Orleans to attend the episcopal ordination of his fellow Vincentian Father Leo Raymond DeNeckere, as bishop of New Orleans. In that see city's beautiful Saint Louis Cathedral on June 24, 1830, Bishop Rosati, assisted by Bishop Michael Portier of Mobile, Alabama, and Vicar General Benoit Richard, consecrated DeNeckere.[4]

The new prelate had been hesitant to accept the miter of New Orleans, mainly because of his weak physical constitution. As an example of this, his ordination for the see originally had been scheduled for May 16 but was delayed until June 24 because in mid-May DeNeckere was suffering from an aneurism in his throat, which caused agonizing episodes of spitting up blood.[5]

Fathers Timon and Odin had been among the several Vincentians invited to the ordination. DeNeckere had consulted Timon, and probably Odin also, about whether or not he should accept the appointment to New Orleans. Timon had urged his Belgian-born fellow Vincentian to return to the Vatican the papal bull naming him bishop of New Orleans, an act symbolizing a refusal. Timon feared that the overbearing responsibilities and demanding workload that were bound to accompany an acceptance of the New Orleans miter would prove dangerously fatiguing for his confrere.

Odin, however, while also concerned about DeNeckere's health, was elated with his elevation to the episcopacy. Back in the spring of 1828, DeNeckere had been named coadjutor bishop to Rosati at St. Louis; and Odin had reacted to the news enthusiastically. At the time of the announcement, from St. Genevieve, Missouri, Odin had written to Timon "the letter from our bishop [Rosati] brings me the good news that Father DeNeckere is named his coadjutor."[6] Odin was not insensitive regarding the state of DeNeckere's health. Rather, the overriding consideration in the heart and mind of the missionary from France seems to have been that he believed DeNeckere's elevation to the see of New Orleans would be excellent for the Catholics of Louisiana. Odin consistently throughout his life, even when his decisions were unpopular, took positions that to him appeared, above all else, most supportive of religion.

Attending the consecration proved to be a joy for Odin also because the occasion served as a reunion that brought together priests from his native Archdiocese of Lyon back in France as well as a number of his fellow Vincentians. Bishop Portier, the assisting prelate at DeNeckere's ordination, like Odin, was from the Archdiocese of Lyon. Portier, who had only become bishop of Mobile a year earlier, on May 15, 1829, was born on September 7, 1795, in Montbrison, France, not many miles from Odin's boyhood home at Hauteville.[7] Father Antoine Blanc also attended the consecration.

A Grave Family Matter: The Death of his Father

After returning to Perryville from DeNeckere's ordination, Odin plunged into the mountain of work that awaited him. As president of the lay college he was well aware that among the American Vincentians opposition to the institution's existence was mounting. Financial strain on the Vincentians had caused discussions to surface in their community centered on the cost of their operation at Perryville. Some of the Vincentians had come to believe that closing the lay college was one way of cutting expenses. Making a strong case for shutting down the college from another perspective, some of the Sons of St. Vincent felt that using seminarians to teach at the lay college violated the apostolic vision of the Congregation of the Mission. While Odin was to keep the college in operation, he soon came to doubt the wisdom of its remaining open. The Frenchman began to realize that the Congregation of the Mission faced a decision on the matter of the college.

In the midst of those developments at Perryville, Odin received news from home that was difficult to bear. His dear *pere* had died. Jean Odin died in late September 1832, but the letter from the Odin family to Jean-Marie announcing the passing of Jean only reached the son on January 27, 1833. On one occasion not long before the arrival of those sad tidings from home, Jean-Marie had written to his parents, proclaiming his love for them and thanking them for all of the affection and kindness they had shown him throughout his life as a missionary. His *mere* and *pere* in the past had regularly sent him clothing and money. In that earlier missive to his parents Odin had urged them "not to spend any more money for me and not to send me anything more."[8] He felt that his parents were sacrificing too much for him.

But on January 28, 1833, a different kind of letter from son and brother to mother and siblings was needed. So, from St. Mary of the Barrens Seminary, Jean-Marie wrote. In one notable paragraph of that message he showed emotion and belief based on both human sorrow over the demise of his father and Christian hope in the Resurrection of Christ and the hope of in the future meeting his father as a citizen of heaven. Jean-Marie's words were those of a son and a priest: "Yesterday I received your letter of last September 28. The death of my father has caused me to shed many tears. This sad news deeply grieves me; write me and tell me if he had the happiness of receiving the Last Sacraments. I shall not cease to pray for the peace of his soul. Oh! If we could all be reunited one day in the house of God!"[9]

Eastward to Baltimore: A Provincial Council

As was to be expected, Odin carried on his shoulders for a long time the weight of the loss of his father. For the missionary from France, though, apostolic beckoning always called. More than a thousand miles eastward across the Mississippi River, through Kentucky, over the Appalachian Mountains, and north through Virginia into Maryland, lay the city of Baltimore. There, in the fall of 1833, the hierarchy of the church convened at America's Second Provincial Council. Jean-Marie Odin was invited to the gathering as Bishop Rosati's theologian.[10]

By the early 1830s Odin's competence in the discipline of theology had matured to a point where Bishop Rosati felt confident in his capabilities. Thus as the prelate made his plans for the Baltimore council, it was only natural that he turn to Odin, his fellow Vincentian, to travel with him as his theologian. In his *Barrens Memoir* Timon recorded that "in September 1833, Fr. Odin, who had labored so much and who was so generally venerated, started for France."[11] The Vincentians at Perryville had decided to send Odin on to Europe following his attendance at the Baltimore council. Odin had not returned to his native land for a visit since leaving there for America more than eleven years earlier, and he was due some time with his family. Moreover, the US Vincentians felt that while in Europe Odin could carry out business for the Congregation of the Mission in the United States. They hoped also that the adventure might have the effect of improving Odin's health by offering him some relief from the taxing schedule to which he had become attached over the past several years on the frontier.

Along part of the way to Baltimore Odin traveled in the company of the Jesuit missionary Father Peter De Smet. The Jesuit likely joined Odin at St. Louis in September 1833. Jesuit records show that De Smet left St. Louis for the Baltimore council in late September 1833, and Vincentian archives reveal that Odin departed Missouri at the same time with De Smet.[12] Unquestionably along their way the two veteran missionaries shared many observations about building the faith on the fringes of the American continent civilized settlement.

De Smet and Odin had similar goals for their respective communities. Father de Smet, after delaying in Baltimore to find out whether the council fathers would assign the mission field of the indigenous peoples entirely to the Jesuits, planned to journey to Belgium. There he was scheduled to labor on behalf of his Missouri Jesuit brothers, working toward their being united with the Belgian province of the Society of Jesus.[13]

The Vincentians of Missouri, on the other hand, had instructed Odin to meet with the superiors of their community at the motherhouse in Paris, in part for the purpose of urging them to form a separate US province of the Congregation of the Mission. It was hoped that the US Vincentian province, if established, would be headquartered at St. Mary of the Barrens Seminary. Odin intended to recommend Father Timon to the Congregation of the Mission superiors as the best possible choice for visitor (superior) of their new American province. Odin also planned to petition the Vincentian officials at Paris to suppress the lay college attached to the seminary at the Barrens. The Frenchman intended to argue strongly that the lay college had proven to be a serious financial drain on the seminary while at the same time surviving as an inconsistency to the principal Vincentian apostolate.

On October 20 from Baltimore Odin wrote to Timon back at the seminary, offering his impressions of the nation's capital, Washington, DC; Georgetown College (America's first Roman Catholic college, founded in 1789); and his own arrival at the Baltimore council: "I returned yesterday evening from Washington City. I have been gratified to see the capital of the US, the capital is beautiful & the president's house handsome. Georgetown college [*sic*] is remarkable for size, location, and cleanliness. The fathers have received me with the greatest affability."[14]

Odin went on to comment to Timon that upon his return to Baltimore from Washington, DC, he had met Father Auguste Jeanjean, a priest whom both the Vincentians had known back in New Orleans. Everybody "expected to salute Mr. Jeanjean Bp. [Bishop] of the indians, but we have been disappointed," Odin reflected.[15] The background to Odin's observation concerned the fact that Bishop DeNeckere, whose consecration as bishop of New Orleans Odin had attended less than three and a half years earlier, had died the previous month. On September 5, 1833, he had fallen victim to yellow fever while ministering to those persons of New Orleans who had contracted the disease. It is not certain that Odin, at the time of his meeting with Father Jeanjean at Baltimore, knew of DeNeckere's death. Possibly even Jeanjean himself was unaware that his bishop had died. Overland communication was slow, with letters regularly taking weeks to arrive at their destination. But Odin had heard of the possibility that the Holy See would name Jeanjean to a special episcopal jurisdiction, perhaps a vicariate apostolic, with hierarchical authority over the mission field of the indigenous peoples populating the vast territory of the western reaches of North America. This would explain Odin's remark about Jeanjean being bishop of the Indians.

Carrying the story further, in 1834 Pope Gregory XVI did offer Father Jeanjean the miter of New Orleans, but Jeanjean refused the proffer and instead went to Cincinnati. Following those developments, on June 19, 1835, the Holy See announced that Odin's close friend Father Antoine Blanc was to be the new bishop of New Orleans. Blanc's consecration took place on November 22, 1835, in Saint Louis Cathedral at New Orleans with Bishop Rosati presiding and Bishops Portier as well as Jean Baptiste Purcell (bishop of Cincinnati) assisting.

Odin ended his comments to Timon about Father Jeanjean by stressing that the New Orleans churchman planned to stop by St. Mary's of the Barrens Seminary on his way back to the Bayou City from Baltimore. Turning to the major reason for his trip to Baltimore, Odin went on to highlight for Timon, "The council will open in a few moments. We do not know as yet what will be discussed, though it appears that the main points will regard the appointment of bishops, the limits of dioceses, etc."[16]

Odin finished his letter to Timon with a few comments explaining that he (Odin) had visited Timon's sister and her family in Baltimore, that he planned to visit them the following day, and that Odin was sending salutations to his fellow Vincentians at St. Mary of the Barrens. Mirroring the mutual respect and friendship that had grown between the two confreres over the past dozen years, Jean-Marie signed his missive "Your obt. [obedient] servt. [servant] and affectionate friend."[17]

Homeward Bound to France

With the close of the Baltimore Council, Odin continued on to Europe, his immediate destination being his beloved homeland, France. He arrived at Paris in late December 1833. From the French capital on December 30 Odin penned another letter to Father Timon back at Perryville. Odin was impressed with the reactions of so many French Catholics to reported miraculous apparitions of the Blessed Virgin Mary in Paris. In that same epistle to Timon, the Frenchman lamented the liberal assaults that he saw being made on the church in his native land.[18]

Following his brief stay in Paris, Odin happily turned his route eastward toward his hometown of Hauteville, anticipating the long-awaited reunion with his family that for some time had been above everything else on his mind and in his heart. There is no extant record of the substance of his visit home, but historical imagination might rightly come into play at this juncture of our narrative. It can safely be assumed that Jean-Marie cherished his brief visit with his mother, brothers and sisters, other relatives, and friends. He must have celebrated Holy Mass often at St. Martin d'Ambierle Church, the parish of his youth. Those occasions would have marked the first times that his *mere*, siblings, and other people he knew in Hauteville would have had opportunities to assist at any of Jean-Marie's masses. He likely offered the masses for them, and most especially for the repose of the soul of his father. What could Odin's thoughts and feelings have been as he walked around his family property— especially the acreage where he had labored as a shepherd in his youth—and into the village, meeting familiar faces from his younger days? How must he have felt when he visited the grave of his dear father so recently deceased? Answers to these and similar questions can probably only be answered in the context of the historical imagination.

Following his brief stopover at Hauteville, Odin journeyed eastward to Lyon for a return to St. Irenaeus Seminary and a visit with former professors. He was no longer the young subdeacon that they had dispatched to America but rather a veteran frontier missionary in his mid-thirties. Father Cholleton in particular was excited to greet their protégé.

Jean-Marie carried with him a testimonial letter to Cholleton from Bishop Rosati, a communication much appreciated at St. Irenaeus because it attested to Rosati's great admiration for Odin and the bishop of St. Louis's thankfulness that the *grand seminaire* had sent the missionary from France to the Vincentians at Perryville. Rosati wrote:

M. Odin has worked with untiring zeal and much success, not only in the education of our seminarians and the students at our school of *Les Barrens,* of which
he has been principal for a long time, but also in the ministry and conversion of
our separated brethren. He has accompanied me to Baltimore and was present at
our second provincial council in the capacity of theologian; there he merited and
obtained the esteem of everyone. He has been entrusted with carrying the acts
and decrees of our council to Rome in order to submit them to the judgment of
the Holy Father. Therefore, Sir M. Cholleton, as it is to you in particular that
I am obliged for having obtained this excellent subject and many others who
work with the same zeal for the salvation of souls, I am very happy to render
this testimony.[19]

Odin's pause at Lyon too was short-lived, especially given his charge from
the bishops of the United States to deliver the proceedings of the Second Provincial Council of Baltimore to Pope Gregory XVI at the Vatican. Nonetheless, during his brief visit to the grand seminaire he was able to inspire the
seminarians themselves to think about volunteering for the American mission
field. Also at this time Odin began establishing the groundwork for his return
to Lyon in a few months, at which time he planned to become engaged in
working for the cause of the Vincentians in America.

Efforts in Italy and Recruitment throughout Europe

All through 1834 and into early 1835 Odin traveled, mainly in Italy, first putting
into the hands of the pope the deliberations of the US bishops at Baltimore
and then seeking aid for his confreres in the United States. He journeyed from
Genoa to Rome, where in August 1834 he met with Pope Gregory XVI three
times and obtained the pontiff's approval of the acts and decrees of the Second
Baltimore Council. He received as well from the Holy Father financial and
spiritual support for the Vincentians in America.

At Rome he met with Cardinal Fesch regularly, the former Archbishop of
Lyon who by that time in his life was living in retirement. Fesch encouraged
Odin, to whom he had administered the Sacrament of Confirmation twenty
years earlier. Fesch also offered Odin prayers and financial help for the Vincentian apostolate in the United States. From the Eternal City Odin wrote to
Father Cholleton back at Lyon: "I am beginning to relax somewhat since my
arrival in Rome. Every moment has been employed in drawing up reports on
the state of the Church in America for the Holy See and for the Propaganda.
Now everything is almost completed. The Sacred Congregation of Propaganda
has approved the decrees of the Council of Baltimore and has found them to
be full of wisdom. It praises considerably the sound judgment and zeal of the
bishops. I have met with the Pope three times; he spoke to me a long time

about our America and wishes very much that we apply ourselves to the mission of the savages."[20]

The year 1835 saw Odin leave Italy and move about through various other nations of central and western Europe, recruiting for the Vincentians back at St. Mary of the Barrens and finally attending the general assembly of the Congregation of the Mission in Paris. At the Paris gathering Odin represented well his brother Vincentians back on the American frontier. His plea for the Congregation of the Mission to erect a separate American province was accepted. Following that decision, Odin urged the Vincentians at the Paris conclave to recommend John Timon for the position of visitor, or superior, of their American province. Before 1835 ended Timon was so named. He was to serve in that capacity until he became the first bishop of Buffalo, New York, in 1847.

Ironically, the meeting at Paris proved to be a disappointment to Odin when it came to dealing with the future of the lay college attached to the seminary at Perryville. The Frenchman originally favored closing the school, but for reasons that he never fully revealed, by the time of his arrival at Paris for the general assembly Odin had changed his mind on the matter. He had come to the conclusion that such an academy could exist as a visible aspect of the Vincentian apostolate. Part of that calling would be to educate Catholic Americans in a predominantly Protestant frontier environment. Still, the decision of the Congregation of the Mission at the time was to go ahead and cease operations at the institution. Jean-Marie then felt frustration that the college of which he had served as president at one time was to be closed. Later, after having returned to Perryville, Odin was happy to learn that the decision to close the college had been reversed at Paris, and the school was to remain open after all.

While still in Europe Odin recruited seminarians and priests from Poland, France, Spain, and Italy, while also garnering material and spiritual support for the Vincentian frontier in the Americas. By late 1835 he realized that it was time to return to the Barrens. Perhaps his greatest lament while traveling in Europe was that he received little correspondence from his brother Vincentians back in America. This vexation in spirit was visible in a letter that he penned from Italy to Father Timon on Christmas Eve 1834: "I feel very much afflicted to see that I am entirely forgotten by every one of you. I have written a great many letters to M—Rosati and to all and have received only a few lines that Mr. Tornatore wrote to me in May. To what must I ascribe that long silence, I cannot say."[21] Before closing his letter to Timon, Odin gave specific directions on how the Vincentians at the Barrens should prepare for the young clerics he had recruited on his trip.

It would be several more months after this letter to Timon that Odin actually departed France once again for America. But when he returned to Perryville, Odin did so with a reinvigorated missionary zeal. He expected to remain permanently at the Barrens, missioning as before in the surrounding vicinity, serving at the seminary, and heading up the lay college until it was closed. Such was not, however, what Providence had in mind for him. One nineteenth-century historian recorded:

> He remained on duty as before at the Barrens, until 1836, when a permanent mission was established at Cape Girardeau [a short distance south of Perryville inland from the Mississippi River], for which he was selected as pastor. On March 24 of that year, the mission was opened by the celebration of Mass by Father Timon, the Visitor, who after Mass introduced Father Odin to the congregation as their pastor, and in doing so [he] paid an exalted tribute to the services he had already rendered to religion, and augured the most favorable results from his mission to the Cape. He labored at this post with unfaltering energy and perseverance for a year or more, to the great benefit of the people there and in the surrounding country, when he was again recalled to the Barrens. For several years he filled various offices and professors' chairs, either at the College, Seminary, or Novitiate.[22]

However, from 1837 through 1840, events were unfolding in Texas in such an historical manner as to ultimately result in Odin being sent to the Lone Star Republic. There, laboring for souls for more than two decades, from July 1840 until the early spring of 1861, Jean-Marie Odin was to gain his greatest fame as a missionary and pioneer bishop extraordinaire, laying a foundation for Catholic Texas that can be seen even today.

5

The Call to Texas

THE SPRING OF 1837 found Father Jean-Marie Odin still stationed at Cape Girardeau as pastor of the new St. Vincent de Paul Church. A synopsis of the story of the Catholic presence at "the Cape" during that period would reveal that five years earlier Father Timon had celebrated the first Mass on the site. He had done so in secret due to a strong anti-Catholic sentiment that dominated the settlers of the locale. By 1836, however, enough Catholics had migrated into the vicinity to warrant a resident pastor being assigned there. Thus it was that Odin was dispatched to the Cape to found a mission.[1] Such an effort was in keeping with the tradition of the Vincentian apostolate.

Within a few months the Vincentians superseded the mission with the parish church of St. Vincent de Paul under the care of Odin as pastor. Odin remained there for a little more than a year before he then returned to St. Mary of the Barrens Seminary to labor in the roles already discussed. St. Vincent de Paul Church and parish were left in the hands of other priests of the Congregation of the Mission.

Catholic Texas: A Foundational Legacy

Meanwhile, several hundred miles southwest from Perryville was the vast land of Texas. As a consequence of the essentially US-influenced movement for Texas' independence from Mexico in 1836, that territory above the Rio Grande eventually came to be known as the Lone Star Republic. Mexico, however, never accepted the Texas claim as an independent republic. Subsequently, severe tensions developed between Mexico and the United States, growing from the independence struggle and the annexation of Texas by the United States almost a decade later, in December 1845. Eventually those difficulties—forming part of the overall imperialistic purview of American foreign policy in the latter 1840s—collectively surfaced as a catalyst for war. In 1846 the United States invaded Mexico and, ratified by the Treaty of Guadalupe Hidalgo in

1848, took from Mexico almost 40 percent of its northern territories. In all of that, the church and its capability for serving its flock in the area suffered dramatically.

Looking back further, for more than a century and a half previously Franciscan friars had labored dedicatedly to build a Roman Catholic religious and cultural base in Texas. But the US-Mexico war encouraged the Holy See to consider altering the church's ecclesiastical structure there. The Vatican was concerned that the church should serve the Mexican Catholics long resident in Texas, those indigenous peoples who were Catholics, and the incoming immigrant Catholics from America and Europe with equal attention. In order that this might be accomplished, Catholic missioning in Texas, having declined noticeably during the early decades of the nineteenth century, needed to be revitalized. Father Jean-Marie Odin (later bishop) was to play the major role in that re-evangelizing as the leading missionary of the period.

In that era Texas could boast of a Spanish Catholic heritage that dated back more than three hundred years. In 1519, the same year that Hernán Cortés initiated the Spanish conquest of the Aztecs in the Valley of Mexico, the Spaniard Alonso Álvarez de Pineda, commanding a fleet of four ships, sailed from Jamaica to the Texas coast of the Gulf of Mexico. Several times he laid claim to territory for the Spanish Crown.[2] Álvarez de Pineda's endeavors are recorded as the earliest contact of Catholic Spain with that vast acreage that was to become known as Texas. Significantly, for the Spanish during their colonial period to Hispanicize meant to Catholicize. Every bit as important, if in fact not even more so, during the following several decades Spanish *conquistadores* from Mexico led *entradas* (exploratory entries) north from the Valley of Mexico into regions, including Texas, that were to become the far northern reaches of New Spain.

In the meantime, the Franciscan friars commenced building their expansive mission system: an enterprise that at one time extended from Florida and Guale (Georgia coastal area) on the Atlantic Seaboard to Alta California on the Pacific Coast, including some thirty-six missions in Texas (some sources claim the figure thirty-eight). Between 1681 and 1793 a string of Texas missions were established from the far western El Paso del Norte vicinity several hundred miles eastward to near French-controlled Louisiana, south to the San Antonio de Bexar municipality, and then eastward again to the Texas Gulf of Mexico.[3]

The three missions founded in the El Paso del Norte area between 1681 and 1684 were under the ecclesiastical authorities of the Spanish province of Nuevo Mexico. In 1690 two missions were established in eastern Texas: San Francisco de los Tejas and Santisima Nombre de María. Even though Texas was erected as an autonomous province of New Spain in 1691, the Spanish failed to occupy the territory on a permanent basis for another twenty-five years. One result of that situation was that the two 1690 missions were abandoned not long after being founded. With the expedition of Capt. Domingo Ramón in 1716, the Spaniards were able to establish their authority over Texas on a more ingrained basis, and within the next two years a number of new missions were founded.[4]

Concomitant with these developments, in May 1718, Spanish governor Martín de Alarcón of Coahuila and "Governor of Texas and such other lands as might be conquered," authorized the Franciscans to construct at San Antonio de Bexar the mission San Antonio de Valero, more famously known to later history as the Alamo. Notwithstanding Governor Alarcón's influence, the actual architect of the founding of Mission San Antonio de Valero was Fray Antonio de San Buenaventura y Olivares.[5]

On the heels of the establishment of San Antonio de Valero came four additional missions in the San Antonio de Bexar municipality, all erected between 1720 and 1731. The most wondrous of those edifices was San José y San Miguel de Aguayo, the "Queen of the missions," built in 1720 and still existing as an active church today. The founder of San José y San Miguel de Aguayo was one of the most beloved and revered Franciscans in the narrative of Texas Catholic history, Fray Antonio Margil de Jesús. Fray Margil, as that Spanish son of St. Francis was affectionately called, was responsible for the founding of several missions and was popularly called the "Apostle of Texas."[6] The three other San Antonio de Bexar missions all were built in 1731: La Purísima Concepción de Acuña, San Juan Capistrano, and San Francisco de la Espada.[7] In addition to Olivares and Margil de Jesús, a number of other Franciscans labored dedicatedly for the Catholic faith in Texas during the Spanish colonial era. Perhaps most prominent among them were Frays Damian Massenet, Francisco Hidalgo, and Juan Gonzales.

The Franciscans brought to Texas a Catholic religion that had historically matured with its roots deeply set in Spain. From the early sixteenth century on, missionary priests, sisters, and brothers had kneaded that Spanish Catholic heritage into the religious, ethnic, and cultural mold that continued to grow during Catholicism's pilgrimage in Mexico among the Mexican and indigenous people. Understanding this would be fundamental to have any appreciation of the Hispanic Catholic world that Jean-Marie Odin was to encounter.[8]

In the late eighteenth century the process of secularizing the Texas missions was initiated as one aspect of a broad reform movement in its administration of northern New Spain that the Spanish Bourbon monarchy of King Carlos III (1759–88) carried out. This endeavor continued for more than thirty years. As secularization in Texas unfolded as part of Spain's overall secularizing of the missions of New Spain, in some missions—San José y San Miguel de Aguayo for instance—Franciscans did remain on the scene for some time. They worked with Spanish royal government officials to oversee matters related to secularization while at the same time ministering spiritually to the populations in the neighborhood of each mission. North of the Nueces River maturation of the mission system had not been accompanied by a healthy growth of parishes. Partly as a result of this, during the early decades of the nineteenth century various forms of popular religiosity surfaced among some of the Catholic Mexicans of the land.[9]

Embedded in the Catholic Mexican life of Texas that Jean-Marie Odin would himself come to love was a deep-seated devotion to Our Lady of Guadalupe (Nuestra Señora de Guadalupe). The cult of Our Lady of Guadalupe (culto de la Guadalupano) originally migrated to Texas with the conquistadores and their entourages in the latter sixteenth and early seventeenth centuries. The Mexican population settled in the *villas* near the missions, in the pueblos and municipalidades, on the ranches, or in the *jacales* settlements of the lower Rio Grande Valley northward to San Antonio de Bexar, thus possessed the legacy of the culto de la Guadalupano. Our Lady of Guadalupe religious feasts were celebrated among the Catholic Mexicans of Texas with intense religiosity and festivity.[10]

Meanwhile, the western reaches of this land bore witness to another religious phenomenon, whose origin could be traced back to more than two centuries before Jean-Marie Odin arrived in Texas, the apparent "miraculous bi-locations of the Lady in Blue" to various bands or tribes of indigenous peoples, most prominently the Jumanos.[11] A recent account of the "Lady in Blue" relates the narrative: "In 1629 a small party of Jumano Indians, painted and tattooed with jagged stripes across their bodies, pounded on the door of a little mission church [the old Franciscan convent at Isleta] near present Albuquerque, New Mexico. They had been directed to go there, the priest in charge later related, by a mysterious Lady in Blue who had several times appeared suddenly in their village for short visits. She told them the story of Christianity with such fervor that the whole tribe had become eager to embrace the new religion. But since she was not ordained, she had sent them to the nearest priest for baptism."[12]

Another historian developed the story in greater detail, recording that: "In July 1629 a delegation of some fifty Jumanos appeared at the Franciscan convent of old located south of present Albuquerque. The Indians had come to New Mexico to request religious teachers for themselves and their neighbors. They demonstrated rudimentary knowledge of Christianity and when asked who had instructed them they replied—the 'Woman in Blue.' Prior to the arrival of the Jumanos, the archbishop of Mexico, Francisco Manso y Zuniga, had written the religious superior of New Mexico requesting information about a young nun's claims of transportations to the frontier of New Spain. The woman in question was María de Jesús de Agreda.[13]

Venerable María de Agreda had taken her final vows as a Franciscan nun in 1620 and had entered the convent of the Immaculate Conception at Agreda,

Spain, a small village in the northeastern region of the country. She became renowned as an advisor to King Felipe IV, as the author of one of Catholicism's most lasting spiritual works, the multivolume *The Mystical City of God,* and as abbess of her convent. Fray Alonso de Benavides, a onetime religious superior of the Franciscans in New Mexico, ventured to Spain and interviewed the nun. Sister Maria acknowledged to him that she had on many occasions fallen into a trance and bi-located to the frontiers of New Spain, where she gave instructions on Christianity to inhabitants of the land. As the Spanish nun described those indigenous people—red-skinned and painted with striped patterns, living in a semi-arid mountainous and plateau-dominated landscape—Fray Benavides became convinced that she was speaking of the Jumanos.[14] Thus was left to Texas a profound Catholic legacy.

Turning to another feature of Texas's Catholic heritage, as such existed at the time that Father Jean-Marie Odin was about to be dispatched to the region, the Lone Star Republic was a grand expanse with yet undetermined territorial boundaries.[15] The Catholic ecclesiastical jurisdictional demarcation was in need of much clearer definitions. On December 15, 1777, Pope Pius VI had set in motion the laying of the hierarchical foundation for Texas by issuing the papal bull *Relata semper.* That papal letter erected the Diocese of Linares in Nuevo Leon, situated between Coahuila and Tamaulipas, Mexico.[16] The Spanish province of Texas to the north existed as part of this new diocese. Establishing the diocese of Linares seems to have been one of the final steps that the royal government of King Carlos III and the church, acting in concert through provisions of the *patronato real* (a royal agreement with the Catholic Church to work together to promote the Catholic identity of the Hispanic world), had devised to strengthen the episcopal structure of the northern provinces of New Spain.[17]

However, the early decades of the nineteenth century witnessed developments in Mexico generally—and Texas in particular—which made it necessary for the Holy See to alter the hierarchical organization of Texas within the international structure of the Catholic Church. A manifestation of late-eighteenth-century radical liberalism swept through much of western Europe, and by the early decades of the nineteenth century it had it had surfaced prominently in the ideologies underlying the independence movements of some of the Latin American nations. With its origins embedded in the anti-Catholic environment of Freemasonry and the de-Christianization—especially regarding Roman Catholicism—views of the Enlightenment and the latter's radicalization of the French revolutionaries from 1789 through 1795, and in combination with English utilitarianism, that extreme liberalism targeted the Catholic Church for assault.

From its earliest days, commencing in 1810, the Mexican struggle to cast away colonial ties to Spain could count Freemasons among its most active adherents. One of the better-known Freemasons was Lorenzo de Zavala, a politician with roots in the Yucatan and later, in 1835–36, a record of active participation in the Texas revolution against Mexico, where he counseled Texans to remain loyal to Mexico but called for reform of the Mexican Constitution of 1824. Zavala, an unhappy Catholic seminarian in his early years, became a Freemason, ultimately moving from the Scottish Rite order to the more radical York Rite lodge. Throughout his adult life he asserted an intense Freemason-oriented anticlericalism.[18]

Mexico claimed its independence from Spain in 1821, and on July 21, 1822, Augustín de Iturbide, a devout Catholic, was crowned emperor in the cathedral at Mexico City. Iturbide's reign proved to be short-lived, however, and by the end of 1824 Mexico was a federal republic with a new national constitution that was much based on the ideals that formed the base of the 1787 constitution of the United States. In the succeeding years, however, an intense struggle erupted between the Freemason-supported radical liberals in Mexican politics, who were determined to diminish the Catholic Church's influence in society, and the church, with its legion of supporters. The Freemason-supported "progressive" liberals in Mexico, misreading the US Constitution's First Amendment, concentrated on separating church from state in the political, societal, and educational spheres. In that political environment, the clergy rightfully decried the negative impact that the confrontation had on the church's mission to bring the "Good News" to the people of Mexico. The Mexican Diocese of Linares, of which Texas was a part, suffered immeasurable damage in that respect.[19]

A similar, but less radical, ideological milieu had surfaced in Texas with the revolution against Mexico in 1835–36. Even though the government of the Lone Star Republic would in the near future welcome Father Odin and his fellow missionaries to its land and help Odin in recovering properties lost by the church during the Texas war for independence, the March 2, 1836, Texas Declaration of Independence mirrored a strong bias against Catholicism. Written mainly—though not entirely—by non-Catholic Americans or Mexicans such as Zavala who admired the US experiment in forming a republic, the Texas Declaration emulated its 1776 US example. But the Texas Declaration of Independence was more extreme regarding religious matters. For example, it denounced the Catholic priesthood with the words, "When the federal republican constitution of their country, which they have sworn to support, no longer has a substantial existence, . . . the whole nature of their government [Mexico's] has been forcibly changed, without their consent, from a restricted federative republic, composed of sovereign states, to a consolidated, central military despotism, in which every interest is disregarded but that of the army and the priesthood—both the eternal enemies of civil liberty."[20]

Blended into that complex set of circumstances for Catholicism in Texas was the previously alluded to Catholic immigration into the Lone Star Republic from the United States and Europe, an historical phenomenon that had mushroomed in the early decades of the nineteenth century. As had been the case in the United States, the Irish led the way, with Germans (including Wends), French, Czechs, Austrians, Slovenes, Slavs, Swiss, and others following (the Polish would first come into Texas later, in 1854). Perhaps no other colony in Texas better exemplifies the Catholic immigrant legacy than the Irish settlement of San Patricio de Hibernia, founded in 1830.[21] Of the San Patricio Irish, their character, and their devotion to the Catholic faith one author wrote, "The San Patricio Irish, having come from diverse counties in Ireland: Sligo, Leittrum, Tipperary, Cork, Donegal, Mayo, and Meath, just to mention a few, each with its own rivalries, its own traditions, songs and dances, were an interesting group. There was moodiness followed by gaiety. In small matters they would squabble, but in the important things they stuck together. There was no discussion concerning their faith and their country."[22]

When they arrived, the Irish of San Patricio de Hibernia and the surrounding settlements of Refugio and Goliad needed to mix with the Mexican population already established in the area. Accepting the reality that ethnic tensions surfaced between both nationalities, the most common bridge that the Irish and Mexicans shared was their Catholic faith. When in 1840 Father Odin would arrive in Texas to lead the revitalization of Catholic life there, he would understand only too well the importance of the church in bringing those peoples, as well as many others, together.

Odin's Reputation Grows

Getting back to Jean-Marie Odin, when he returned to St. Mary's of the Barrens Seminary in the spring of 1837, after having served as pastor of St. Vincent de Paul Church at Cape Girardeau, he assumed once again his duties as treasurer of the seminary. The next year he was named treasurer-procurator, which effectively gave him responsibility for the seminary's entire financial operation. Meanwhile, he resumed his missioning journeying and probably once again began to teach at the seminary (the record here is unclear).

By the late 1830s, conditions for the Congregation of the Mission in the United States had improved. Odin had been present on August 20, 1835, in Paris when Father Jean-Baptiste Nozo had been elected Vincentian superior general. Immediately he showed himself to be supportive and wise in his dealings with the Vincentians in America. One of his most important decisions regarding the Vincentians at Perryville was that of leaving the lay college attached to the seminary, a development, as we have already observed, with which Odin eventually came to agree. Then just a few months after Odin returned to the Barrens from Cape Girardeau, on October 29, 1837, the new St. Mary's of the Barrens Church at Perryville was dedicated. Eight days earlier Bishop Rosati had officiated at the transfer of the relics of his confrere and co-founder of the Vincentians in America, Father Felix De Andreis, from the old church to the new one. Odin enthusiastically participated in all of the ceremonies and celebrations surrounding these events.[23]

Meanwhile, under the leadership of Father Timon as visitor of the Congregation of the Mission in the United States, the Vincentian apostolate expanded up and down the Mississippi River Valley, all the way into Louisiana. For example, in 1838, the Sons of Saint Vincent, although already involved in parish work in the Diocese of New Orleans, accepted an invitation from Bishop Blanc to take over the running of the diocesan seminary.[24] The Vincentians enjoyed a long-standing tradition of decision-making on a community basis, wherein all members of the house were encouraged to voice their views on issues. Odin would have participated in the collective determinations of his community regarding any expansion of Vincentian efforts at evangelization. Given Odin's unshakable friendship with Timon, his influence with the visitor relative to the future direction of the Congregation of the Mission in America was great.

At the same time, it often was the case in the United States during that era that bishops rose from the ranks of priests who were missionaries. It is hardly surprising then that as the end of the 1830s approached, Odin's name surfaced frequently within US ecclesiastical circles as a possible candidate for the episcopacy. Among the several testimonies for Odin were the following. On August 29, 1838, Bishop Blanc wrote to Bishop Jean Baptiste Purcell of Cincinnati, who was in Rome at the time, regarding the selection of a coadjutor bishop for Blanc's Diocese of New Orleans: "Bishop Francis Patrick Kenrick [coadjutor and apostolic administrator of the Diocese of Philadelphia] is thinking of making a new presentation [for New Orleans] and since Father Thomas Heyden has refused, Kenrick thinks only of Odin or Father [Peter] Richard Kenrick [Bishop Francis Patrick Kenrick's brother]." Before a few months had passed, Purcell sent a letter back to Blanc from Rome, assuring his brother prelate that he would not ignore the recommendation of Odin for the Diocese of New Orleans.[25]

Almost a year later in a letter to Blanc at New Orleans dated April 8, 1839, Archbishop Eccleston of Baltimore wrote of the episcopal vacancy in the See of Natchez, assuring Blanc that he, Eccleston, would prefer either Odin or Father Kenrick for that diocese. However, Eccleston went further to reveal that he believed that Kenrick would decline the appointment and Odin was being held in reserve for the miter of Detroit. Among the clergy and bishops who kept abreast of such hierarchical concerns, it was commonly known that Bishop Simon Brute wanted Odin for the Diocese of Vincennes. Shortly before his death on June 26, 1839, Brute "charged his episcopal colleagues to have Odin elected his successor in the Vincennes See."[26] The US episcopacy made other overtures regarding Odin being named a bishop, but Texas was to be the French missionary's destiny.

6

⟡⟡⟡

Send Us Some Priests

In the spring of 1837, other events had begun to unfold that would eventually draw Father Jean-Marie Odin to Texas. At New Orleans a small band of Irish Catholics from the Lone Star Republic had gathered to purchase building materials for use back home in repairing their residences, which were damaged during the Texas war for independence from Mexico during 1835–36. Those settlers authorized John Joseph Linn of Victoria, Texas, to write a letter over their signatures to "Archbishop Samuel Eccleston and the Bishops in Counsel [*sic*] at Baltimore," urging the US Catholic hierarchy "to send us some priests."[1]

Linn was a stalwart Catholic who would live his faith for more than a half century in Texas. At the same time he matured as a noted Texas patriot who labored to build up his adopted land. Throughout his life in Texas Linn regularly supported priests, and nuns as well, especially after Father Odin and his missionaries arrived in 1840. He served as hosts to the clergy, helped them to find dwellings, and offered them his services in countless other ways. Upon his arrival in Texas with three Spanish confreres in 1840, Odin would stay five days at Linn's roomy but unpretentious home in Victoria. During that visit, Odin celebrated Mass for several of Victoria's Catholics. Throughout his more than twenty years in Texas Odin would find in John Joseph Linn a steadfast friend of the church. Linn was born on June 19, 1798, in County Antrim, Ireland, into a family whose ancestral property had been stripped from them by the English during the suppressions of Oliver Cromwell back in the seventeenth century. John Linn, the father of John Joseph Linn, came to identify himself with Irish patriotism against the English government and eventually joined the United Irish Brotherhood. When John Joseph was a small child, the family emigrated from Ireland to the United States, settling in New York. In the younger Linn's own words, "Several years were spent in that city, and fourteen subsequent years in Dutchess County of that State, when the family again returned to New York City." During that early period of his life, John Joseph Linn main-

John. J. Linn. Courtesy UTSA Libraries Special Collections,
Institute of Texan Cultures, #79–268.

tained a close acquaintanceship with other Irish Catholic immigrants in New York, which helped him to mold more deeply his own Hibernian and Catholic identities.[2]

At age twenty-four, Linn departed New York to settle in New Orleans. There, for seven years, the Irishman found himself engaged in various aspects of the merchant trade business. In 1829, he ventured westward into Texas as an entrepreneur in the enterprise of selling tobacco and other products. Settling inland from the Gulf of Mexico at Victoria on the Guadalupe River, Linn began to build up his business. In the context of developing his economic interests, he frequently made trips south from Victoria to Matamoros (recall that in those years Texas was still a co-province of Mexico with Coahuila). In the meantime he married and established his wife, parents, and siblings with him at Victoria. It was during one of those journeys to Matamoros that Linn observed a Mexican family's devotion to their Catholic faith in such a way as to make a lasting impression upon the already strongly Catholic Irish immigrant. In his own book, *Reminiscences of Fifty Years in Texas* (published many years later, in 1883, when he was over eighty-five years of age), Linn recalled that:

> During one of my journeys to the Rio Grande I was accompanied by a Mexican. Stopping one night about fifty miles from the Rio Grande, we pitched our camp in close proximity to that of a shepherd. Feeling fatigued, I retired early to bed and was soon wrapped in refreshing slumber. I awoke with the early dawn; but the old shepherd was already calling his family up for their customary morning devotions. I heard them recite their prayers and sing a hymn; and being moved by curiosity—if, indeed, I was not actuated by a deeper interest—I crossed the intervening space that separated us, and confronted them. The patriarchal head of the family was fully sixty years of age, his wife about fifty, and the children, two boys of about fifteen and twelve, and a daughter of ten. What an instructive lesson was thus presented by this poor man in the primeval wilds of Nature! With the earliest dawn his first duties were rendered to his God. Here, then, were some of the fruits that had germinated from the sacred seed sown by consecrated messengers of the Church in early Texas. This little episode made a lasting impression on my mind. How, like the patriarchs this man appeared! What a glorious commentary upon the blessed work of the Church![3]

It was this immigrant Catholic of a deeply religious character who composed the March 20, 1837, letter to the US Catholic hierarchy pleading that priests be sent to Texas. Urging the US bishops to give their attention to Texas, Linn went on to explain to the prelates his concerns, as well as those of the Irishmen for whom he was writing: "Because of the war we have had to leave our homes in western Texas. But, since the [US] government has recognized us as independent, we expect to return to our homes soon. We will return with only one regret, we have no priests who speak English. We will be annoyed by sectarian preachers who swarm about. We ask for two priests who are accustomed to the western missions."[4] Linn identified Father James Mullen of New Orleans; Father Robert A. Abell of Bardstown, Kentucky; Father Edward McMahon, also of Bardstown; or Father Timon as possible missionaries for Texas.

Further, he forthrightly described the generally poor condition of the Catholic religion in Texas, as he and his fellow Irishmen assessed it. In the words of one Vincentian scholar, "In an honest effort to depict physical and economic conditions for the pastors whom they sought to acquire, they went on to sketch the country. It had no equal for soil and climate, and the general aspect of the landscape was 'beyond description.' The inhabitants, for the most part, were from western American states like Missouri and Kentucky. Their manners and customs were the same—so much so that every house was open to travelers. For this reason, pseudo-shepherds could, and did, abuse hospitality, making unwary Catholics the prey of their perverting influence. Most of the settlers were 'ignorant of the truths of our religion; in fact, most having no religion at all.'"[5]

Linn's plea for priests apparently never reached the bishops meeting in Baltimore. Bishop Blanc, to whom Linn delivered the letter, realized that Texas was not under the episcopal jurisdiction of the US hierarchy and therefore he likely left the epistle in New Orleans as he journeyed to the Baltimore Council. Linn may actually have met Odin and some of the Vincentians at the Barrens in the mid-1830s; there is a reference to a Mr. Linn in the Vincentian archives that had previously been located at Perryville.[6] While he may have or may have not met any of the Vincentians, and while his undelivered letter cannot be credited with having been the impetus that prompted the Holy See's actions regarding the Catholics in Texas at the time, Linn's initiative was of the moment. His communication was significant because it made a convincing argument for priests being sent into Texas, and it was at the same time reflective of the immigrant Catholics' perception of Catholicism's situation in the Lone Star Republic north of the Nueces River in those days.

A need for priests was common to settlement on the fringes of American society where Catholics made up all, or at least a noticeable portion of the population, whether the need existed on the frontiers of the Hispanic world or on the cutting edge of the expanding westward movement from the Atlantic Seaboard. When Linn's letter expressed the desire for English-speaking priests, it simply brought attention to the reality that missionaries needed to be fluent, or at least conversant, in the language the people they served. Sermons had to be preached, confessions had to be heard, and catechesis given in the vernacular of the locale. From the broadest view, churchmen and nuns with abilities in a variety of languages were sought for Texas.

Some weeks after the Linn letter, as Odin continued his priestly labors back in Missouri, other developments began to evolve that bore directly on Odin's eventual assignment to Texas. The activity of Count Charles Farnese, an entrepreneur from France visiting Texas during 1837, drew the Holy See's attention to the plight of Catholics and their religion in Texas.[7] Farnese proposed to Sam Houston, the first president of the Lone Star Republic, who served in that office from October 22, 1836, to December 10, 1838, a grandiose scheme aimed at erecting a Roman Catholic archbishopric for Texas.

Farnese reasoned that such would, if the pope established it, lay the groundwork for reinvigorating Catholic life in the land. Moreover, the French visitor argued, a development of that nature would free Texas of Mexican Catholic hierarchical authority and at the same time imply papal recognition of Texas independence. While President Houston, duly impressed by the hint of papal acceptance of Texas independence and an ecclesiastical breakaway from the Mexican bishops, found the count's plans attractive and gave them his support, the Holy See failed to seriously consider them. When Farnese returned to Europe later in the year and laid his design before papal authorities, it was rejected. Still, his initiative prompted the Holy See to begin to look more closely at the situation for Catholics in Texas.

While the Holy See's focus was being brought to bear more directly on Texas in 1837, Odin continued with his responsibilities at the seminary, the lay college, and missioning throughout the vicinity of Perryville. During the fall of that year, Father Timon was in Paris attending to affairs of the American Vincentians. From the Barrens Seminary on September 18, Odin wrote a long letter to Timon reporting on a number of matters. Odin reminded Timon that the American Vincentian community was in desperate need of funds. Odin was simply offering a gentle reminder, as Timon realized, even before he departed the Barrens, that throughout his trip he would have to seek out financial help for his Sons of St. Vincent in America. On a more positive note, Odin was able to comment on the progress of several of the Vincentians at the seminary: some priests and the others seminarians.

On the other hand, there also existed difficulties. The missionary from France was particularly concerned about two of the priests. Both clerics talked too much, Odin lamented, annoying not only the parishioners but colleagues in the Congregation of the Mission as well. They had developed a gift of the tongue in an exaggerated manner. One of the priests regularly spoke in a "flippant and disrespectful" tone; the other one, to the dismay of his flock, consistently delivered excruciatingly long sermons.[8]

Then Odin turned to other concerns. There were the usual requests for sacramental vestments, chalices, holy pictures, furniture, and similar items that frontier missionaries made of their brother priests touring Europe. But Odin made a special plea to Timon that the US visitor search out certain materials for the community of nuns recently established at St. Genevieve. These sisters especially needed French spelling books, wrote Odin.

On a more personal note, Odin was pleased to inform his confrere that word had reached the Barrens that Timon's father had recovered from a recent illness. Beyond these items, the Frenchman happily confirmed to his partner that the new St. Mary's of the Barrens Church at Perryville was to be dedicated on the twenty-ninth of October; so also was the mission church at St. Genevieve the following Sunday.[9]

By the spring of 1838, Father Timon had returned from Europe, enthusiastic about the accomplishments of Odin and the other Sons of St. Vincent in his absence. More significantly, 1838 proved to be a pivotal year for the Vincentians regarding their future labors in Texas. It was then that Bishop Blanc of New Orleans received the first response from the Holy See concerning Catholic evangelization of the Lone Star Republic. One Catholic historian recently recorded the Vatican's reaction in this way: "On January 16, 1838, Cardinal Ciacomo Fransoni, prefect of the Sacred Congregation for the Propagation of the Faith, wrote to Bp. Antoine Blanc of New Orleans informing him of Rome's knowledge of the Texas situation and that he himself had been informed that the Texas president was very friendly to the Catholic church. He [Cardinal Fransoni] requested Blanc to send some priests to Texas to ascertain exactly what conditions were like there and to make a full report to Rome of their findings so that a decision could be made as to appropriate actions.[10]

As a result of that letter it was to be only a matter of time until Vincentians would be dispatched to the Texas mission field. Jean-Marie Odin would have been aware of the situation as it began to develop. After all, he was by that time one of the most respected Vincentians on the American frontier. Close to both Bishop Blanc and Father Timon, he was highly regarded within the Congregation of the Mission and informed about much of that community's affairs. Nonetheless, for another two years the Frenchman contentedly occupied himself with his service in and around Perryville, from St. Genevieve to Cape Girardeau.

At about the same time that Cardinal Fransoni's letter to Bishop Blanc at New Orleans arrived there, Odin wrote from St. Genevieve to Timon who had returned to St. Mary's of the Barrens Seminary: "We were looking for you yesterday, but were disappointed. Our little mission still goes on. We cannot judge as yet of the fruits. Great many attend mornings and evenings, still those who need it the most seem to keep away and show themselves rarely.[11]

That his focus remained steadfast on the work of the Congregation of the Mission in Missouri, even to the point of giving his attention to small details, can be seen in another letter that Odin, from the Barrens Seminary, sent to Timon at St. Louis, in the late spring of 1839. Among other matters, Odin complained that, "Mr. Daily tells me that the college is without quilts, not having seen any among the articles sent by Mr. Paquín [Vincentian Father Joseph Paquín, who later was to follow Odin to Texas]; you are requested to procure some few thousand.[12] "Some few thousand" would have been an extraordinarily large quantity for Odin to have solicited, so that number could have been a translator's error in studying Odin's letters. Still, that piece of correspondence revealed Odin's tendency to take care of persons under his charge. Such an attitude in him would remain consistent when he assumed the task of leading the Catholic reevangelization of Texas a short time later.

Acting upon Cardinal Fransoni's instructions from January 16, 1838, that he send priests to Texas to survey the condition of Catholicism there and then report back to the Holy See, Bishop Blanc turned to Father Timon and his Vincentians. Six weeks after receiving Fransoni's letter, on March 30, 1838, Blanc wrote to Timon, "I think that such a mission can suit only a religious order or congregation, and your own in particular." Blanc went on to suggest to Timon that he could sail from New Orleans to Texas and quickly discover the state of Catholicism in the Lone Star Republic and its future prospects. Following such a jaunt, Blanc assured him, the best possible decisions for the good of the Catholic faith in the region could be made.[13]

That Father Timon was eager to expand Vincentian activity, especially in Blanc's New Orleans diocese, was well known within the Congregation of the Mission.[14] A few years earlier, just as the American province of the Vincentians was erected with Timon named as visitor, the Vincentian motherhouse back in Paris was anticipating that Pope Gregory XVI might ask that some Sons of St. Vincent be made available for the mission field of Africa. With that in mind, the Congregation of the Mission superior general, Father Jean-Baptiste Nozo, had cautioned Timon about taking on new assignments for his American community. The African possibility, however, never materialized. This, as well as the Vincentians' great respect for Bishop Blanc and their own zeal for evangelization made it certain that Timon would agree to the New Orleans ordinary's plea.

Father Timon presumed, though, that inasmuch as his readiness to travel to Texas might imply that the American Vincentians' willingness to commit their congregation as missionaries there might be exactly what Bishop Blanc desired, Father Nozo back in Paris would have to grant permission for the trip. Communications from Blanc and Timon not only to Father Nozo in Paris, but also between Blanc and Cardinal Fransoni in Rome, and from Fransoni to Nozo as well, eventually gained Father Timon needed authorization. But the approval for his Texas journey came to Timon only on October 20, 1838, several months after Fransoni and Blanc had started the whole initiative. After Timon, accompanied by a young Spanish Vincentian priest named Juan Francis Llebaria, completed the reconnaissance into Texas during late December of 1838 through January 1839, the eventual obligation to oversee the rebuilding of Catholicism in Texas fell on the shoulders of Jean-Marie Odin.

7

꧁꧂

On the Shoulders of Odin

I N THE FALL-WINTER OF 1838–39 two events occurred that affected Jean-
Marie Odin. First, there was the unexpected death of a young confrere at
the Barrens Seminary, Father Francis Simonin, on September 15, 1838.[1] Then
three months later came Timon and Llebaria's excursion into Texas. The passing away of Father Simonin touched Odin deeply, but the Timon-Llebaria
tour had a more lasting impact by changing his future as a missionary priest
dramatically. The culmination of what Timon saw firsthand as the needs of
Catholics in Texas during his trip to the Lone Star Republic, further refined by
Bishop Blanc's perceptions, ultimately resulted in Odin being uprooted from
Missouri and transferred to Texas. In that land the missionary from France was
to spend the majority of the remainder of his life.

In reference to Father Simonin's death, Odin wrote to Father Jean Baptiste
Etienne, procurator general of the Congregation of the Mission in Paris, "It is
with a heart filled with the most profound grief that I announce the severe loss
which our mission of America has suffered. . . . Providence has just exacted of
us a very great sacrifice. On the 15th of this month, we had the misfortune to
lose our confrere Fr. Francis Simonin, after an illness of seven weeks. All hearts
were attached to him here because of his good spirit and noble manners, both
engaging and affable."[2]

Father Simonin, a young French Vincentian born in 1810 at St. Vincent de
Boisset, Canton of Perreux, Department of Loire, appeared to be one of the
bright lights on the horizon for the US Congregation of the Mission. Odin's
letter to Etienne expressed with real emotion the bereavement that he and
his fellow Vincentians on the Missouri frontier felt. The jaunt into Texas of
Fathers Timon and Llebaria came while Odin was still trying to recover from
the loss of his colleague Simonin.

Timon and Llebaria spent most of their days in Texas at Galveston and
Houston or traveling between the two settlements. Leading Catholic personages of the new republic whom the Vincentians met at Houston dissuaded the
two churchmen from journeying farther inland, pleading inclement weather
as well as the presence of marauding Comanches in the area, both situations

posing serious threats to the missionaries' safety.[3] Had Timon and Llebaria been able to expand the trip to include territories to the west and south of Houston toward San Antonio de Bexar, they would have seen firsthand the sad conditions of catechesis in that most historic and significant of all of Texas' Catholic municipalities and the location of five eighteenth-century Franciscan missions.

But Father Timon's decision that he and his Spanish confrere not continue beyond Houston made sense. The dangers were truly menacing. Besides, those same men who made the warnings were able to summarize for Timon and Llebaria what seemed to be in their views Catholicism's situation in Texas at the time. Those men represented both the Spanish-Mexican legacy of Texas as well as the growing Catholic immigrant presence. Those citizens, moreover, were among the most respectable in Texas. Foremost among them were Juan Nepomuceno Seguín, state senator from San Antonio de Bexar; Judge John Dunn, senator from Goliad, Refugio, and San Patricio; James Kerr, representative from Jackson; José Antonio Navarro, also from San Antonio de Bexar; and John Joseph Linn himself from Victoria.[4]

The Catholic Texas demography that these people represented and knew only too well was unique. It was a population that had developed originally in a frontier region evangelized through the influence of the Spanish and Mexican Catholic culture that had been carried north from the Valley of Mexico and offered to some of the indigenous peoples of Texas. By the second and third decades of the nineteenth century, that original Catholic identity had begun to knead with a non-Hispanic Catholic religiosity entering Texas from the United States and Europe. Whoever ultimately was assigned to the Lone Star Republic to shore up the faith there eventually would have to understand the nature of the challenge to evangelization that such an ethnically and religiously diverse demographic region offered.

The Catholics at Houston who advised Father Timon of the status of the church in Texas brought to his attention the problems existing in San Antonio de Bexar that weakened Catholic life there. The Houston Catholics reported to Timon that two priests residing at San Antonio, or in the neighborhood thereof, Father Refugio de la Garza and José Antonio Valdez, both were living unpriestly immoral lives. In addition, the two clerics were ignoring the sacramental, catechetical, and social responsibilities to the people that their vocations demanded of them. Father de la Garza, since 1820, had served as pastor of San Fernando Church in San Antonio. Father Valdez was residing on the outskirts of the village in retirement from his earlier tenure as priest at Mission La Bahia del Espiritu Santo in Goliad.

With San Antonio de Bexar located within the ecclesiastical jurisdictional boundaries of the Mexican Diocese of Linares, both de la Garza and Valdez were serving with their priestly faculties granted by the ordinary of that bishopric, Bishop Francisco José María de Jesús Belaunzarán y Ureña, a Mexican Franciscan who had been named to head up the diocese in 1831. Bishop Belaunzarán y Ureña had written to Bishop Blanc at New Orleans on February 21, 1839, that he had withdrawn the priestly faculties from Fathers de la Garza and Valdez, pointing out that in so doing he was "putting an end to the scandal of the faithful."[5]

Of the several individuals at Houston who drew Father Timon's attention to the unfortunate developments at San Antonio de Bexar, Juan Nepomuceno Seguín complained in the most emphatic manner. Seguín, himself a Catholic Mexican, was baptized as a baby only seven days old on November 3, 1806, in San Fernando Church. On January 5, 1839, he presented Father Timon with an "Affidavit on Parish Priests of Bexar and La Bahia." In this report Seguín averred that:

> This gentleman [Father de la Garza] is a native of the city of San Fernando de Bexar for which he was elected priest in a competition of curates in 1820 and authorized to function as priest by the See of Monterrey [actually at the time Linares]: he took possession of his office that same year. At the beginning he carried out his duties with great care and decency, and much zeal and dedication to the divine cult. He made notable repairs and improvements to the parish church, for which he gained the appreciation and respect of all the residents. In 1824, when he returned from Mexico City, where his parishioners sent him as a deputy to the General Congress, he began to abandon the obligations of his post entirely. It is shameful to see how filthy the temple remains after it caught fire because of the carelessness in leaving it in charge of a too young, careless, and licentious boy. As far as his religious and moral life, he has done it with so little discretion that almost no one in Bexar is ignorant of his having lived during his entire tenure as priest with various lovers, by whom he has had the following illegitimate children: Concepción, José de Jesús, and Dorotea. He is an enlightened and cultured man.[6]

Regarding Father Valdéz, Seguin simply said that "I know that he is the priest of La Bahia del Espiritu Santo, by the authority of the Bishopric of Monterrey [again, Linares]. He is a man of an entirely depraved conduct: who has lost the public's faith in his private contracts; whose behavior is so scandalous that he takes his two illegitimate daughters (whom he had by a young maiden he seduced) hanging from his arms down the middle of the parish church, and who enters the sacristy by the altar to change in order to say mass. He has been prosecuted various times by the justices for his scandalous life."[7]

Father Timon likely had already decided to delegate to Jean-Marie Odin the task of rebuilding Catholic life in the Lone Star Republic, as he, Timon, and Father Llebaria were making their way into Texas. That meant that it would fall on the shoulders of Odin to settle matters with the two incorrigible *sacerdotes* (priests) at San Antonio. Departing Galveston for his return to Missouri on January 12, 1839, Timon had by that time commenced writing his report on the condition of Catholicism in Texas for Father Nozo in Paris.[8] Reaching New Orleans on the fourteenth of that month, Timon discussed his observations with Bishop Blanc.

Following his visit with Blanc, Timon headed back up the Mississippi River to St. Mary's of the Barrens Seminary. In his conversation with Blanc, and also in his summary sent to Father Nozo, Timon recommended that Texas be erected a diocese. Bishop Blanc, on the other hand, in his correspondence with the Holy See, urged that a prefecture apostolic over the land be established with Timon named as prefect apostolic. The bishop's view prevailed.[9]

Odin's Nomination and Departure for Texas

The first mention of Odin being destined for the Lone Star Republic is contained in a letter dated March 12, 1839, that Timon wrote to Blanc from St. Louis, where he had gone to preach a two-week mission soon after arriving home from his Texas jaunt. In that missive, Timon informed Blanc that at the time he was unable to dispatch Odin to Texas. Instead, wrote Timon, he planned to send Father Paquín to Nacogdoches, Texas, for the purpose of conducting a mission there. Timon was especially anxious that the Catholics in that settlement enjoy the opportunity of making their Easter Duty. Timon commented further to Bishop Blanc that "by the time it becomes more prudent to fix on something more permanent, other arrangements can be made."[10]

In the meantime, Blanc had already turned his attention to the delicate matter of corresponding with Bishop Belaunzarán y Ureña of Linares about the issue of the transfer of episcopal authority over Texas away from his Diocese of Linares. On January 15, 1839, while Timon was in Texas, Blanc wrote to the Mexican prelate that "the Texas revolution has come to the attention of the pope as well as Propaganda." Enclosing with his letter a copy of the papal instructions authorizing him to send priests into Texas for the purpose of assessing the situation there, Blanc indicated to Belaunzarán y Ureña that he intended to delegate the task to Vincentians. Assuring the bishop of Linares that he in no way desired to interfere with his position as the ordinary of Linares, Blanc asked Belaunzarán y Ureña to "reply right away."[11]

At the Convent of St. Cosme of Mexico, Belaunzarán y Ureña composed his February 21 reply to Blanc. In addition to his already-discussed comments about Fathers de la Garza and Valdéz, the bishop of Linares wrote much more. He could not deny the just request of the Holy See, he affirmed, but he made bold to insist that permission be obtained from the Mexican government through the United States plenipotentiary for any involvement in Texas by a member of the US hierarchy. Belaunzarán y Ureña was well aware of the potential international and domestic tensions that might erupt over these developments, given that while the United States recognized Texas independence, neither the Mexican government nor most of the Mexican population had as yet accepted this circumstance.

Belaunzarán y Ureña complained to Blanc that "disgraceful revolutions" in Mexico had prevented him from making his planned pastoral visits back in 1833. And, the bishop lamented, the wars were still going on! Here Belaunzarán y Ureña was referring not only to the continued struggles between Texas and Mexico but also to the assault on the church in Mexico engineered by Mexican liberals. Finally, Belaunzarán y Ureña, using the title of bishop of Monterrey (which title the diocese eventually would attain), assured Blanc that he felt the latter's course of action regarding Texas would safeguard the integrity of his diocese.[12]

April 1839 brought two other developments that were to bear on, at least indirectly, Jean-Marie Odin's assignment to Texas as vice prefect apostolic. In a communication to Propaganda Fide, Vincentian Superior General Nozo discussed the possibility of assigning some of his clergy to Texas, with a Vincentian being named prefect apostolic. But the superior general opposed Father Timon becoming a bishop at the time. In the meantime, French concerns about the church in Texas unexpectedly surfaced. Abbe Matthew Bernard Anduze, chaplain of a French naval fleet under the command of Charles Baudin that was present in Mexico on waters as a part of France's military presence in the region, had become curious about the church's situation in that country and Texas as well. On February 20, 1839, from Vera Cruz Anduze wrote to Bishop Blanc in New Orleans explaining his interest and commenting that while in Mexico he had unsuccessfully tried to meet with Bishop Belaunzarán y Ureña. Shortly thereafter Anduze sailed from Vera Cruz to New Orleans and then back to Galveston, Texas. Arriving at Galveston on April 17, Anduze was elated to learn that "the pope had placed the spiritual administration of Texas in Blanc's hands." The French chaplain perceived that this news was well received by the Texas cabinet.[13]

Concomitantly, word came to the Barrens Seminary on June 11 of that year that both Odin and Timon "were proposed to Rome for episcopal sees." However, neither of the two Vincentians became bishops immediately. For Odin such was premature. Timon was indeed offered the miter as Bishop Rosati's coadjutor at St. Louis, but he refused the nomination. As these developments were taking place, Odin continued with his duties at Perryville and the surrounding vicinity.[14]

Following an extended missioning trip through Louisiana during the winter of 1839 and spring of 1840, Father Timon, in April of 1840, returned to the Barrens to find awaiting him "letters appointing him prefect apostolic of

Texas." But Timon could never have hoped to move to Texas on a permanent basis given his many responsibilities, including those attached to his serving as visitor of the American Vincentians. Guided by his own earlier inclination and adhering to the advice of his council—one of whom was Father Odin—Timon named his French confrere vice prefect apostolic and called upon him to set out for Texas as soon as possible.[15]

One unfortunate aspect of Timon's and Odin's appointments was Bishop Rosati's reaction. Depending on what appeared to be his focus as he reflected on these developments, Rosati's mood changed. Usually it fluctuated between frustration, profound disappointment, and anger. It was never agreeable. On the very day that Timon returned to the Barrens Seminary from Louisiana to find the papal documents with his appointment to Texas, April 12, 1840, Rosati, who already knew of the assignment, had written to Propaganda Fide strongly protesting the action. Six days later, having heard that Odin too was destined for Texas as vice prefect apostolic, the bishop of St. Louis wrote a similar letter of protest to Propaganda Fide in reference to his missionary from France.[16]

Rosati was upset that Father Timon earlier had refused the bishop's miter as his own coadjutor for the Diocese of St. Louis. Then, believing that he was going to lose both Timon and Odin to Texas, the ordinary of St. Louis, whom it will be remembered was a Vincentian, became visibly irritated. Rosati had no way of knowing at the time that while Timon would occasionally return to Texas for a visit, it was Odin who would be permanently stationed in the Lone Stare Republic. Furthermore, Father Timon served as Bishop Rosati's vicar general and Odin acted as his provicar general, causing Rosati to feel even more betrayed that he had not been informed about the assignment of his priests to Texas.[17] The bishop of St. Louis seems to have borne no resentment toward Odin, who for so many years had worked closely with him, and who after all was never in a position to communicate with his bishop about what was developing for Texas. And Rosati's anger at Timon, who could have and should have consulted with his diocesan ordinary, was relatively short lived.

However, Rosati was greatly agitated with Bishop Blanc for his role in the affair. Rosati knew that his brother bishop from New Orleans, a prelate with whom he had labored side by side for years, was the one ecclesiastic in America who was integrally part of the maneuvers. Yet Blanc had kept Rosati in the dark. A sincere letter that Blanc later wrote to his friend at St. Louis in which he apologized for any misunderstanding helped to smooth over matters as time passed. Even so, Rosati suffered that ill feeling against Blanc for quite some time.

Odin had much to do in order to get ready for his new assignment, so much preparation needed in so little time. He had been at the Barrens Seminary for more than seventeen years; the institution had been his home. But now he had to move on, to a mission field on a frontier hundreds of miles distant, in a land about which he knew pitifully little. It was to be another adieu!

"On May 2nd, 1840, I left St. Mary's Seminary, Perry County, Missouri, for Texas."[18] This was a simple Odin entry in the daily journal that he had decided to keep during his impending venture into Texas. The French priest opted for a travel route that would carry him down the Mississippi River to New Orleans and then by packet to sail along the eastern rim of the Gulf of Mexico to the Texas coast. He planned his trip, with considerable help from Father Timon, in such a way as to traverse the Texas coast past Galveston Bay towards Matagorda and then enter La Vaca Bay Pass and proceed inward to Linnville (named after John Joseph Linn).

New Orleans

It was a Saturday morning, May 2, when Odin, accompanied by a fellow Vincentian, Peter Doutreluinue, departed St. Mary's of the Barrens Seminary for Cape Girardeau and the continued voyage downriver to New Orleans. Doutreluinue was bound not for Texas but for Natchitoches, Louisiana, situated on the banks of the Red River. As a missionary and then first pastor of St. Vincent de Paul Church, Odin had made the journey from Perryville to the Cape several times before. He knew well the verdant terrain characterized by rolling hills abundant with trees and other flora that dominated the landscape lying only a short distance westward from the great river. Unfortunately, though, as he and Doutreluinue left Perryville, Odin was suffering from one of his periodic migraine headaches.[19]

Arriving at Cape Girardeau that evening, Odin, his migraine headache having by then subsided, enjoyed a good night's sleep. On the following day he celebrated Sunday Mass at the recently established sisters' convent there. On Monday the vice prefect apostolic made a simple entry in his daily journal: "Mass at Cape at 12 O'clock. Left the Cape to go on board the 'Meteor.'"[20] Even though Odin mentioned no such send off, surely his former parishioners at St. Vincent de Paul Church would have gathered to wish him well as he and Doutreluinue prepared to board their vessel for New Orleans. If so, the St. Vincent de Paul flock would have done so with heavy hearts, as he had been a beloved pastor for them.

At Cape Girardeau several other people boarded the *Meteor*. Among those passengers were a Mr. Paris and three nuns from the Bethlehem convent near the Barrens Seminary, whose chaplain Odin had been earlier. They were headed for Arkansas. In addition, the list of travelers included a Mr. O'Neill, who was scheduled to join Father Doutreluinue at Natchitoches; three seminarians destined for Assumption Seminary at Lafourche, Louisiana; and two young Spanish Vincentian priests bound for Texas with Odin: Fathers Miguel Calvo and Eudald Estany.[21] Calvo and Estany, along with Vincentian Brother Raimundo Sala, another Spaniard who would join the group three weeks later at Donaldsonville, Louisiana, were essential to Odin's Texas mission because they spoke Spanish.

Calvo, Estany, and Sala had traveled from Spain to France for their Vincentian formation and studies. With the resurgence and radicalization of Spanish liberalism's assault on the church in Spain in the 1830s, and tensions and violence associated with Spain's First Carlist War (1833–40) escalating, liberals influential in the government targeted the Vincentians as one of the several religious communities to be suppressed. The three Spaniards thus found themselves unable to return to their homeland.[22] Within a short time all three volunteered for the Vincentian foreign missions, where they ended up in America on the Mississippi River frontier and available for service in Texas.

That Odin insisted upon taking with him the Spanish-speaking priests and brothers to labor among the Catholic Spanish and Mexican population reflected in him a sincere concern for those earliest Texas Catholics, those who had opened up New Spain's northern frontier, established the Catholic missions, and built presidio and municipal settlements. That dedication to the Spaniards and Mexicans then under his spiritual charge made up an intrinsic aspect of the French missionary's devotion to all Catholics of Texas throughout his many years of succoring Catholic life in the land.

As the *Meteor* cleared port at Cape Girardeau and began to edge its way slowly but steadily down the Mississippi River, Odin, Calvo, and Estany must have sensed the permanence of their new assignment. En route Odin organized religious exercises on board for his Vincentians. That attention given to their norms and devotions likely relieved the three churchmen of some of the anxious feelings they were experiencing. The ship chugged its way past the riverine settlements of New Madrid, Randolph, Memphis, and Commerce as it headed for New Orleans.

On the morning of May 6, Mr. Paris and the three nuns from the Bethlehem convent, Sisters Aloysis, Julian, and Philomens, disembarked the *Meteor* at the small river enclave of Napoleon to continue their journey overland into Arkansas. The next afternoon, a Thursday, the ship almost ran headlong into a destructive storm two miles north of Natchez. Odin called the natural disaster a hurricane, but his description of the destructive winds was more suggestive of a tornado: "That day will never be forgotten by the inhabitants of Natchez. Between 2 and 3 P.M. a dreadful hurricane swept off almost all the houses; great many lives lost; sight frightful; trees torn down; S.B. Prairie all torn into pieces; S.B. Hind sunk; a great many flatboats destroyed; people drowned; young Emanuel Blanc, from St. Louis University, killed [Odin does not comment whether young Emanuel was related to Bishop Blanc]. Rainy day and hail storms. Our escape from the hurricane was certainly miraculous, as we were within a short distance from the region of it, and would have been in it had we not stopped for a few moments."[23]

Just how long memories of that frightening encounter with one of nature's most devastating forces remained entrenched in Odin's mind can never be known. But he did describe it to a number of people as the months passed. On prime example of this was that at the beginning of his first letter written to Bishop Rosati from Texas, the French missionary went into detail about the experience. Composing his missive in San Antonio de Bexar on August 27, 1840, Odin wrote, "I left the Barrens on May 2, and during our trip we escaped as by miracle the terrible hurricane which desolated the city of Natchez. We were only two miles from the unfortunate city when it was destroyed, and we would have been in the middle of the region that the destructive wind passed over if the captain had not stopped the boat for several seconds to shelter us from frightful hailstorms that broke the windows of our cabin."[24]

Delayed for some time in the Natchez vicinity due to the havoc of the storm, the *Meteor* eventually was underway once again for New Orleans. They passed Point Coupee, where on board the ship Odin may have nostalgically reminisced about the occasion of almost eighteen years earlier when at the parish there he visited with his friend, the future first archbishop of New Orleans, Antoine Blanc. The packet ship churned beyond Baton Rouge and anchored on Friday evening at Donaldsonville. There all of Odin's traveling companions, including Fathers Calvo and Estany, disembarked. A nighttime continuation of the voyage down the Mississippi River brought that leg of the French Vincentian's adventure to an end.

Early the following morning, Odin spotted in the distance the spires of New Orleans's St. Louis Cathedral, a religious edifice whose origin as a parish church dates back almost to the founding of the city of New Orleans in 1718. Using New Orleans as his base of operations, for several weeks Odin busied himself throughout the region as far east as Mobile, Alabama, as he made his final preparations for the move into Texas.

Odin first turned himself to the onerous task of trying to collect monies due the Congregation of the Mission from various persons or groups in and around New Orleans. Such were mainly parents of students attending Barrens Seminary or the lay college. Whatever income he might collect would help defray the expenses of the Vincentian venture into Texas. After several days of effort, however, Odin was compelled to write to Father Timon back at Perryville that "on Saturday morning I arrived at this place. From that time I have endeavored to collect *accts*. but without success."[25]

Ready money was scarce on the frontier, and parents who wanted to pay tuition often did not possess the means to do so. In all, out of several hundreds of dollars owed to the Vincentians, Odin was able to collect only $225. One father gave him some sugar to send upriver to the Barrens Seminary as payment in kind.[26] The Panic of 1837, an economic depression of major proportions which hit the nation right after Martin Van Buren assumed the presidency of the United States, was still showing its impact in 1840.

A week after his arrival in New Orleans, Odin began a round of visits to convents, churches, seminaries, and other religious establishments in the lower Louisiana-Mississippi Valley. Among the institutions he visited were the Jesuit Spring Hill College at Mobile, Alabama, only recently founded in 1830, and the Seminary of the Assumption at Donaldsonville. During that month-long sojourn he celebrated Mass, preached, heard confessions, gave instructions to children, and engaged in other forms of catechesis. In the course of those activities Odin, at various locales, met with a number of priests, nuns, seminarians, and laypersons and offered them spiritual direction and encouraged them to seek support for his missioning venture to Texas. While little was forthcoming in the form of financial aid, some religious communities presented him with other kinds of gifts. For example, the sisters of the Religious of the Sacred Heart at St. Michael's Convent in St. James Parish, Louisiana, not only promised him their prayers but presented him as well with two albs (full-length white linen vestments secured with cinctures and used in celebrating Mass). Others—sisters, priests, and lay persons—bestowed upon Odin similar offerings for his mission.

When preaching sermons during his Masses Odin often used English, a language in which by 1840 he had become reasonably fluent. On other occasions, however, such as while delivering a sermon in Mobile's Cathedral of the Immaculate Conception, where the Catholic population was heavily French, he spoke in his native tongue. In giving sermons and spreading the "Good News," he was doing what his vocation as a priest asked of him.

The deeply spiritual churchman understood fully well that the most lasting help coming to him for his assignment to Texas would be the grace that he received through faithfulness to his prayer and sacramental life. As always, he celebrated his Masses with a profound dignity, which expressed both his Sulpician and Vincentian formation. His sermons were delivered in a humble but incisive and convincing manner. Those characteristics of religiosity were a mark of Jean-Marie Odin that remained with him throughout his life as a priest.

While Odin was making those rounds, he at the same time eagerly sought the most advantageous way to transport himself and his missionaries to their ultimate destination of Linnville, Texas. Two weeks after his arrival at New Orleans, he returned to Donaldsonville to make arrangements for Fathers Calvo and Estany as well as Brother Sala, to accompany him back to New Orleans. On the evening of May 27, all four Vincentians were in the Bayou City. It would, however, be another five weeks before they would again be en route to the Texas coast: Odin spent the month of June seeking a ship on which they could book passage.

Showing his anxiousness to get on with the trip, Odin, on June 26, wrote to Father Timon back at the seminary: "We are still at New Orleans, but tomorrow morning we shall leave onboard the schooner *Henry* commanded by Capt. Auld. You cannot imagine how tired we are of waiting for our departure. Regret that we did not take the S.B. for Galveston, we would have been long before now in Texas. There will be 33 German passengers on board with us, all are Catholics. But the Vincentians were unable to leave on Captain Auld's ship on June 27, and the vessel's departure was delayed five additional days, until July 2. Finally, however, they were underway. The schooner passed the balize (a floating navigational guide for ships at the outer rim of the harbor) at 9:00 A.M. and headed out into the Gulf of Mexico, leaving New Orleans in the distance.[27]

Ahead for the four Vincentians were ten days of navigating the gulf south-by-southwest and then due south at an agonizingly slow pace. After sighting the Texas coast, Captain Auld set the *Henry* on a course for Cavallo Pass at Lavaca Bay. Entering Cavallo Pass, the vessel then negotiated a difficult passage along the inland bay to Linnville. At that small port settlement, situated just north of Indianola and east of Victoria, on the evening of July 12, Father Jean-Marie Odin, the future first bishop of Galveston and second archbishop of New Orleans, appeared on the scene with his small band of missionaries. They had reached Texas.

A Vice Prefect Apostolic Arrives

JULY WEATHER ON THE TEXAS GULF COAST is regularly hot and humid, with relief from the heat coming mainly with breezes from the sea or rains that intermittently appear and temper the heat somewhat. It was early in the morning on just such a warm and humid Monday, July 13, 1840, that Odin and his Spanish Vincentian confreres first stepped ashore on Texas soil, at Linnville. After arriving the night before aboard Captain Auld's ship *Henry,* the Vincentians and other passengers had made preparations for disembarking the following day.[1]

Linnville had been established only a few years earlier, in 1831, mainly due to John J. Linn's selection of that site for the warehouse that he needed for his mercantile business. On his second trip into Texas from Louisiana Linn had purchased a schooner named *The Opposition* that he planned to use in his enterprises. And even though *The Opposition* was lost at sea a short time after Linn bought it, the Irishman remained determined to construct a warehouse at a locale somewhere on the shores of Lavaca Bay and use it to continue to build his trade interests. Linn's family home was established inland a few miles at Victoria on the banks of the Guadalupe River. The warehouse site, "Linn's Landing," soon came to be known as Linnville. Odin, upon his disembarkation at the tiny port settlement, estimated that it consisted of no more than a dozen houses. The entire population of Linnville at the time may not have exceeded two hundred people.[2]

The Vincentians' voyage from New Orleans to Lavaca Bay had been a difficult one. The exceedingly warm daytime temperatures at sea sometimes seemed unbearable to the passengers aboard the *Henry*. To make matters worse, after the vessel entered Cavallo Pass, it was grounded for three days at Indianola before being able to move on up the coast of Lavaca Bay to Linnville. In a letter written to Bishop Blanc the day after he landed at Linnville, Odin described the voyage thus: "Six days after our departure from New Orleans we sighted the territory of Texas, and with a favorable wind we cleared the difficult passage of Cavallo. Having entered the Bay of Lavaca, we had to reopen a passage through the mud and sand. The ship ran aground constantly; it was even necessary to unload a small part of the cargo. Sunday evening we cast anchor opposite Linnville. The dead calm rendered the first days of our voyage rather painful; however, every night there arose an excellent breeze which made up for the excessive heat of the day." Odin went on to point out to Blanc that aboard the *Henry* "our various traveling companions were Catholics for the most part; and the others, though Protestants, showed us a great deal of affection."[3]

Linnville to Victoria

The time had come for Odin to commence his own survey of the situation for Catholicism in the Lone Star Republic and begin laying the foundation for the reinvigoration of Catholic life in the region. Upon the Vincentians disembarking the *Henry* the vice prefect apostolic immediately began to move around Linnville, introducing himself and his fellow missionaries to the inhabitants of the settlement and seeking out whatever Catholics he might find residing in the vicinity. Among those whom he chanced upon were Judge John Hayes; W. G. Ewing, a local merchant; Ewing's sister (no name recorded), "who was raised in Nazareth, Kentucky," and who was to be married the following Sunday to a Major Watts; as well as a few others not mentioned by name.[4]

Odin happily reported to Blanc that among the residents at Linnville, he had found a few Missouri merchants whom he had known for a long time and an Irish Catholic (Judge Hayes) who had lived at the landing for several months. "I have been told that there are several Catholic families in Victoria and a small Mexican establishment 18 miles from this city; I am going there," Odin added. After three days at Linnville, he and his fellow Vincentians had finalized their plans for continuing on to Victoria situated twenty-five miles to the west. Following the 1835–36 Texas revolution against Mexico, the new Texas legislature had officially recognized Victoria as a municipality and county. The site had previously existed for a few years as a town named after President Guadalupe Victoria of Mexico.[5]

Early in the morning on July 16, Odin, Estany, Calvo, and Sala, in the company of a Colonel McDonald—whom Odin identified only as a Catholic—struck out for Victoria. Traversing the route that featured a picturesque setting of "rolling prairies intersected by many streams," the missionaries arrived at Victoria that same evening. John J. Linn and his family hosted Odin's party for the next five days.[6]

It took Odin only a short time to decide upon his initial steps aimed at rebuilding the Catholic presence in Texas. During his stay at the Linn home, he settled on assigning Father Estany as pastor at Victoria. Estany was asked to serve the Catholics of Victoria—mainly immigrants with a heavy Irish

John J. Linn's home in Victoria, Texas, where Jean-Marie Odin celebrated his first Mass in Texas. Courtesy UTSA Libraries Special Collections, Institute of Texan Cultures, #79–269.

identification—as well as Mexicans in the surrounding area.[7] There already existed at Victoria a small church, one which Odin described as "a little wooden church of 20ft. by 40." An Irish Dominican priest who had studied in Spain, Argentina, and Mexico before settling in Texas, Father Thomas Molloy reportedly had been stationed at Victoria during part of the latter 1830s. Earlier Father Molloy had labored at San Patricio and possibly also at Goliad. However, Odin made no mention of Father Molloy, and there is no extant record of Linn having mentioned the Irish cleric to Odin during the latter's stopover at the Linn home. Since it is assumed generally that Father Molloy was still living when the Vincentians made the visit to Victoria, his whereabouts at the time remains a mystery.[8]

The title to church property in Victoria had been assumed by the Texas government after the 1836 revolution. Nonetheless, the Catholics living in or near the area bounded by Victoria, San Patricio, and Goliad, including some Mexican families living near Coleto Creek less than fifteen miles southwest of Victoria, were now Father Estany's charge.[9] Odin, Calvo, and Sala then had to venture on to San Antonio de Bexar.

On the Road to San Antonio

One can only imagine the substance of the conversations that Odin and his confreres engaged in with John J. Linn, his family, and other Catholics while visiting at Victoria. Odin himself recorded little about the nature of his talks with Linn. What the French churchman did have to say centered on Linn's urging him to reclaim title to that Catholic Church in Victoria from the Lone Star Republic government at the new capital in Austin. In his own book, *Reminiscences of Fifty Years in Texas,* published decades later in 1883, Linn spoke hardly at all about his work with Odin, although he did write a two-and-one-half page complimentary summary of Odin's years in Texas and his decade as the second archbishop of New Orleans, concluding that "The memory of Bishop Odin is revered by the Catholics of Texas."[10]

It is certain that Odin was focused on the critical situation for the Catholics in and around San Antonio de Bexar. Father Timon, before Odin departed for Texas, back at St. Mary's of the Barrens Seminary, had taken his vice prefect apostolic into his confidence regarding the complaints of Juan Nepomuceno Seguín and the other Catholics whom Timon had met at Houston relative to the sad behavior of Fathers de la Garza and Valdéz. The vast majority of San Antonio de Bexar's Catholics were Mexicans of long-standing faith who had formed a religious identity with the municipality that could be traced back more than a century. The secularization of San Antonio's missions and Fathers de la Garza and Valdez's scandalous neglect of the municipality's Catholic faithful in the more recent years had contributed to an undermining of Catholic life throughout the San Antonio de Bexar neighborhood. As a result, the Catholic Mexicans in the Bexar city vicinity, with their culturally based quiet dignity, would accept that *un cambio de la guardia* (changing of the guard) was needed.

On the morning of July 21, Odin, Calvo, and Sala bade farewell to Father Estany and their hosts the Linn family and set out for San Antonio. The Bexar city was a journey of several days from Victoria southward and then southwest along the Goliad Road. For the adventure the three Vincentians joined a caravan of merchants, mainly Mexicans, who were transporting twenty carts of merchandise from Victoria to San Antonio.[11] Odin and his confreres had good reason to believe that crossing the more than one hundred miles of rolling, brushy, sometimes wooded, sunbaked terrain, where they would be constantly exposed to the elements as well as the threat of roaming bands of bellicose Comanches, would be undertaken more safely in the company of the merchants than on their own. A few German immigrants also made up part of the entourage.

How correct the Vincentians' decision proved to be! A mere two weeks later, in San Antonio, they would hear the frightening news of a destructive

Comanche raid on Linnville, during which Major Watts was killed, and his new bride of just a few days, Ewing's sister, was taken captive. The Comanches also attacked Victoria.

On the evening of July 21, Odin's caravan arrived at Coleto Creek. The next day Odin and his Vincentians delayed along their way to visit the rancho of Don Maria Fernández. There the vice prefect apostolic, Father Calvo, and Brother Sala were able to attend to the religious needs of the Fernández clan as well as those of five other Catholic families living in the vicinity of that rural estate. Odin assured those people that Father Estany would soon be visiting them. In the meanwhile, Don Maria informed Odin that "a few days earlier the Indians (likely Comanches) had taken all the horses."[12]

The end of Wednesday's jaunt found the travelers camped six miles from Goliad. The following partial long quotation from Odin's daily journal of that date is worth citing, though it contains some misinformation (corrected where necessary in the notes). It mirrors the French missionary's impressions and perceptions of a Texas at that time new to him. Odin wrote:

> We visited in the morning *La Bahia,* or Goliad, a town built in the year, or about the year 1715. . . . The patron of the church is Our Lady of Loretto. There are only seven Mexican, two Irish, and two American families living at Goliad. Goliad stands on a beautiful eminence on the bank of the San Antonio River. The prairies around are vast and fertile. From a distance, the traveler is struck by the view of the few buildings still standing, and imagines himself approaching the ancient cities of Italy. Near Goliad on the opposite side of the San Antonio River stands [*sic*] an old ruined church, convent, and fortification known by the name of Mission *Espiritu Santo.* It was erected by the King of Spain for the Indian mission and was under the care of religious of Guadalupe [Franciscans from the Colegio de Nuestro Senora de Guadalupe at Zacatecas, Mexico]. Five miles west of Goliad there are, likewise, the ruins of a church and convent called Mission Rosario. The Mission Del Refugio is eight miles distant from Goliad.[13]

According to those comments of Odin, on July 22 the caravan had halted for a two-day stopover near the ruins of the old Mission Nuestra Señora del Espíritu Santo de Zúñiga, allowing the three Vincentians to visit Goliad the following day. On July 24, camp was broken, and Odin, Calvo, and Sala once again found themselves on the road to San Antonio de Bexar. That leg of the journey would prove to be a most difficult one for them, however: persistent summer heat with temperatures above ninety degrees, a scarcity of food and water, illness, tiredness, oxcarts breaking down, and other obstacles prevailed. "We traveled then slowly. Carts were often breaking. Oxen lost. Fever among us," Odin entered in his daily journal. He himself suffered attacks of fever along the way, and he was thankful to be able to later write to Bishop Blanc that "our Brother Sala had provided himself with some bottles of Celinian balm, and he worked wonders among us."[14]

In spite of the hardships, as Odin and his troupe pushed on toward San Antonio, they enthusiastically turned their attention to evangelization. They devoted themselves with particular care to seeking out Mexican families. For example, an entire day was spent at the Rancho San Bartoloméo located fifty miles east of San Antonio. Beyond that, before entering the Bexar city the three missionaries visited several additional spreads, a number of them being Mexican ranchos whose origins could be traced back to the Spanish and Mexican eras of Texas.[15] Meanwhile, the vice prefect apostolic, well experienced in missioning among the indigenous peoples from his many years in Missouri and Arkansas, spent time with about 160 Lower Lipan Apaches.[16]

On the same day that he met with the Lipan Apaches, July 28, Odin made the acquaintance of Don Juan José Maria Erasmo Seguín, father of Juan Nepomuceno Seguín. Erasmo invited the three churchmen to breakfast with the Seguín family at their rancho, a grand range of several thousand acres named Casa Blanco, situated a few miles west of Floresville, a day's ride from San Antonio on the Goliad Road. Erasmo Seguín, born on June 2, 1782, in San Antonio and baptized in the San Fernando Church there, was prominent among Catholic Tejanos (Texans of Mexican ethnicity).[17] Don Erasmo was to remain a steady supporter of Odin and the church in Texas until his death in November 1857.

Matters to be Settled

"On July 30, we arrived in San Antonio de Bexar, a city pleasantly situated on the banks of the river by the same name," Odin wrote to Father Etienne at the Vincentian motherhouse in Paris. When Odin first reached the Bexar city it existed as an attractive settlement with most of its buildings "centered about the horseshoe bend in the San Antonio River."[18] San Antonio was the most important center of population north of the Rio Grande. It was significant first as the heart of a Franciscan missions cluster, maturing in the years 1718–31; then as the official seat of the Spanish government over Texas beginning in 1773 (though the municipality had served as the unofficial focus of Spanish government in Texas for decades before 1773); and finally as the seat of local Texas provincial government for the Mexican province of Coahuila-Texas. However, as we know, Odin, Calvo, and Sala were gravely concerned that since the late 1820s the town had witnessed a discouraging weakening of Catholic life under the lax leadership of Father de la Garza and, ultimately, Father Valdéz.

In his Houston deposition to Father Timon eighteen months earlier, Juan Nepomuceno Seguín had confirmed that Father de la Garza had rejected his vow of clerical celibacy as a *sacerdote* (priest) and was openly consorting with women. Equally discouraging, daily masses no longer were being celebrated at San Fernando Church, and the offering of catechism classes for the faithful had ceased. Moreover, Father de la Garza had begun demanding outrageous fees for administering the sacraments of baptism and marriage as well as for presiding over funerals and giving the dying the church's last sacrament, that of anointing of the sick. Finally, shortly after the Texas war for independence in 1836, de la Garza ceased making entries in the San Fernando Church parish records.[19] With the appearance on the scene at San Antonio of Odin and the other Vincentians, *un cambio radical* (a radical change) seemed imminent.

It was early in the morning on that Thursday when Odin, Calvo, and Sala entered San Antonio de Bexar, following their trek from Victoria. Fatigued and facing another hot day, the three Vincentians were eager to get settled into their quarters. San Antonio presented a larger and more historical setting than did Linnville, Victoria, or Goliad, and it was unfamiliar to the clerics. Fortunately, José Casiano, a Catholic businessman in the municipality who dealt in real estate, had made arrangements for the churchmen to stay at one of his houses. The Casiano home proved to be quite satisfactory for the missionaries, so much so that within just a few months Odin would purchase the residence from Casiano for three thousand dollars.[20]

Dominating Odin's thinking throughout the whole journey from Victoria was the prospect of his unavoidable confrontation with Fathers de la Garza and Valdéz. "On the day of my arrival I paid them a courtesy visit," Odin wrote to Bishop Rosati. Odin knew about Bishop Belaunzarán y Ureña's February 1839 letter to Blanc, wherein the Mexican prelate said that he had withdrawn their priestly faculties from the two San Antonio clerics. Moreover, Odin carried with him papers from Father Timon ordering the removal of de la Garza and Valdéz from active sacerdotal endeavors in the Bexar city, an authority that Timon possessed as the new prefect apostolic of Texas. Beyond that, several Catholic Texans, including Judge Hayes at Linnville, had also advised Odin of de la Garza's and Valdéz's shortcomings as priests.[21]

But what did Father Odin himself observe firsthand regarding the two priests and their behavior? And how did he react to the situation regarding Catholic life that he found at San Antonio? It must be remembered that Odin was a dedicated missionary steeped in the spirituality of St. Vincent de Paul. He had long been weaned from any possible evangelistic naiveté through his more than a decade and a half of laboring on the frontier of the Mississippi River Valley. Such an understanding of Odin is fundamental to coming to grips with his handling of Fathers de la Garza and Valdéz. This is true in particular when considering that occasionally the argument is made that Juan Nepomuceno Seguín and José Antonio Navarro may have had political feelings against Father de la Garza in particular, which, it sometimes is averred, negatively influenced their views of him as a priest. Odin would have dis-

San Fernando Church (later Cathedral). Front view, showing Carolan's Auction House next door. Probably taken between 1856 and 1867. Courtesy UTSA Libraries Special Collections, Institute of Texan Cultures, *San Antonio Light* Collection, #0010-A.

regarded any such polemics, inasmuch as the Frenchman was above all else simply a man of the church.[22]

Odin realized that generally among the Mexican people of San Antonio their Roman Catholic allegiance was deeply cemented, if not regularly practiced due in part to the condition of the Catholic religion in the neighborhood during that period of San Antonio's history. At the same time the vice prefect apostolic feared that as a Frenchman he might be considered a "foreign priest" sent to a locale where the local pastor was Mexican surrounded by family and supporters. As it developed, however, his concerns failed to materialize with any real depth. Many of the Bexar city's Catholic Mexican citizens were overjoyed to see Odin initiate a religious revitalization in their community.

Odin left several accounts of what he found at San Antonio and how he responded to the situation. From his letters and daily journal it is learned that on that Thursday he first tracked down Father Valdéz and visited with him for a while. Later in the day the vice prefect apostolic sought out Father de la Garza, locating the pastor in the "priest's house" near San Fernando Church.

Odin's discouragement at what he encountered was reflected in an August letter of that year that he wrote to Etienne: "Seeing them [de la Garza and Valdéz] in the midst of their wives and children, one dressed in a calico frock with white pants and the other in a small jacket of the same color, I felt so distressed that I could scarcely utter a word."[23]

But Odin did inform Father de la Garza that he himself would celebrate Mass at San Fernando Church the following Sunday and deliver a sermon in English, while Father Calvo would preach in Spanish. On the Friday and Saturday following the visits with de la Garza and Valdéz, Odin and Calvo walked around San Antonio surveying the Catholic situation in the neighborhood. So disheartened was Odin with what he observed that he wept. In a letter to Bishop Blanc, the Vincentian lamented, "In what a sad state I found the matter of religion! The church is half exposed and the haunt of a thousand swallows by day and thousands of bats at night. The ornaments that were once rich are all in such a state of filth and decay that it makes one sick. Never a word of instruction, no catechism, Mass mumbled every Sunday and attended by a half dozen old women and children; imagine the picture." How he must have felt! The missionary priest who for years back at St. Mary's of the Barrens Seminary and College had made it a practice to hear confessions for the seminarians and lay college students well into the night after returning from his fatiguing missioning rounds on Saturdays, in San Antonio learned that confessions had not been heard on a regular basis at San Fernando Church for five years.[24]

It soon became clear that the church's entire sacramental structure, from baptism to the anointing of the sick, had to be restored for the Catholics of San Antonio. Odin would be able to assume the leadership in this revival of the faith in the Bexar city because as vice prefect apostolic he possessed certain ecclesiastical jurisdictional faculties similar to an ordinary bishop in territories where normal Catholic hierarchical structure was nonfunctional.

"The curiosity of seeing two new priests attracted a large crowd," Odin reported to Bishop Rosati in reference to the Mass celebrated that first Sunday in San Antonio's San Fernando Church. The Vincentians were determined, however, that the Mass attendance on that August 2, 1840, Sunday was not to be viewed merely as a demonstration of the curious. Rather, Odin, Calvo, and Brother Sala saw that gathering of the faithful for Mass as the beginning of a new era in Catholic worship in the church. With the support of Brother Sala and the spiritual strength of their Vincentian formation, Odin and Calvo set about rebuilding. The result of their effort was that in his missive to Bishop Rosati of August 27 Odin was able to report: "We fixed the hours of Holy Mass, and a good number of people attend every day; we began catechism in English and French [in his daily journal Odin emphasized that Father Calvo also taught catechism in Spanish]. More than one hundred and twenty children flock to it every day. Already we have heard confessions; we are also working to repair the church."[25]

From the first day of his arrival at San Antonio Odin had realized only too well that relieving both Fathers de la Garza and Valdéz of their priestly authority and responsibilities in the Bexar city could not be delayed. After all, had not Bishop Belaunzarán y Ureña withdrawn the two priests' faculties more than a year and a half earlier? "I therefore presented myself to the parish priest and showed him the various letters with which I was provided," Odin told Rosati in his August letter. The vice prefect apostolic was referring to a meeting he had scheduled with Father de la Garza on Monday, August 3, following the Sunday Mass at San Fernando Church. During the course of his explaining to de la Garza that the latter was no longer the pastor of San Fernando Church, Odin announced that Father Calvo, "a more active and zealous priest," was to assume that position instead.[26]

While visiting with de la Garza on that occasion Odin witnessed an example of the former pastor making excessive financial demands on his poor parishioners. The incident is best narrated in Odin's own words: "He [Father de la Garza] was so troubled that he could scarcely understand them [the papers that Odin presented to the priest affirming the ecclesiastical changes in San Antonio]. Just as I was speaking to him two women came begging him to go and baptize a child likely to die. 'Do you have two *piastres* to give me?' he asked. 'No,' they answered, 'the mother is too poor.' 'Go get the money and then I will baptize the child.' [Odin then speaking] I felt so indignant that I immediately told these good women to go to our dwelling and there they would find a priest who would without charge."[27]

On the heels of that unpriestly display of behavior of Father de la Garza, Odin informed the San Fernando Church pastor that his ecclesiastical authority had ceased, and in the future any appeals to have it restored would have to be made to the vice prefect apostolic himself. By the end of that week, Odin, accompanied by José Antonio Navarro, José Flores de Abrego, John McMullen, and the Protestant mayor of San Antonio, John W. Smith, had completed an inventory of the church's properties and collected silver vessels and other church possessions stored in Father de la Garza's home. During the same period Odin also relieved Father Valdéz of his duties. On his second Sunday in San Antonio de Bexar Odin again celebrated Mass, with a good number of the municipality's Catholics in attendance and some Protestants as well. As during the Mass of the previous Sunday, Odin again preached in English and Calvo in Spanish.[28]

But all was progressing too well, and Odin, the experienced missionary that he was, sensed this. In his August 27 letter to Bishop Rosati the Frenchman expressed as much. He wrote, "[K]nowing that the work of God is well established only when it rests on tribulations, I was frightened seeing that every-thing was prospering beyond our hopes."[29]

Comanche Raids and the Church Tower Bells Controversy

Problems were about to surface, the first being the previously mentioned Comanche raids on Linnville and Victoria, and the second being tensions for the three Vincentians that erupted at San Fernando Church over Odin's refusal to allow the church's tower bells to be rung for a Protestant funeral. "On the fourth day of August, 1840, we of Victoria were startled by the apparition pre-sented by the sudden appearance of six hundred mounted Comanches in the immediate outskirts of the village," wrote John J. Linn about the Comanche attack on Victoria. Linn went on to describe how between the fourth and eighth of August, the Comanches threatened Victoria, killed numerous set-tlers in the vicinities of that town as well as Linnville and then attacked the latter community and burned it. As already mentioned, among those persons killed was Major Watts. Mrs. Watts, W. G. Ewing's sister and recent bride of Major Watts, was captured and then later escaped under the protection of her brother, even though a Comanche arrow struck her. The Comanches raided John J. Linn's warehouse at Linnville and inflicted much damage on the port settlement before finally setting the torch to it.[30]

Odin was shocked and dismayed when he learned of the catastrophe. "We heard that the Indians had attacked and burned down Linnville and taken many horses and cattle. They also attacked Victoria," he entered in his daily journal on August 13.[31] The missionary, who back in Missouri and Arkansas had cherished laboring among the indigenous peoples, and who less than three weeks earlier had visited with Lipan Apaches along the road from Victoria to San Antonio de Bexar, was now beginning to sense the threat posed by the presence of bellicose Comanches. This was a new and different experience for him. It is unclear whether Odin, when hearing about the raids, realized that Major Watts had been killed and his new bride taken captive at Linnville. The vice prefect apostolic, as would have been expected of him, simply grieved for all of the people who suffered from the raids.

Yet in an understandably special way he immediately feared for the safety of Father Estany at Victoria. The Frenchman soon found out that his confrere's life had been spared, although the new pastor had lost his and many of the church's possessions, including some sacred vessels. In his August 27 letter to Rosati, Odin described the situation in this manner: "Savages in the number of 500 recently attacked Linnville, and after seizing everything they set fire to all the houses. From there they fell upon Victoria, where they killed fifteen to twenty people. They were successfully repulsed, but they retreated only a short distance and the next day they reappeared. The first house they attacked was where Rev. Estany lived. He had the good fortune to escape their weapons, but they stole all his linen, his altar vessels, and even his books. Horses, mules, oxen, cows, everything was seized and carried away in these parts. We live here in constant fear."[32]

Meanwhile, a confrontational situation had erupted at San Antonio, one that forced Odin to defend Catholic Church tradition against the lax practices that Father de la Garza had allowed to creep into everyday life in the Bexar city during his years as pastor at San Fernando Church. Under de la Garza the custom had grown of allowing the church tower bells to be rung to announce public events such as cock fights, horse races, and so forth. It also had become common to ring the bells to take notice of Protestant funerals. However, according to Catholic precedent, the tower bells of a Catholic church could be rung on a regular basis at dawn, at noon for the Angelus (El Angelus in Spanish-speaking San Antonio) or Regina Caeli for Easter Time (Regina Coeli for Spanish-speaking areas), and at night. Beyond that, in communities where Catholics made up a noticeable presence among the population, it was the custom to sound the church bells at the elevation of the Host during the consecration in the Mass. At the same time, the bells might also have been employed to call parishioners to Mass. Those usages of the church tower bells remain common today in many areas. On special occasions, such as the death of a pope, archbishop, bishop, or some other prominent church figure, the church tower bells might also be rung.

In mid-August Odin was invited to a Saturday evening meeting of the trustees of San Fernando Church, a get-together organized for the purpose of addressing the issue of planning church repairs. During the course of the gathering's discussions, Odin queried Mayor John W. Smith, a Protestant, as to whether or not the municipal government at San Antonio had in the past ordered the ringing of the San Fernando Church tower bells for public functions and Protestant funerals. In the context of developing his question, Odin informed the mayor that such use of the bells was contrary to the rules of the Catholic Church. In his reply to Odin, Mayor Smith assured Odin that the municipal government had never requested that the church tower bells be rung in the manner indicated. Smith then urged Odin to put into place whatever plan of action he, as head of the Catholic Church in Texas, would deem necessary for the future regarding the issue.[33]

However, the mayor proved to be unfaithful to his word. Within two days of the Saturday evening meeting, on August 16, Col. Henry Wax Karnes, a Texian hero of the revolution against Mexico, died. Karnes claimed no religious affiliation, and his funeral was scheduled for August 18. On the day following the colonel's death a deputation of San Antonio citizens, with the support of Mayor Smith, approached Vice Prefect Apostolic Odin with a request that the San Fernando Church tower bells be rung for Karnes's funeral. Odin expressed to his visitors his own respect for the memory of Colonel Karnes, but nonetheless he refused their petition. Odin carefully explained to the group, as he had earlier at the church trustees' meeting, that the ringing of the bells on the occasion of a Protestant funeral would violate Catholic Church traditions.[34]

In his discussion with the citizens, Odin recalled that while Christianity had first entered Texas through the efforts of Franciscan friars and their missions, even before the revolution of 1835–36 Americanist and Protestant attitudes were becoming increasingly influential in the land.[35] That reality, along with Father de la Garza's lax approach to ringing the San Fernando Church's tower bells, lay at the heart of the tensions that the Karnes funeral affair ignited. On the day of Colonel Karnes's funeral, a Wednesday, tempers flared. Eventually, as the hours of the day passed, a coterie of San Antonio men—Catholics and Protestants alike—fueled agitation against Odin. As anger increased, two of the men, a doctor and a lawyer, climbed the church belfry and rang the bells as best they could. A couple of US judges tried to calm the situation, and several Catholic Mexican citizens defended their new priest.[36]

It appears that Mayor Smith not only had agreed with the agitators against Odin, but he had himself acted as the ringleader of the provocation. Odin described the end of the squabble in a letter to Bishop Blanc, lamenting that "After the funeral the mayor wished to convene an assembly in order to censor my actions; he had been most eager to arouse tempers by means of two so-called Irish Catholics. He had even boasted about giving me my walking papers, but he could bring together only nine people between the ages of 18 and 20. And when they organized their meeting it was impossible for them to phrase a single resolution. However, they entrusted a lawyer to draft something. At the end of two days I was sent some resolutions signed by five individuals only, accusing me of narrow-mindedness, intolerance, etc. I immediately answered them with civility and firmness. I was told that my answer confounded them and they were exceedingly sorry to have displayed the bad humour."[37]

Mayor Smith did not give up easily. He subsequently attempted to float a petition against Odin among San Antonio's Mexican population. Seeing through his ploy, they would have no part of it. The incident was reported on in the newspapers of the new Texas capital, Austin. But Father Odin satisfactorily responded, muffling the excitement against him. The Karnes funeral affair passed into history, and Odin and his Vincentians were once again able to turn their attention to strengthening Catholic life in Texas north of the Nueces River.[38]

9

The Mission beyond San Antonio

IT HAD BEEN A CHALLENGING AUGUST for Father Odin and his Vincentians in San Antonio. As the weeks passed and summer gave way to fall, Odin, Calvo, and Sala began to sense a flame of religious fervor igniting once again among the Bexar city's Catholic population. September was marked by the appearance of rains and hope for milder temperatures. With October and November would come the Indian summer so well known to that area of the Lone Star Republic. Perhaps the expected pleasant weather might be seen as a symbol of better developments to come for the Catholic re-evangelization of the land.

Building Up the Faith from Horseback

During this first month in the city, Fathers Odin and Calvo, with the considerable help of Brother Sala, inaugurated a revitalization of Catholic life at San Fernando Church. Catechism classes in both Spanish and English began on August 10. The following day Father Calvo "carried, publicly, the Blessed Sacrament to a sick man."[1] Many Catholics reverently accompanied Father Calvo and the Blessed Sacrament through the streets of the city. It had been fourteen years since the people of San Antonio de Bexar had been able to participate in such a procession. In the meantime, repairs to the church were started, and the two priests began celebrating Mass daily, with sermons usually given in Spanish, although occasionally they were in English. Moreover, the sacraments of baptism, confession, marriage, and the anointing of the sick as well as the preparation of the youth for First Holy Communion once again became part of the lives of San Antonio's Catholic families. A renewal of catechism classes for the young, taught in Spanish, and when necessary in English or even French, gave Father Odin a special sense of apostolic achievement.[2]

While all of this was developing, Father Odin installed Father Calvo as the new pastor of San Fernando Church and completed, along with José Antonio

Navarro, an extensive survey of the condition of each of the former Franciscan missions in the San Antonio vicinity. The noted Vincentian historian, the late Father Ralph Bayard, commented on that inventory more than a half century ago, writing that "With Navarro he [Father Odin] had made an assessing visitation of the four missions, located from three to nine miles south of the town. The remains of San Juan Capistrano and San Francisco de la Espada, choked by cactus, huisache, and mesquite and swarming with geckoes and spiders, were beyond restoration. San José and Nuestra Señora de la Purísima Concepción, though leaky and otherwise worse for disuse, could be renovated without prohibitive expenses."[3]

Feeling secure that the reinvigoration of the deposit of faith among the Catholics in San Antonio de Bexar was well underway and set firmly in the capable hands of Father Calvo, Odin then turned his attention more clearly to his mission beyond the Bexar city. On November 9, bidding a temporary farewell to the people of that municipality, he departed for other locales of the vast region of Texas now under his ecclesiastical jurisdiction. As the vice prefect apostolic took his leave early in the morning, he joined eight other travelers, again for the sake of protection from marauding Comanches still in the area.[4]

The troupe slowly nudged their horses and carriages eastward, passing just south of Mission San Antonio de Valero, the Alamo, and heading out of the city toward the settlement of Gonzalez some seventy-five miles distant. As had been his custom since those early days of riding the mission circuit in Missouri and Arkansas, Odin planned to visit as many isolated ranches, farms, town (*villas*), and villages (*pueblos*) as possible. He would labor among Mexicans, Irish, Germans, Czechs, French, Belgians, and other nationalities with historical Catholic identities, showing an equal enthusiasm for all. At the same time he would do what he could for the indigenous peoples.

In the course of that evangelizing, which would ultimately consume the next two decades of his life, Father Odin would travel either on horseback or on foot. Experiencing extremes of weather—often pleasant and other times harsh—he would barely survive floods, struggle over parched lands, traverse undulating hill country, make his way through wooded tracts, and find himself sometimes ill, while bringing the Gospel and the church's sacraments to Texas' scattered Roman Catholics. In so doing, Jean-Marie Odin would lay the foundation for Catholicism's nineteenth-century renaissance in Texas and establish the base for the Catholic Church's future development in the land for decades to come.

That November trek of Father Odin beyond San Antonio de Bexar took him northeast across the Guadalupe and San Marcos rivers, through the settlements of Seguin and Gonzalez, and southeast back to Victoria. En route to Victoria from Gonzalez the vice prefect apostolic stayed over at the Flores rancho on the banks of the Guadalupe River. There he took delight in

San José y San Miguel de Aguayo Mission, San Antonio, Texas, 1860s. Exterior of the mission showing front and south side elevation. Courtesy Catholic Archives of Texas.

catechizing many people. Some twenty-three miles from Victoria Odin and his traveling companions came upon a Catholic Irishman from Missouri named Patrick Dullen.[5] That chance encounter proved to be another illustration of how Texas was developing as a demographic and religious junction, kneading together the Catholic Mexican world with the vanguard of a Catholic immigrant westward migration from the United States and Europe into the Lone State Republic.

Four days out from San Antonio de Bexar, and after he had reached Victoria and enjoyed a reunion with Father Estany, Odin recorded in his daily journal, "Traversed very extensive prairies. Large pecans grow on the banks of the Guadalupe. Early in the morning we arrived at Victoria. I spent time with Mr. Estany, found him quite thin; he had been sick during all the fall."[6] Father Estany's physical condition caused Odin great concern, and he spoke with his

Spanish priest about it during their visit. The two Vincentians unloaded supplies that Odin had brought from San Antonio, spent some time rejuvenating their Vincentian spirituality, and discussed developments at Victoria, Linnville, and San Antonio. Odin and Estany also devoted time to reviewing the latter's evangelization among the Mexican and immigrant Catholics in the vicinity of Victoria.

"Rev. Estany has been ailing for nearly two months. Two other priests from Kentucky who had come to settle in Texas have had serious illness." These words Jean-Marie Odin wrote to Father Etienne back at Paris on December 13, 1840. Aside from mirroring Odin's continued worry about Father Estany's health, this message contained the vice prefect apostolic's first mention to the procurator general of the Congregation of the Mission of the two clerics from the faculty of St. Joseph's College at Bardstown, Kentucky, who had ventured to Texas to serve among the Catholics there almost a year earlier: Fathers George W. Haydon and Edward Clarke.[7]

At the time of his letter to Etienne, Odin had not as yet actually met Haydon and Clarke, but he was aware of their dedicated missioning in the area since their arrival in Texas in late December 1839. From January 1840 to June 1841, with the exception of several weeks during the early period of their excursion when Father Clarke had fallen ill and remained at Richmond on the Brazos River, the two Kentucky priests had visited Catholics in the region bounded on the south by Refugio, on the west by San Antonio de Bexar, and on the east by the settlements along the Brazos River.

At one point during his labors, at San Antonio de Bexar, Father Haydon had presented himself to Father de la Garza, who received the Kentucky priest cordially and even gave him a badly needed set of vestments as well as a chalice. Nonetheless, Haydon soon came to conclusions about the unpriestly life of de la Garza that supported the later observations of Jean-Marie Odin. Convinced that in the Bexar city he had come upon an irregular clerical situation, Haydon wrote to Bishop Blanc back at New Orleans, urging that a Spanish-speaking priest be sent to San Antonio to replace Father de la Garza at San Fernando Church.[8]

Father Haydon carried on his ministry in Texas into the fall of 1841, when he died of yellow fever at Morgan's Point, on the shores of Galveston Bay, while administering the sacraments to and consoling the victims of the dreaded sickness at that settlement. Father Clarke continued to labor in Texas until 1856, at which time he departed for Louisiana.[9]

Following Jean-Marie Odin's brief stay with Father Estany, the vice prefect apostolic devoted almost two more weeks among Catholics in the environs of Victoria. A particularly joyful part of Odin's jaunt proved to be his catechizing among a number of families along the Lavaca River, some of whom he found that he had known back at Perryville, Missouri, as parishioners of Saint Mary's of the Barrens Church. The vice prefect apostolic buoyantly described his happy reunion with those Catholics to Father Etienne back at Paris: "Nearly 4,000 Catholics live west of the Guadalupe River. Ascending the Lavaca, I discovered 112. Several among them belonged to our parish at the Barrens. My arrival among them caused a very responsive pleasure: all approached the holy tribunal and 32 presented themselves to the holy table. They are busy constructing a wooden church under the protection of Mary, in memory of our church in Missouri.[10]

Within a few days of his appearance among the former Missourians, Odin met with Father Clarke at Brown's Settlement. In his conversations with Clarke, Odin voiced his own clear approval of the labors that the two priests from Kentucky had been doing. Offering Clarke encouragement for his future efforts in Texas, Odin renewed the Kentuckians' priestly faculties for service in Texas.[11]

But there existed a matter of major importance to which the vice prefect apostolic now had to turn his attention: reclaiming for the church title to several of its missions, churches, and attached lands and properties previously owned in Texas under the Spanish and then Mexican governments but subsequently lost to the Republic of Texas in the aftermath of the 1835–36 revolution against Mexico. If the Texas civil authorities could be persuaded to return ownership of these holdings to the church, then the foundation for a Catholic rebuilding in the Lone Star Republic would be noticeably strengthened. Thus, Odin's eyes were turned north toward the capital of the republic, the city of Austin on the Colorado River. Of added importance, the vice prefect apostolic's trip to Austin would make up part of his overall plan to survey the western areas of Texas, as he knew the republic at the time, "in search of Catholics scattered throughout the immense land."[12]

The Challenge to Odin in Austin

After spending five days at Brown's Settlement, Odin mounted his horse and, leading his mule, struck out for Austin. He made good headway along the banks of the Colorado River on that first day, covering thirty-eight miles. By the end of the second day the French priest had reached a site out in the open terrain approximately a mile beyond the settlement of Bastrop. There he camped overnight. Then after having carefully guided his horse and mule along the ground of the Colorado River route through the eastern reaches of the Texas hill country for three days, Odin was able to record in his daily journal that he "spent the night eight miles this side of Austin." On November 29, having traveled about one hundred miles from his original point of departure, the vice prefect apostolic entered the city of Austin, itself little more than a frontier community. Of Austin at that time one historian recently wrote,

"Austin. . . was selected as the site of the permanent capital in 1839. In the spring of that year Edwin Waller surveyed the townsite and construction commenced on the public buildings. At an auction sale on August 1, 1839, over three hundred lots were sold; the officials of government arrived in October, the city was incorporated in December, and Edwin Waller was elected mayor in January 1840."[13]

Fortune seemed to smile on Odin shortly after his appearance at the capital city, when he met an acquaintance whom he had come to know earlier while in New Orleans on his way to Texas, the *chargé d'affaires* of France to the Texas republic, Jean Pierre Isidor Dubois de Saligny. The Catholic diplomat invited Odin to the French Legation House, Saligny's temporary residence in Austin. On that same day that he met Saligny, Odin participated in the first of several "discussions of congress" to which he would be invited while making Austin his haven. The following morning Saligny suggested to Odin that the churchman use the French Legation House for the duration of his sojourn to the capital city. In the context of making his offer, Saligny promised Odin whatever aid he might be able to muster in support of the vice prefect apostolic's attempt to reclaim for the church from the Texas government titles to Catholic properties. In addition, Saligny made a gift to Odin of "two or three acres for a church and convent."[14]

The joining together of Odin and Saligny to serve the church's interests in the young Texas republic was a visible manifestation of the Roman Catholic legacy of France. At the time the vice prefect apostolic knew nothing of another and apparently less than admirable side of Saligny's character that seems to have existed. Saligny's behavior in Texas, and later in Mexico as well as back in France, was criticized as having been self-centered and sometimes dishonorable. It drew severe condemnation from both the Texas government and Saligny's superiors in the French ministry. Unaware of that situation, Odin only found in Saligny a friend of the church.[15]

Just how prominent was the vice prefect apostolic's role in the negotiations in Austin that ultimately returned to the Catholic Church the titles to its Texas properties? Odin's efforts in fact proved to have been quite significant. He possessed some familiarity with how and why the church had lost churches, missions, and other holdings. Moreover, Odin understood fully well that by right those religious edifices, lands, and other properties belonged to the church and should be returned to the proper ecclesiastical authorities. "My main purpose in coming to Austin was to obtain from Congress a decision which secured for Catholic worship all churches built under the Spanish government," wrote Odin to Cardinal James Fransoni, cardinal-prefect of the Sacred Congregation de Propaganda Fide back in Rome.[16] With that focus, Odin entered into the political and social orbit of Austin, endeavoring to work through the

Texas legislature a bill designed to restore to the Catholic Church title to its lost properties.

Unbeknownst to him at the time, the vice-prefect apostolic was soon to enjoy in that effort the on-site help of his friend and religious superior, Father Timon. Before the end of December, Odin and Timon would be reunited in Austin. On the very day that he had started writing his latest letter to Cardinal Fransoni, December 14, Odin entered in his daily journal, "I read in a Galveston paper of the arrival there of Revs. Timon and Stehle [Vincentian Father Nicholas Stehle had accompanied Timon on his trip to Texas from Louisiana]."[17]

Father Timon, as visitor of the Congregation of the Mission's American province and prefect apostolic of Texas, had planned his second trip to the Lone Star Republic for some time. He realized clearly that his Vincentians were linked directly to any possible revival of Catholicism in Texas. So, even though Odin would be the leader of the Catholic revitalization there, and Timon was confident that his confrere was already doing an outstanding job, the visitor felt a need to inspect the situation himself. That second journey to Texas was important to Father Timon also because he was scheduled in the near future to undertake a voyage to Europe, primarily for the purpose of reporting to his Congregation of the Mission superiors at the Paris motherhouse on the status of the Vincentian missioning effort in America. The situation in Texas was bound to loom prominent in that account.

Another urgency prompted Timon to take on the Texas jaunt. In October of 1840, he received a letter from Cardinal Fransoni, written in July, directing him personally to deliver a friendly communication from the Holy See to the head of the government of the Lone Star Republic, Pres. Mirabeau B. Lamar. That Vatican initiative might be interpreted as a virtual papal recognition of the Lone Star Republic's stature as an independent nation. Since succeeding Sam Houston as president of the Lone Star Republic on December 10, 1838, Lamar had pursued vigorously a policy of encouraging European governments and Mexico as well to recognize Texas independence.[18] Therefore the papal greeting that Father Timon was to carry to Lamar was of considerable historical importance. And it promised to serve well the interests of the church in Texas.

On December 1, Timon and Stehle sailed from New Orleans for Texas, arriving at the port of Galveston four days later. Spending a short time at Galveston and then Houston, the two priests soon set out for Austin, where they arrived on December 21. However, well before Fathers Timon and Stehle made their appearance at the Texas capital, Odin had already begun the process aimed at attaining passage of a church properties title bill in the Texas legislature. At the same time the vice prefect apostolic visited with and catechized among Catholic families in the area, purchased lots for the church, opened a subscription for the construction of a church in Austin to be under the invocation of St. Louis of France, and made himself visible around the Austin community for the sake of missioning.[19] On December 6, for example, Odin traveled fifteen miles south of Austin to the settlement of Comanche. There he found two Catholic families, whom he served through the morning of December 8, and stayed with a Belgian couple, Napoleon Alex Van Hamins and his wife (no name available for her).

Returning to Austin, Odin immediately turned to preparing his petition to the Texas congress.[20] Working tirelessly from a plan that Father Timon (with Odin's help) had designed earlier, and taking advantage of the expertise and support that Saligny and a few leaders of the Texas community offered him, Odin wrote his petition to the House of Representatives. Meanwhile, Saligny hosted a lavish dinner in his home for Odin and a select group of dignitaries whom the *chargé d'affaires* felt might be prevailed upon to move the petition through the legislature. Among those guests were Gen. Sam Houston; Gen. William Harrison; Cornelius Van Ness, senior representative from San Antonio de Bexar, and Mrs. Van Ness; and Representatives James Mayfield, George Blow, James Byrne, and Michael Menard, a close friend of Odin's from Galveston.[21]

Additional banquets at the Saligny residence brought Odin into contact with other influential Texans, some of whom were professing Catholics. From discussions with those personages the vice prefect apostolic soon formed the opinion that the church properties bill would attract its most ardent supporters from among Houston, Byrne, Menard, Mayfield, Senators William Daingerfield and James Miller, and Rep. William Porter. During that time Odin came increasingly to appreciate Saligny for his support of the church. This was clearly seen in letters the French priest mailed to other ecclesiastics including Etienne and Fransoni. To the latter the vice prefect apostolic wrote and suggested that the Holy See honor Saligny with a title of Roman count.[22]

On December 21 Odin presented his finished petition to Representative Porter, who introduced it in the House of Representatives that same morning and saw it referred to a Select Committee of the House. In the process of the bill being worked through that legislative body, Representative Van Ness moved to have Mission San Antonio de Valero, the Alamo, excluded from the list of missions being considered for return to the church. Van Ness argued that around the Alamo had grown an historical identity associated with Texas independence and the Battle of the Alamo that demanded that the mission remain a possession of the Republic of Texas. The senior representative from San Antonio ignored the historical reality that Franciscan missionaries had established Mission San Antonio de Valero 118 years before the battle of the Alamo and had missioned from it for more than a century. From that perspective Mission San Antonio de Valero had its place enshrined in the historical narrative of Texas long before the Battle of the Alamo. Van Ness, though, convinced a majority in the House of Representatives, and Mission San Antonio de Valero was removed from the inventory list of those properties being considered in Odin's petition.

On January 13, 1841, two weeks after Fathers Odin and Timon had departed Austin for East Texas, the vice president of the Lone State Republic, David G. Burnet, a Calvinist who had dined with both Odin and Timon during their stay in Austin and had engaged in vigorous but friendly discussion about religion with the two Vincentians, signed into law the Texas congress's act approving the following:

> An act confirming the use, occupancy, and enjoyment of the churches, church lots, and mission churches of the Roman Catholic congregation living in or near the vicinity of the same. Sec. 1. Be it enacted by the Senate and House of Representatives of the Republic of Texas, in Congress assembled. That the churches of San Antonio, Goliad, and Victoria, the church lot of Nacogdoches, the churches at the Mission Concepción, San José, San Juan, Espada, and the Mission of Refugio, with out-buildings and lots, if any belong to them, be, and they are hereby acknowledged and declared the property of the present chief pastor of the Roman Catholic Church in the Republic of Texas, and his successors in office in trust forever, for the use and benefit of the congregations residing near the same, for religious purposes and purposes of education, and none other; provided that nothing herein contained shall be so construed as to give title to any lands except the lots upon which churches are situated, which shall not exceed fifteen acres.[23]

Ironically, the day following Burnet's signing of the bill into law, Representative Van Ness experienced a change of heart in reference to exempting from the list of church properties Mission San Antonio de Valero. Likely influenced in that direction by Sam Houston, Van Ness unexpectedly introduced a second bill in the House of Representatives that returned ownership of the Alamo mission to the Catholic Church. The legislation was quickly pushed through both houses of the Texas congress and signed by Burnet on January 18.[24]

Riding the Circuit with Timon Once Again

"The journey down to Houston was a continued mission," recalled Father Timon years later regarding the early stages of his five-week missioning trip with Odin after the two Vincentians departed Austin. It was on the day that Odin's petition regarding church property titles was carried to the Texas Senate, December 31, that both Sons of Saint Vincent left the Texas Capitol to begin evangelizing eastward.[25] They both were informed later of the successful passage of the Texas congressional acts mentioned above. In the meantime, Odin was intent upon finishing his survey of the status of the Catholic faith in those lands he understood made up the territory assigned to him as vice prefect apostolic. The missioning trek with Timon east, ultimately to the region of San Augustine near the Sabine River, was planned as the final leg of that adventure.

From a physical perspective, the tour developed as one of the most demanding of either Odin's or Timon's missioning experience. Undertaken in the dead of winter, the expedition had to be endured in cold and wet weather. Roads along the route—sometimes mere paths—were muddied and deteriorated. It was not uncommon for the two priests to paddle upriver or make their way across water bodies (we recall that Odin could barely swim), sometimes sleeping out of doors regularly exposed to the chill and damp conditions.

The reality of a Catholic Texas short on clergy gripped Odin and Timon. They soon concluded that the greatest need was churches for both the incoming Catholic immigrants and scattered resident Mexicans. But with the exception of the churches that the Texas government had recently returned, few were to be had. Added to this, the republic's Catholics possessed little money for the building of churches. During their travel, Odin and Timon celebrated Mass each day, often in private homes but sometimes in public buildings.[26] Along their route they regularly catechized, baptized, heard confessions, reconciled marriages, and preached.

Odin and Timon labored among long-neglected Catholics but sometimes conversed with Protestants as well, some of whom were anti-Catholic and negative and others who were friendly and respectful. That period in the narrative of the United States was one where intense phobia against immigrants, especially Catholic ones, was emerging throughout Protestant America. This was noticeably true of the American South, and thus Texas. The vehemently biased nativists were becoming more radical in their denunciations of Catholics at every level of society. However, on a number of occasions Protestants received the two Vincentians in a courteous manner. One such example of this was a Reverend Miller and his family, Presbyterians who lived near Cummings Creek. They hosted Odin and Timon overnight in their home on January 4, and 5, 1841, engaged in friendly and constructive dialogue, and bid the two missionaries a good trip.[27]

From December 31, 1840, to January 8, 1841, Odin and Timon journeyed first to the Van Hamins home at Comanche where Odin had visited earlier and then on to the community of Bastrop, the Miller residence near Cummings Creek, the German settlement of Industry, San Felipe, and beyond Bayou Creek to Houston. It was on a Friday that the pair entered the former capital of the Lone Star Republic. As had been their custom since their earliest days riding the missionary circuit together in Missouri and Arkansas, Odin and

Timon sought a place to set up an altar for the celebration of Mass. Having made such arrangements by Saturday evening, on Sunday, January 10, Odin was able to record in his daily journal, "We celebrated Mass at Mr. Bernard Careher's store. Father Timon preached on the Eucharist, and in the evening he preached in the old Senate room. Large audiences. We opened a subscription list."[28]

On his initial visit to Houston with Father Llebaria back in late December 1838 and early January 1839, Timon had formed a church building subscription committee. The "energetic young politician" John Fitzgerald, along with John J. Linn, had headed that earlier group. But due to the depressed economy of Texas during that period, and also because no resident priest was stationed in the vicinity to offer encouragement, the committee's efforts had produced few results. Now a new subscription committee was formed. Chairing it was the merchant who had made available his store for Mass, Bernard Careher. Joining the storeowner were a French Catholic, Mr. De Chene, and an Irishman named Donellan. Even though poverty still dominated the Texas economic scene, seven hundred dollars were pledged immediately.[29]

In the unfolding of those developments, the early contour of a parish structure began to take shape, the first of many parish church foundations that Father Jean-Marie Odin would inspire during his more than twenty years laboring in Texas. The church that was to be constructed in Houston would be placed under the protection of St. Vincent de Paul. Odin himself, on January 11, baptized the first person of the envisioned new parish, a two-month-old baby boy named William Pascall.[30]

With that aspect of their trek completed, Odin and Timon arranged to have their horses stabled, bade farewell to Mr. De Chene, who had acted as their host in Houston, and departed for Galveston aboard the ship *Dayton*. Soaked from the rainy weather, the two missionaries arrived at their destination the next morning. During the week that they spent in Galveston, Timon invested his confrere Odin with the appropriate authority as chief pastor of the Catholic Church in Texas. It may have been at that time also that Timon granted Odin special ecclesiastical rank to administer the sacrament of confirmation, inasmuch as, in Timon's words, Odin "was in fact Prefect Apostolic of Texas."[31]

At Galveston Odin and Timon happily were reunited with Michael and Peter Menard and their families. There they also met an old friend from St. Mary of the Barrens Seminary at Perryville, Dr. Nicholas Labadie. The doctor introduced the two clerics to his second wife, Agnes Rivers. The two Vincentians involved themselves at Galveston in much the same manner as they had at Houston: celebrating Mass, catechizing, preaching, administering various sacraments, and starting a subscription for pledges designed to finance the building of a church.

On January 19, the pair again boarded the *Dayton* and commenced the final lap of the journey in eastern Texas. They endured a difficult trip back to Houston that included the voyage up the channel on the *Dayton,* an attempt to negotiate a segment of the waters on a skiff, a trek of nine miles knee deep in mud, and a final segment of the journey on horseback. Arriving at Houston late on the night of January 21, the two churchmen waited there until the morning of January 23, when they then set out for Nacogdoches.

Missioning all along the way, the two Sons of St. Vincent again encountered demanding travel conditions, threading their way beyond Huntsville to Nacogdoches and finally on to San Augustine. At the latter settlement, having concelebrated Mass the previous day, Odin and Timon parted company. Timon headed his horse northward toward Natchitoches, Louisiana, anticipating his return to St. Mary's of the Barrens Seminary at Perryville. Odin, on the other hand, turned back in the direction of San Antonio to begin another chapter in the Catholic evangelization of Texas.

࿔

He Is to Be Vicar Apostolic

"FATHER TIMON STARTED FOR NATCHITOCHES and I went to Mr. McDonald's, four miles from San Augustine on the Irish Bayou. . . . I baptized and catechized," Odin wrote in his daily journal on February 8, 1841.[1] That stopover at the home of Donald McDonald was just the first of several such evangelizing initiatives that the missionary from France made during his thirty-two-day itinerary from San Augustine back to San Antonio de Bexar. His journal entries covering the period of the trek consistently highlighted Masses celebrated, baptisms administered, confessions heard, preaching, and catechizing carried on.

The amalgamation of the names of people Odin served en route to San Antonio, as he presented himself along the way, could be seen as a veritable catalogue of the Mexican and immigrant Catholic population to be found in Texas during that period of history. To mention just a few from among a good number, there was the family of Mariano Sanchez; that of Maria Cassilda Lasarina; the clan of Joseph Maria Procella; John Durat and his large household living on the banks of the Angelina River; Refugio Valenzuela; David Shelby and his kin residing in Austin County; John Kerr and his relatives; and another Irishman named Fagan (first name not given) settled near Victoria.

With his return to the San Antonio, Jean-Marie Odin had concluded his survey of those areas of Texas under his jurisdiction, as he understood his assignment at that point in his tenure in the Lone Star Republic. But, regarding Catholic ecclesiastical boundaries, the expansive land lying south of San Antonio to the Rio Grande and extending eastward and westward from the Gulf of Mexico to El Paso del Norte, remained a question mark in his mind and would remain so for years. As a decade later Odin would explain to Cardinal Alessandro Barnabo, prefect de Propaganda Fide at the time, the French missionary was inclined to accept the view that the Texans "in their declaration of independence. . . . requested as the western border of their domain the Rio Grande from its mouth to its source."[2] Odin's interpretation of the Texas boundary line issued proved accurate. But, as he seems to have sensed, problems clearly existed with such a broad claim. As one respected source commented on that topic, "It is a well-known fact that on December 19, 1836, the first Congress of the Republic of Texas adopted an act defining the southern and northwestern boundaries of the Republic to be the Rio Grande from its mouth to its source, then due north to the 42nd parallel, east along the 42nd parallel to the Adams-Onis line, then south to the source of the Arkansas River, along the Arkansas to the 100th meridian, and south along the meridian to the Red River. This western and northern boundary line, adopted apparently on the suggestion of Stephen F. Austin and others, is almost beyond comprehension in its exaggerated final form."[3]

That distorted perception of the boundary lines of the Texans in 1836 left Odin unsure about the extent of the territory of his own ecclesiastical jurisdiction in 1840. Of special concern to him was whether or not he should try to exercise authority over the area south and west of the Nueces River to the Rio Grande. Odin wondered if that vast acreage might not actually fall under the jurisdiction of the bishop of Linares, or possibly even Durango, Mexico. It was to be more than thirty years later that the ecclesiastical boundary question finally would be resolved, with the erection of the Vicariate of Brownsville in 1874.[4] If Odin assumed, and he seems to have done so, that his jurisdiction existed from the Nueces River northward, then he determined to work that spacious area with dedication.

No Miter for Detroit

Before bidding farewell to Odin at San Augustine, Father Timon had asked his friend to travel to the Barrens Seminary in May to confer with him "to perfect arrangements for the Texas mission."[5] Following up on Timon's request, less than three weeks after he returned to San Antonio de Bexar Odin started out on the journey. He headed for New Orleans, with an ultimate destination of Perryville and the seminary for his meeting with Timon. It would be during that trip, in New Orleans, that Odin would learn from Bishop Blanc that Pope Gregory XVI had named him coadjutor bishop of Detroit, Michigan, and bishop of Claudiopolis, *in partibus infidelium.*

The news disturbed Odin greatly. At that point in his life as a frontier missionary he had become focused on rebuilding the foundation for the church in Texas. Twice earlier he had bid his adieus: from his beloved homeland, France, and from Missouri, a territory he had come to love. How difficult it would be for him to recast his attention away from Texas, where so much needed to be done, to go to Detroit, where the church could already boast of a bishopric. Moreover, being the humble priest, the Frenchman had never shown any inclination toward aspiring to the Catholic episcopacy.

On March 10, 1841, Odin departed San Antonio de Bexar in the company of several citizens of the municipality: José and Ignacio Casiano; John Connally; José Antonio Chávez; and the sons of José Antonio Navarro, Ángel and Luciano. Five years later Ángel Navarro would graduate with his bachelor of arts degree from the Vincentian College at Cape Girardeau, Missouri. He had elected, in concert with his parents' wishes, to obtain his formal college education from priests who belonged to the same congregation as did the man he had come to admire greatly, Father Jean-Marie Odin.[6]

Eight days after leaving the San Antonio, during which time they had dined at the Navarro ranch and had camped overnight at several locations, the Odin entourage reached Houston. Two days later Odin was aboard the ship *Albert Gallatín* en route to Galveston. On April 11, at Galveston, he celebrated Easter Sunday Mass and then penned a long letter to Father Etienne at Paris. From Galveston Odin booked passage to New Orleans on the *Savannah*, stepping ashore at ten o'clock in the morning on April 16. Arriving almost in rags, as soon as he disembarked the *Savannah*, Odin headed for Bishop Blanc's residence. Blanc first scolded the Texas missionary for depriving himself of anything more than the barest of clothing. Then the bishop informed Odin of the Easter Sunday death of Father Auguste Jeanjean, the vice prefect apostolic's friend of earlier years and recently the vicar general of the Diocese of New Orleans.

Another surprise from Blanc awaited Odin. In the Frenchman's own words, "During High Mass the bishop handed me bulls appointing me Bishop of Claudiopolis and coadjutor of Detroit. [I] was so much frightened that I could not read them."[7] Bishop Blanc entreated Odin to remain in New Orleans until he could consecrate the Frenchman in beautiful and historic St. Louis Cathedral. Odin, however, assured his friend and bishop that he would be unable to accept consecration until he had conferred with Father Timon up at Perryville, a conference that Odin felt was essential since Timon was the US Vincentian superior.

Timon, meanwhile, had learned of Odin's episcopal nomination a couple of days prior to Odin himself having heard the news from Bishop Blanc, and he too was dismayed at the announcement. On April 29, even before Odin arrived at the Barrens Seminary with the news from New Orleans, Timon wrote to Blanc voicing his opposition to the recent turn of events. There can be little doubt that Timon anticipated the day in the near future when Jean-Marie Odin would be named a bishop for Texas. Informing Bishop Blanc in his letter that only a few months earlier Odin had been granted special authority to administer the sacrament of confirmation, Timon admitted to the New Orleans ordinary that Odin "was in fact Prefect Apostolic" of Texas.[8]

Lamenting the apparent appointment of his friend to the See of Detroit, Father Timon complained to Bishop Blanc that it would be easier to find

someone else for Detroit than another Odin for Texas. Moreover, the head of
the American Vincentians made known his fear to Blanc that if Odin accepted
the miter for Detroit, that new assignment might very well work to shorten
the French missionary's life.[9] Timon failed to develop this concern in detail,
but unquestionably he had in mind the potentially devastating impact that the
severe weather associated with the Detroit area—especially the cold—might
have on Odin's physical constitution.

Less than a week after receiving the papal bulls naming him coadjutor
bishop of Detroit, and accompanying letters from Cardinal Fransoni urging
him to accept the nomination, Jean-Marie Odin bade farewell to Bishop Blanc
and boarded the ship *Maid of Kentucky* to continue his voyage upriver to the
Barrens and his meeting with Father Timon. At daybreak on May 1, Odin and
his traveling companions, among them José Casiano, arrived at Pratt's Landing
near the Barrens. Odin and Casiano immediately proceeded on to the seminary, where Casiano stayed for five days and then returned to New Orleans.
Odin, on the other hand, remained for more than five weeks in the vicinity of
Perryville, St. Louis, and St. Genevieve. It was during that period of time that
he finalized his decision to reject the miter for Detroit.[10]

However, unknown to Jean-Marie Odin, those weeks were also marked by
the maturing of a conviction in Timon's heart and mind that Texas should be
raised to the hierarchical stature of a vicariate apostolic, with Odin named vicar
apostolic. Such a change would then mandate that Odin be ordained a bishop.
Father Timon recorded those developments in his *Barrens Memoir* decades
later, writing that:

> On the night of 5 May, [Odin] gave his bulls and urgent letters from Cardinal
> Fransoni to Fr. Timon, leaving the subject to his [Timon's] decision. The Visitor
> said "No Odin, I beg of you to say the Mass tomorrow morning for my inten-
> tions that God may guide me to the fitting answer, and I will offer the holy sac-
> rifice for the same intention." After Mass the next morning, the visitor gave his
> decision. "Fr. Odin good men can easily be found for the bishopric of Detroit,
> where things are already in a prosperous way; but it would be difficult to find
> a competent person now to take so poor and difficult a post as yours in Texas.
> Hence, I think it more for the glory of God and the good of souls that you send
> back the bulls and return to your post." Odin immediately refused the sacred
> office in Detroit and returned to Texas. The visitor, without letting Fr. Odin
> know of his intentions, wrote to Rome and to Paris urging the nomination of
> Fr. Odin as Vicar Apostolic of Texas and bishop *in partibus infidelium*. This was
> soon affected to the great benefit of that country.[11]

Timon's *Barrens Memoir* account failed to lay bare certain facts and perceptions of developments as they mirrored Odin's own deepest feelings in

the unfolding of events. Significantly, Odin held strong feelings that he was unworthy of becoming a member of the Catholic episcopacy. This is clear from the substance of a letter he composed to Bishop Blanc from St. Mary's of the Barrens Seminary on May 9, enclosing with his correspondence the bulls for return to the Holy See. To Blanc the missionary from France wrote, "It has been impossible for me to submit to the acceptance of the office that His Holiness has deigned to entrust to me. I perform so poorly some tasks of a simple clergyman, so what would become of me raised to a dignity of which my incompetence and my lack of virtues render me so unworthy." Odin ended his communication to Blanc with a plea that the New Orleans ordinary write to Pope Gregory XVI urging that he [Odin] no longer be considered for an appointment to the Catholic hierarchy.[12]

A few months later, in February 1842, the Texas vice prefect apostolic expressed similar concerns about his feeling poorly qualified to become a bishop to Father Jean-Baptiste Etienne, who at the time served as secretary general of the Congregation of the Mission in Paris. Explaining to Father Etienne the circumstances of his having received the bulls from Pope Gregory XVI back in the late spring of the previous year, Odin related to Etienne that at first he was unable to make up his mind about accepting the nomination. But, Odin wrote, his sense of unworthiness and his awareness of his lack of abilities had caused him to return the bulls to the Holy See.[13]

Vicar Apostolic of Texas

Having resolved the Detroit miter issue while at the same time missioning throughout his old neighborhood centering on the vicinity of St. Mary's of the Barrens Seminary, Odin, on June 8, 1841, boarded the ship *Meteor* at Pratt's Landing and headed back down the Mississippi River to New Orleans, with his ultimate destination being Texas. Three weeks later, on a Tuesday late in the afternoon, he arrived at Galveston from New Orleans aboard the steam packet *Savannah*.[14] As would be expected, the vice prefect apostolic immediately turned his attention to his flock in the Lone Star Republic.

One of the highlights of Odin's first few days back in Texas was an opportunity to preach in Galveston on the Fourth of July. But it soon became apparent to him that matters had become more unsettled in his adopted land since he had left for New Orleans in the late spring. Tensions between Texas and Mexico had intensified, with the possibility of war being talked about seemingly everywhere. A treaty between Texas and Mexico had never been signed after the Battle of San Jacinto back on April 21, 1836, and the Mexican government had refused to recognize Texas independence. The threat of hostilities remained constant. The Texans had recently dispatched Judge James Webb to negotiate a settlement with the Mexican government, but shortly before Odin set foot back on Texas soil Judge Webb had returned without having been allowed to meet with Mexican officials.

In a July 8, 1841, letter to Bishop Blanc, Odin shared what he had witnessed as he made his way around Galveston: "The affairs of Texas seem to look bad. Judge Webb having left for Mexico in order to negotiate with the government, had come back without having obtained admission. Such a great insult was keenly resented by our good Texans; one speaks of nothing but war and invasion." But the French priest perceptively added to Blanc that he hoped that all the Texan talk about conquering Mexico would be limited to meetings. Revealing his understanding of the true nature of matters regarding Texas, Odin included in his correspondence to Blanc an opinion that "to hear these grand speakers one would be tempted to believe that Texas is the most powerful nation in the universe."[15]

During those first few days back in Texas—mainly at Galveston and Houston—Odin busied himself writing letters to his mother and several confreres, celebrating Mass, hearing confessions, and generally serving again as a missionary priest was called to do. He was especially concerned about his mother, now almost a decade without her husband, but he often thought of his brothers and sisters as well. In addition, Odin paid particular attention to urging the Catholics of Galveston and Houston to persist in their commitment to build a church in each city. More than merely encouraging those Catholics verbally, at both Galveston and Houston the vice prefect apostolic donated one hundred dollars from his own purse toward the cost of constructing the two churches.[16]

At the same time, Odin had to endure a major disappointment that surfaced during the summer of 1841: the fleeing from missioning in Texas of one of his Vincentian colleagues, Father Nicholas Stehle. When Stehle had entered Texas the previous December in the company of Father Timon, the Congregation of the Mission had envisioned that he would serve primarily among German Catholics. As a native of the Lorraine on the German-French border, Stehle, it was hoped, would be able to take advantage of his knowledge of the German language and familiarity with German customs and traditions to evangelize.[17] However, after laboring only four months among the Catholics along the Brazos and Colorado Rivers, Father Stehle decided to leave Texas. In a letter to Father Timon dated April 12, 1841, he poured out his heart about the discontent he felt with his assignment to Texas. In that letter, which ironically Odin likely carried with him to St. Mary's of the Barrens on his April–May trip to visit with Timon, Stehle pleaded to be relieved of his duties on the frontier and returned to a more disciplined Vincentian establishment. Father Stehle's inability to adjust to frontier life had brought about the worst in his disposition. He increasingly became coarse and bad tempered when dealing with people, which ultimately resulted in his being seen as an unwelcome priest among the faithful of his assigned station, alienating Catholics and non-Catholics alike. In such a situation, Stehle was proving useless as a missionary.[18]

Odin realized that the decision to withdraw Father Stehle from Texas was Timon's to make, and he accepted that reality with no qualm. But nonetheless, he was upset with Father Stehle. Three days after Stehle departed Galveston for New Orleans aboard the steamship *Kingston* on July 13, Odin wrote a lengthy letter to Timon. Regarding Stehle's behavior, Odin complained, "Mr. Stehle started last Monday for the States. I did my best to make him stay until my return from my little tour, but could not prevail upon him. It is true, at the same time I was begging him to continue here, I felt embarrassed on account of his not going to confession. Since we separated from him, he has not discharged that duty. I spoke to him on the subject, but could never get any satisfactory answer. I never saw a man more hidden and more difficult. Since I came to Houston, I found that he is more unpopular here than at Galveston. Though he showed himself willing to return, I think it is more advisable for him to remain in the States, and especially in a community.[19] And so the disappointment of Father Stehle for Odin and the Vincentians in Texas came to an end.

In the meantime, in June 1841, Father Timon departed Missouri for a voyage to Europe, bent upon seeking support for the American Vincentians and planning to attend the sexennial conference of the Congregation of the Mission at Paris. Before leaving Missouri, Timon wrote both to the Holy See and the Congregation of the Mission superior general, Father Jean-Baptiste Nozo, urging that Texas be elevated to the ecclesiastical status of a vicariate apostolic and that Father Jean-Marie Odin be named vicar apostolic. Timon remained in Europe until December 2, participating in the sexennial conference, visiting several Vincentian establishments, recruiting for his American province, and generally promoting the needs of his confreres from Missouri to Texas.[20]

Well before the American visitor took his leave from Marseilles, France, in December 1841, to return to New Orleans, his requests regarding Texas and Odin had been acted upon.[21] While in residence at the Congregation of the Mission motherhouse Saint-Lazare at Paris in July, Father Timon learned that the Holy See had accepted Odin's refusal of the Detroit miter. But at the same time he was informed that by the papal bull *Universi dominic gregis*, dated July 16, 1841, Texas had been created a vicariate apostolic. A second bull of the same date, *Pastorale officium*, named Odin vicar apostolic of Texas and bishop of Claudiopolis *in partibus infidelium*.[22]

Vincentian Father John Boullier, traveling with Timon to Europe, and procurator of the Texas mission (he handled financial matters), wrote to Bishop Blanc on July 27, confirming these developments.[23] Boullier also informed Blanc that Father Peter Paul Lefevere, an alumnus of St. Mary's of the Barrens

Seminary and a priest of the Diocese of St. Louis, would be named coadjutor bishop of Detroit instead of Odin.

Meanwhile, Odin had been in Texas just a year. He had brought into the land badly needed priests and a brother speaking the Spanish language of the region's original Roman Catholics and had invited and supported clergy knowledgeable in other tongues. He had settled matters at San Antonio de Bexar, helped to recover Catholic Church properties at Austin, and had surveyed and missioned Texas as he knew it at the time. Now his feet were to be firmly set in the turf there to build up the faith as a Vincentian missionary bishop.

II

A Missionary Still

FROM ROME, ON JULY 31, 1841, Cardinal Fransoni dispatched a letter to Jean-Marie Odin informing him of Pope Gregory XVI's naming him vicar apostolic of Texas and bishop of Claudiopolis *in partibus infidelium*. Fransoni enclosed in his mailing, by way of Bishop Blanc at New Orleans, for transmittal on to Odin, the papal bull erecting Texas a vicariate apostolic and the materials formalizing Odin's appointment. In his comments to Odin the cardinal indicated that the Frenchman was expected to accept the nomination "for the good of religion."[1] There would be no refusal this time.

The Vatican communications arrived at New Orleans on October 11, and Bishop Blanc immediately forwarded them to Odin at Galveston, along with his own instructions about ordination plans. The new bishop-designate, however, had left Galveston almost immediately following his return to Texas from New Orleans back in July, three weeks before Cardinal Fransoni had sent his mailing. Venturing westward to Houston, Victoria, and the vicinity, and then on to San Antonio, Odin had spent the entire second half of 1841 and early 1842 laboring among the Catholics throughout that area.

As so often happened to him in his adult years, the French priest's health broke down during those months. The summer heat and humidity and then the fall showers consistently made demands on Odin's stamina. In August, as he was missioning in the area south and west from Houston to Victoria, he suffered a serious attack of fever accompanied by vomiting that felled him for more than two weeks, from the eighth to the twenty-fifth of the month. Struggling on, he made his way into Victoria and rested at John J. Linn's home. In that town now so familiar to him, Odin enjoyed a much welcomed reunion with Father Estany.[2]

And then it was on to San Antonio, where the vicar apostolic designate stayed several months, laying claim to the mission properties that the Austin government had returned to the church the previous December and January. At the same time, in the Bexar city Odin endeavored to become more aware of the area's historical Catholic Mexican heritage, which included trying to learn as accurately as possible the Spanish of the Hispanics. As a part of this, Odin participated in the December 12, 1841, celebration for La Virgen de la Guadalupe. The *Guadalupana fiestas religiosas* had matured over many years as jubilees deeply set—religiously, culturally, and socially—in the lives of the Catholic Mexicans of the Bexar municipality.

Regarding Odin's developing interest in the Mexican culture and this aspect of the Catholic world at San Antonio de Bexar, one scholar recently wrote, "Odin . . . participated in *Tejano* religious feasts like the 1841 San Antonio celebration in honor of Our Lady of Guadalupe and . . . spoke enthusiastically of the religious zeal demonstrated in these celebrations. Odin learned Spanish and was insistent that those coming to minister in Texas do the same."[3]

Upon his return to Galveston in the first week of February 1842, Odin found the letter from Cardinal Fransoni and the accompanying instructions from Bishop Blanc awaiting him. After reading them, he realized that plans for a trip to New Orleans must be worked out immediately. The setting for Odin's ordination and consecration as a bishop was to be the old St. Louis Cathedral of New Orleans. One of the most beautiful and historic Catholic edifices for worship in the United States, St. Louis Cathedral (now a basilica) had its origins as a church dating back to 1727.[4] Jean-Marie Odin knew the cathedral well. He had often celebrated Mass and heard confessions in it as a missionary. Undoubtedly, as a young subdeacon having just arrived in New Orleans back in July 1822, he would have attended Mass, gone to confession, and made visits to the Blessed Sacrament in the cathedral during his several weeks' stay in the city at that time. We have already seen that he spent much time in the cathedral awaiting his trip to Texas in the summer of 1840.

Before departing Galveston for New Orleans and his ordination and consecration, however, Odin had to direct his attention to recent developments in the Texas port city. A new church of St. Mary's—a plain and unattractive building—had just been completed in Galveston to the point where Mass could be celebrated in it. Thus, on February 6, the vice prefect apostolic offered the first-ever Mass at St. Mary's for an overjoyed Galveston gathering of Catholics. Odin himself paid approximately $460 of the full cost of $900 for the construction of the church. In the meantime, the missionary from France initiated the sacrament of confession (penance) at St. Mary's, a part of the sacramental schedule to be implemented on a regular basis when he returned to Galveston from New Orleans as a bishop.

Three days after that first Mass at St. Mary's Church, the ship *Atalanta* arrived at Galveston from La Havre, France, with a number of French immigrants aboard.[5] Father Odin happily welcomed to Texas those settlers from his homeland. He was well aware that they could prove important to the future maturation of the Roman Catholic religion in the Lone Star Republic.

Having managed as best he could on such short notice to see that all was in order regarding his responsibilities at Galveston, Odin boarded the steamship *Neptune* at noontime on the seventeenth of the month for a two-day voyage to New Orleans. After a quick and uneventful passage, the ship docked at the Louisiana bayou city in the evening of the nineteenth. Odin stepped ashore circumspectly, anticipating his upcoming ordination as a bishop scheduled to take place a mere fifteen days later, on March 6. For a time he had remained reluctant about the episcopal stature thrust upon him, continuing to feel a strong sense of unworthiness. But in obedience he came to accept his appointment, believing that if he refused the miter once again he would be acting against the divine will. Jean-Marie made known those feelings in two letters, one written to his mother back in France sometime after his ordination and the other to Father Etienne at Paris on March 28.[6]

There was much to prepare and so little time! Taking precedence over all else for the soon-to-be bishop was his desire to make a religious retreat, which had long been the tradition for a priest about to be elevated to the dignity of the episcopacy. And Jean-Marie Odin realized only too well that in his new role as a bishop he would need all the spiritual strength that a well-made retreat could offer. Thus, five days after his arrival at New Orleans the bishop-elect began a ten-day retreat at the Old Ursuline Convent in the city. Ursuline sisters had first come to New Orleans from Rouen, France, more than a century earlier, on August 6, 1727. Their temporary home was "the large, two-story Kelly House at the corner of Bienville and Chartres streets." After remaining at that location for seven years, in 1734 the Ursulines moved into their first convent. Almost two decades later, in 1752 or 1753, they once again settled into a new convent, the first one having deteriorated badly from exposure to the elements. Finally, in 1824, the Ursulines occupied their third convent, a building situated downriver from the original site but still set within the boundaries of New Orleans. It was in that convent that Odin made his retreat.[7]

On March 5 Odin emerged from his retreat spiritually refreshed and prepared for his episcopal ordination the following day. Meanwhile, Father Timon had departed St. Mary's of the Barrens Seminary on February 17 for his trek down the Mississippi River to be with his longtime friend and confrere at the ordination and consecration.[8] There Timon would join a representation of Odin's fellow Vincentians, other clerics, sisters from different female religious communities, and lay personages to witness the ordination and consecration of Jean-Marie Odin as bishop to serve on the Texas frontier.

In his *Ordinations of US Catholic Bishops, 1790–1989: A Chronological List* (1990), Charles N. Bransom Jr. recorded of Odin's consecration that "1842, March 6, at New Orleans, Louisiana, Saint Louis Cathedral, Anthony Blanc, Bishop of New Orleans, assisted by Michael Portier, Bishop of Mobile, and John Chanche, Bishop of Natchez, consecrated John [Jean]

Mary [Marie] Odin, C.M., Titular Bishop of Claudiopolis, Vicar Apostolic of Texas."[9]

Jean-Marie Odin was the fortieth prelate ordained and consecrated to serve in lands that ultimately merged as part of the United States, and his ordination and consecration at St. Louis Cathedral was a solemn and grand celebration. All eyes seemed fixed on Odin as the procession of altar boys, clergy, and bishops made its way into the sturdy stone cathedral—itself showing signs of decay but nonetheless inspiringly topped with three light grey spires—and proceeded down the center aisle of the cathedral's interior to the main altar. Father Timon happily participated in the procession with the clergy, proud that his closest friend was being elevated to the Catholic hierarchy but also undoubtedly thinking of the promise that such held for Catholic Texas.

The ordination and consecration were worked around the central celebration, the Holy Mass, with Bishop Blanc as the main celebrant. The entire rite lasted more than two and a half hours and was conducted in Latin. At the beginning, Odin was presented kneeling facing Bishop Blanc, who was seated near the main altar. Before everyone present the missionary from France took his oath as bishop and pledged his fidelity to the teachings of the church and to the pope as vicar of Christ. Bishop Blanc then administered an examination of faith to Odin, fulfilling the centuries-long mandate of the church that every man being elevated to the dignity of the episcopacy undergo a charitable but intense public examination of his faith.

Following the examination, Odin received his pectoral cross, the insignia of a bishop and gift of Bishops Blanc and Portier.[10] Then began the celebration of the Holy Mass. At the *Allelulia* Odin once again knelt before Blanc, and the latter, along with Bishops Portier and Chanche, laid the Gospels on the back and neck of Odin, symbolizing the authority a bishop possesses as custodian of the word of God.

Then came the most profound part of the ordination and consecration ceremony, the laying on of the hands. Blanc, Portier, and Chanche each approached Odin and solemnly laid their hands on his head, with Blanc reciting the words "Receive the Holy Ghost." Thus was recalled the ancient tradition of the Roman Catholic Church traceable back to the laying on of the hands of St. Peter and the investing of bishops with ecclesiastical authority as successors of the original twelve apostles of Jesus. The celebration of the Mass continued with the preface intoned. Blanc anointed Odin on the head with the chrism, blessed a crozier (an ornamental staff shaped like a shepherd's crook that symbolizes a bishop's role as shepherd of his flock), and presented it to Odin. Then Blanc placed the episcopal ring on the fourth finger of Odin's right hand, the symbol of the prelate's espousal to the church. At the end of the Mass Blanc solemnly placed a blessed bishop's miter on the head of Odin. Jean-Marie Odin was then bishop of Claudiopolis and vicar apostolic of Texas—he was

Bishop Odin.[11] What might Bishop Blanc have been thinking at that time? How personal must have been his feelings! Jean-Marie Odin, the man whom Blanc, a newly ordained priest, had first met more than a quarter of a century ago as a sixteen-year-old parishioner back at Ambierle, France, had just been ordained and consecrated a bishop for the Texas frontier.

A Missionary Still

"Don't go imagining that with this title your poor son will be obliged to live in an episcopal palace, to go out in a carriage, etc. A bishop of Texas must always lead the life of a missionary," wrote Odin in that aforementioned letter to his mother following his ordination and consecration.[12] His next few years in Texas were to demand from the new bishop as much missionary zeal and determination as had ever before been required of him.

As a bishop, Odin now possessed authorities and responsibilities that far exceeded what he had enjoyed as vice prefect apostolic. The most unique of those powers was that of ordaining priests, an authority that Odin would use many times during his nineteen remaining years in Texas. In addition, Odin would be able to ordain and consecrate as bishops priests named by the pope. This he would do slightly more than twenty years later for his successor as bishop of Galveston—a status given to Odin in 1847—Father Claude Marie Dubuis. From that point on he could also administer the sacrament of confirmation, that sacrament through which Catholics already baptized "are strengthened by the Holy Spirit in order that they may steadfastly profess the faith and faithfully live up to their profession."[13]

Of immediate importance regarding the anticipated growth of Catholicism in Texas, Odin now enjoyed an ecclesiastical prominence that assuredly would help him in his labors to seek out priests, brothers, and sisters for service in the Lone Star Republic. For some time clerical and religious recruitment for Texas had been a major topic in his discussions with Father Timon and Bishop Blanc. Those conversations brought into the open Odin's awareness that at that particular point in history the Catholic Church in Texas was being called upon to catechize and evangelize an increasingly broad range of nationalities and varying heritages.

For two decades Texas had witnessed an ever-increasing migration into the land not only of Catholic immigrants of assorted ethnic backgrounds from Europe and the United States, but also Protestants and the unchurched as well. This situation had first developed in part as a consequence of the Mexican government's opening Texas to colonization, beginning with that of Moses Austin and Stephen F. Austin at San Felipe, as well as Texas maturing as a final destination for some Americans and Europeans forming part of the westward movement in the United States during the first half of the nineteenth century.

Thus, the complex demography taking shape in Bishop Odin's vicariate apostolic of Texas in the 1840s and afterwards demanded of him that he seek priests, brothers, and sisters from wherever he could find them in Europe, the United States, Canada, and Mexico. Attracting Mexican clergy and nuns, however, would prove to be difficult. This was due mainly to a tension-filled political, social, military, and economic environment that had come to dominate relations between Mexico and Texas in recent years. The roots of this situation were grounded in Mexican and Texan memories of the 1835–36 Texas revolution against Mexico and lingering antagonisms about that struggle. At the heart of those ill feelings from Mexico's perspective was a collective conviction that Americans, reflecting views supportive of manifest destiny, and a few Mexicans, such as for example Lorenzo de Zavala, saturated with Enlightenment ideals, had instigated the rebellion of Texas against Mexico. Most Mexicans in Mexico proper, and certainly the Mexican government, believed that the Texas independence proclaimed on March 2, 1836, was invalid and that Texas remained a part of Mexico.

Many Tejanos (Texans of Mexican ethnicity) were loyal to the Republic of Texas but lived just across the Rio Grande from their mother country, where deep-seated family legacies and attachments remained. For those people anxieties seemed almost always present. Perhaps the most noted of those personages was Juan Nepomuceno Seguín, a member of the Texas Senate during the fall of 1840 and *alcalde* (mayor) of San Antonio de Bexar in the early spring of 1841, a period when Odin was so active missioning in the area. Since Texas independence Seguín seemed consistently to find himself embroiled in the tensions between Mexico and Texas. Playing the roles of supporter of Mexican federalism, mediator between Mexico and Texas after Texas independence, and military leader, Seguín was equally viewed with respect and suspicion on both sides of the Rio Grande because of what at times seemed to be loyalty to both Mexican federalism and the Lone Star Republic.[14]

Adding to the fearful mood of the time was the impact on Mexican and Texan attitudes of the ill-fated Santa Fe expedition that the Republic of Texas president Mirabeau Lamar, on his own and without the support of the Texas congress, had sponsored in the spring of 1841. That development vexed people from Austin to Santa Fe to Mexico City. In addition to all of these, the severe anticlerical onslaught against the church in Mexico itself by the liberals in the political and other areas of public life of that Catholic nation continued to push made it unlikely that Bishop Odin would be able to count on much help from south of the Rio Grande.

More than two months were to pass before Bishop Odin was able to return to Texas from New Orleans following his episcopal ordination and consecration. During the several weeks' delay in New Orleans he spent his time busy in a number of ways, fulfilling his duties as priest and bishop. Just three days following his ordination and consecration, he started preaching a five-day retreat for the Sisters of Charity at their Female Orphan Asylum in New Orleans.[15] The new bishop also officiated at various confirmation rites, celebrated Mass and preached in St. Louis Cathedral as well as other churches, spent considerable time hearing confessions, and offered various aspects of catechesis in and about New Orleans. He also visited the Vincentian-run seminary and parish at Donaldsonville, Louisiana.

But on May 11 of that year 1842, at 11:00 A.M., Bishop Odin boarded the packet ship *New York* bound for the port of Galveston. Even before he had departed New Orleans, he had learned of a Mexican military incursion into Texas under the command of General Rafael Vásquez, with Goliad, Victoria, and—on March 5—San Antonio de Bexar having been temporarily occupied. Odin had heard the news of the invasion nine days after his episcopal ordination and consecration. Of the situation Odin wrote to Father Etienne at Paris, "a few days after my consecration I received some very bad news about our mission in Texas. Mexico, which had never wanted to recognize her [Texas'] independence, has just attempted to reconquer it."[16]

It is unclear, however, as to whether Bishop Odin realized at the time of his departure from New Orleans on May 11 that Vásquez's ingress into Texas was a brief one and that the Mexican general had withdrawn his army back across the Rio Grande after only two days in San Antonio. But without a doubt, Odin's concern for the safety of the people in Texas and the Catholic mission there dominated his feelings.

Back in Texas Rebuilding the Faith

"Our voyage was short and much more pleasant than I dared promise myself," Odin wrote to Blanc on May 16 about his return to Galveston five days earlier aboard the *New York*.[17] But the Catholic Texas to which the new bishop returned was already different from that which he had left in February, given the fact of his having become a bishop and the new stature of Texas as a vicariate apostolic. The changes in the altered hierarchical status of the church there were far-reaching. Texas no longer existed as a mission of the American Vincentians but was now a separate ecclesiastical jurisdiction with Bishop Odin, as vicar apostolic, responsible directly to the Holy See.

Thus, while the Congregation of the Mission *maison mere* at Paris and Father Timon, as visitor of the American Vincentians, both felt compelled to help the new Bishop Odin as much as they could, Texas administratively had been removed from the worldwide scope of the Vincentian missioning vision. Odin would therefore be required to seek assistance beyond the circle of his Vincentian community.[18] Complicating matters, the political boundaries of Texas were not clearly defined, and that added to the difficulties that the new bishop could be expected to encounter, since the territorial reaches of the new vicariate apostolic were to be defined as those identical to the boundaries of the Republic of Texas. But how far south beyond the Nueces River and west into the area that New Mexico historically claimed did the parameters of Texas extend? In that early summer of 1842 Bishop Odin was simply unsure of the answers to these questions.

General Vásquez's recent March 5 occupation of San Antonio de Bexar had intensified tensions between Texas and Mexico. And that incursion, which Bishop Odin saw as a reminder of the ever-present threat of a more serious invasion from Mexico, along with the continuing danger that the bellicose Comanches posed throughout the region, were prominent among Odin's fears and concerns. Of the latter threat he commented to Father Etienne in his March 28 letter, "the savages will not fail to profit from this general confusion by making their raids, and many unfortunate families will be sad victims of their cruelty.[19]

But Bishop Odin realized only too well that amidst these difficulties his task was to begin to lay the foundation for the future development of the church there. One situation that the new bishop hoped to improve upon as soon as possible after his return to Texas was to correct the unstable circumstances regarding his residence that he had been forced to endure since his arrival in the republic almost two years earlier. During that entire period Bishop Odin had been unable to call any home his own. Now a more permanent dwelling for him was urgently needed.

This situation required an immediate resolution not only because Odin had become a bishop but also because he wanted to build a Vincentian community life for those Sons of St. Vincent already serving with him in Texas and those who would come to Texas in the future. Father Calvo and Brother Sala, joined eventually by Father Estany, were already trying to do so in San Antonio. Odin hoped to do the same for Galveston.

Beyond these considerations, the new vicar apostolic wanted to obtain for Galveston a priests' residence, a rectory, for the good of Catholicism in the city and its environs. Galveston, looming increasingly prominent as a receiving port for immigrants to Texas, many of whom were Catholics, and San Antonio, the most historic municipality of Texas characterizing the Mexican Catholic tradition, were both seen as potentially notable in the hoped-for ripening of Roman Catholicism in that vast land. Thus, less than a week after his return to Galveston, Bishop Odin purchased and moved into a small house with four rooms, a kitchen, and a hall and located "in the most peaceful part of the city."[20]

Odin's buying that property reflected also his continued commitment to promoting catechesis among the Catholics under his charge. Providing instruction in the faith had been central to his missioning since his early days in Missouri. Odin wrote to Bishop Blanc shortly after attaining the Galveston property, "On the back of the lot I also have a large house that used to serve as a shop for the owner and that I shall convert into a school." As the teacher for the school Odin selected his sacristan, James P. Nash, an Irishman whom the new bishop observed to Blanc "has already taught here with much success."[21]

The next few years would find Bishop Odin's schedule filled with catechetical activity, offering the sacraments and building churches and mission stations for the thousands of Roman Catholics he was to serve within the geographical boundaries of Galveston, Houston, the Lavaca Bay region, San Antonio de Bexar, north to the Colorado River and Austin area, to the northeastern reaches of Texas, and finally back to Galveston. In 1849 that missioning circumference would be expanded to include the territory south of the Nueces River to the Rio Grande.

Bishop Odin, however, would have to carry out his labors in an environment of tensions and uncertainties even beyond those already mentioned. Several developments were to converge to influence this: the annexation of Texas as a state on December 29, 1845, with all of the political ramifications that surrounded that event; the traumas and ill feelings on both sides of the Rio Grande associated with the US-Mexican War of 1846–48; and a growing Protestant aggressiveness in Texas that surfaced concomitant with a maturing nativism that was imported from north and east of the Red and Sabine Rivers, which agitated prejudices against Catholics.[22]

Finally, Bishop Odin would be forced to encounter slavery once again, that institution that he had come so much to abhor. Of special repugnance to him was that following Texas' annexation to the United States slavery was now legal in the Lone Star State.

Bishop Odin was well aware that as midcentury approached, Texas remained very much a frontier region with wild and sometimes dangerous societal elements. While it was true that such a situation offered challenges for missioning, the darker side of some of the roustabout maverick population in certain locales could only be tolerated. Odin had become particularly concerned about the number of killings that occurred in some towns, on occasion taking place right out in the open. On June 12, 1842, for example, while still in Galveston, Odin recorded in his daily journal that "a man was killed this morning on the streets. There was another a few days ago." A week later he added the comment in his daily journal that "we have had three men killed in the course of a few days."[23]

In spite of such a perilous environment, the responsibility for continuing Roman Catholic missioning throughout Texas was Odin's. As always, it was a challenge that he relished. He plunged himself into laboring in those uncharted waters with dedication and zeal. It was to be only a few years until the revival of Catholic life in Texas was a reality—Bishop Odin's main legacy to Catholic Texas.

The Search for Priests and Nuns

B Y THE MID-1840S IT HAD BECOME APPARENT to any number of persons within the Catholic Church's inner circles that the region making up the Lone Star Republic, soon to be annexed by the United States as that nation's twenty-eighth state, was destined in the near future to be raised to the ecclesiastical status of a diocese. It appeared likely also that Jean-Marie Odin would be named the bishop to head up the anticipated new diocese. While the site of the episcopal see city (diocesan seat) for the expected bishopric was left open to conjecture, the port city of Galveston seemed the likely choice.

Several reasons existed for such expectations. In reference to Jean-Marie Odin being named the bishop for whatever diocese might be erected, the Frenchman's reputation as a dedicated missionary throughout Missouri and surrounding vicinity prior to his arrival in Texas carried much weight. He was well known up and down the Mississippi River from Illinois to Louisiana. Moreover, many Catholics, clergy and religious as well as laypersons, knew that the missionary from France had brought great enthusiasm to his labors in the Lone Star Republic. Further, all evidence suggested that the period immediately following Bishop Odin's return to Texas from New Orleans as vicar apostolic in May 1842 was proving to be one of great evangelistic enthusiasm on his part. Odin and his clerics were continuing to strive vigorously to strengthen the faith among the growing Catholic population of the land. Finally, after his trip to the Baltimore Council a decade earlier Jean-Marie Odin was highly admired in both Rome and Paris. The Vincentian, then, appeared the obvious choice to head whatever new bishopric might be created.[1]

Writing more than a century ago, Father Claude Jaillet, a priest from Odin's own home archdiocese of Lyon in France, who had first arrived in Texas in 1866 and then enjoyed several years laboring in and around San Diego, in south Texas west of Corpus Christi, spoke of Odin and the evangelizers serving with him in this manner: "A new era began for the Church with the appointment of Rt. Rev. Dr. Odin as the first Vicar Apostolic of Texas. So few were his clergy that he could count them on his fingers. Their field of action was an immense one. . . . Those were trying times, and the Church of Texas was truly an apostolic mission. But let it be said to the honor of our dear ancestors in the holy ministry that they were equal to the task. The names of the saintly Odin and his zealous successor, Bishop C.M. Dubuis, and of Fathers [Louis] Chambodut, [Charles] Padey, Timon and several others will always be held in great reverence by the Catholics of Texas."[2]

In regards to Galveston looming on the horizon as the possible see city for the desired new bishopric, the picture was not quite so clear. It will be remembered that San Antonio de Bexar had served as the religious and political center of Texas under both Spanish and Mexican rule. For more than a century that municipality had been considered the heart of Texas' Catholic life north of the Lower Rio Grande Valley. And the Bexar city in the 1840s continued to boast of a dense Catholic population, most of it a legacy of that Spanish and Mexican heritage. Still, Galveston, as has been indicated, was a port city situated so as to be emerging as an entry point of growing importance for countless Catholic immigrants from the United States and Europe. This consideration would prove to be fundamental to the future development of the Church and its ability to carry out its mission to all Catholics in the region.

Early on Odin came to realize that the steady incoming Catholic migration played a significant role as a catalyst for much of that Catholic growth and expansion. On February 4, 1841, responding to *empresario* W. S. Peters's request for a colonial grant to be located in north central Texas bordering the Red River, the government of the republic had passed a land grant law for immigrants. That piece of legislation would serve as the "basis for all empresario land grants made under the auspices of the Republic of Texas."[3]

Such awards of land and attached privileges had influenced the Texas historical narrative in a major way since 1820 and had acted to make more complex the ethnic and religious character of the region. The grants issued as a result of the 1841 initiative added a new dimension to the ever-widening panorama of nationalities settling in Texas. This situation too created great demands on the Catholic Church, reinforcing its centuries-old mission of bringing the "Good News" to all peoples. Such loomed prominent in Bishop Odin's mind as he struggled to determine clearly the needs of the Catholics and the church in Texas during those foundational years.

The communities established in the 1840s pushed European immigrant settlement in Texas westward and southward beyond San Antonio to the far reaches of the republic. In 1842, not long after the immigrant land grant initiative, Henri Castro, a fifty-five-year-old French citizen, began organizing a movement of colonists from Europe to Texas. Although it took Castro two years to establish a colony in Texas, over a five-year period he recruited more than two thousand French, German, Belgian, Dutch, Hungarian, and English settlers to the land. Given that a high percentage of those migrants were Catholics, Bishop Odin offered Castro his steadfast encouragement and support. Not only did Odin work with those immigrants when they began arriving in Texas during the late summer of 1842, but he also advanced money to a few of them for their subsistence as they awaited the arrival of Castro in San Antonio. In January of the next year, Castro repaid Odin one thousand and sixty-three francs.[4]

Between the first and third of September 1844, the initial results of Castro's efforts came to fruition when the entrepreneur, sometimes in a driving rain, successfully led a group of his colonists west from San Antonio to the Medina River, where he founded Castroville. Bishop Odin immediately set out to visit the settlement. There on September 12, a mere nine days after the establishment of Castroville, the vicar apostolic laid the cornerstone for a planned Catholic Church to be placed under the patronage of St. Louis. By 1847 Castro had founded the settlements of Dhanis, Quihi, and Vandenburg. In addition to the European migrants already identified, Castro's colonies attracted some Mexican residents.[5]

While the populating of the Castro settlements was developing, German life in Texas, which dated its origin back to 1831, began to assume greater prominence in other locations in the republic.[6] The leadership of Prince Carl of Solms-Braunfels, John O. Meusebach, and the German Adelsverein (the Society for the Protection of German Immigrants in Texas founded in Germany in 1842 and the agency that oversaw German migration to Texas from 1844 through 1847) provided the inspiration for much of that colonization. Prince Carl and the Adelsverein were responsible for the establishment of the town of New Braunfels north of San Antonio on the banks of the Guadalupe River on March 21, 1845. It remains today unclear as to whether the prince himself was Roman Catholic or Protestant, but he tried to make his colony attractive to both for the sake of settlement in Texas.[7]

In late April 1846, under the auspices of the Adelsverein, Meusebach led the Germans from New Braunfels eighty miles northwest to found the colony of Fredericksburg. The colonists arrived at their destination on May 8, 1846. Soon a lay teacher named John Leyendecker began the practice of regularly leading Fredericksburg's Catholics in prayer, with Leyendecker himself reading from the Bible. In 1847, a French priest arrived whom Odin had recruited from the Archdiocese of Lyon in his homeland a year earlier. A churchman eventually to become almost as prominent in the Catholic Texas narrative as Odin himself, Father Claude Marie Dubuis was accompanied by a Spanish *sacerdote* (priest), Father Pedro Salazar. Together they visited Fredericksburg, celebrated Mass, heard confessions, and catechized.[8]

Meanwhile, reports had surfaced of another priest laboring in some of the colonies west of San Antonio, a Bohemian secular cleric named Gottfried Menzel. The actuality of his presence at such locales as Castroville and

New Braunfels remains a mystery however. A rumor that he served in New Braunfels in 1846 has been shown to be false. It appears, moreover, that Bishop Odin never incardinated him for service in Texas. Menzel disappeared from the scene likely during the 1850s, never to be heard of again in the Catholic Texas story.[9]

From Where Will He Attain Priests and Nuns?

Between the years 1842 and 1846, the number of priests assigned to Texas increased from the small handful stationed there when Jean-Marie Odin was made vicar apostolic to fifteen.[10] Odin himself, with the support of Father Timon as well as various bishops and heads of religious orders, societies, and congregations throughout America and Europe, lead the recruitment effort that brought those additional priests to Texas.

At the same time during those years, Odin had come to realize only too well that as much as priests, Catholic nuns were needed for Texas. Over the centuries Catholic sisters had played a leading role in educational, charitable (including hospital and orphan foundations), and social initiatives that were essential to the mission of the Church throughout the world. Attesting to this missioning spirit that countless communities of female religious exhibited in venturing to Texas at the beckoning of Bishop Odin in the latter 1840s and beyond, the late Sister M. Monica LaFleur of Houston wrote, "A century after the 1841 designation of Texas as a Vicariate-Apostolic, an organized missionary area of the Catholic Church, Most Rev. Lawrence J. Fitzsimon of Amarillo, Texas, remarked that while the pioneer 'French Sisters' who came to Texas did not receive public acclaim as did the French clergymen, they did experience similar hardships."[11]

While Odin was unable to attract a community of nuns to Texas until January 1847, he had begun working to lay a foundation for their coming much earlier. On June 17, 1842, slightly more than a month after he returned to Texas from New Orleans and his ordination and consecration as bishop and vicar apostolic, Odin sent a letter to Father Etienne in Paris regarding his search for priests and the difficulties involved: "I left New Orleans on May 11 to go again to Texas. I was to take several priests with me, but the disturbances that have befallen the land [the trouble between Mexico and Texas as well as the Texian militiamen's disruptive behavior in several Texas towns] made me judge that it would be better to wait until peace was perfectly reestablished. Therefore I came back alone." Three days after mailing his letter to Etienne, Odin voiced similar hesitations in a communication to Father Timon at the Barrens Seminary, asserting that "I would like to have a priest for Houston and one for Galveston, and still [I] dare not write to you to send them in the present unfavorable circumstances."[12] The priests who were originally scheduled to accompany Odin on his return to Texas had been made available as a result of the vicar apostolic having entreated Father Timon and others for help.

Odin's purview of matters related to his seeking clerics and sisters for his vicariate apostolic stemmed from his understanding that while Father Timon and the Vincentians would offer as much assistance to Texas as possible, once Odin had become the ecclesiastical head of a vicariate apostolic he would be expected to find priests and nuns on his own, beyond the Vincentian community. Thus it is no surprise that in December 1842 he wrote to his mother back at Hauteville, commenting that "It is possible that I will be obliged to make a trip to Europe, as soon as Mexico recognizes the independence of Texas. I need priests, nuns, and it is only in France that I will be able to find them. Pray the good God to bring peace to the country, and I will then have the hope to go see you."[13]

Setting aside for the moment the topic of recruiting priests and nuns, Jean-Marie's letter to his mother also included his reaction to the sad news that he had received from a priest in France, the Abbe Botton (the first name of the priest was not noted) on or about December 14 of the recent death of Odin's younger brother, who had been residing in Lyon. That brother—though Odin failed to identify which one of his siblings it was who had died—must have been one of the last three children born to Jean and Claudine Marie Odin more than three decades earlier. Heartbroken, Jean-Marie lamented to his *mere* that "Heaven has just exacted from us all a great sacrifice and required our resignation to a new and bitter trial. Oh! How grieved I am to learn of the death of my dear brother!" Jean-Marie, just a short time prior to hearing the unhappy news about his brother's death, had been overjoyed to receive a letter from his sister Josephine. In his words to his mother the Texas missionary expressed how that very welcome communication from his sister almost immediately was overshadowed by the grief he found in Abbe Botton's news: "It was only a few days since I had received Josephine's letter when that of M. the Abbe Botton arrived; the first one filled me with joy, and suddenly here I am plunged in the deepest sorrow by the second one. How rapidly the days of this life go by! Let us redouble our fervor, dear mother, in order to merit the solid rest and joys of heaven."[14]

Following the correspondence to his mother, Odin wrote to Father Stephen Rousselon at New Orleans, Bishop Blanc's vicar general and a longtime friend of Odin, and announced the passing of his younger brother. In that mailing Odin packaged materials for a power of attorney needed for settlement of the younger Odin's will and inheritance back in France. Over the years Odin had increasingly come to depend upon Father Rousselon for financial and legal advice. Jean-Marie asked Rousselon to prepare the power of attorney and forward it on through the port of New York to the proper legal authorities in his homeland.[15] Odin offered his Masses and other prayers for the soul of his deceased brother and for the comfort of his *mere* and the rest of the Odin family, bearing his personal sadness with deep spiritual strength.

Odin, however, soon turned his attention once again to serving the needs of the Catholics under his care and building the church throughout his Texas vicariate apostolic. This meant that, except when he was ill, he had a daily routine of celebrating Mass, hearing confessions, sacramentalizing marriages, presiding over confirmations, administering extreme unction, catechizing, overseeing various aspects of building churches and missions, and seeking out Catholics wherever he could find them. And as well his search for priests and nuns had to go on.

The vicar apostolic spent most of the spring of 1843 laboring among the Catholics of Galveston, Houston, and the lower Brazos River region. He had at the time only three priests with him in Texas: Fathers Estany, Calvo, and Clarke. Father Haydon, as we know, had died, and, also as we know, Father Nicholas Stehle had departed Texas in the summer of 1841. Father Estany, responding to Odin's urgings, had gone to San Antonio. But he regularly traveled back to his original pastorate at Victoria to be with the Catholics of that locale and its nearby settlements. Father Calvo remained with Brother Sala among the people of San Antonio and its environs. Father Clarke worked the Lavaca River settlements. However, within a year additional priests would begin to arrive in Texas.

Before that development could unfold, Odin's attendance at the fifth Provincial Council at Baltimore, scheduled to convene on May 14, 1843, had taken precedence. He departed Galveston for New Orleans and the arduous trip to Baltimore aboard the boat *New York* on March 29.[16] Odin entertained hopes that this journey would make better known to the American prelates the status of Catholicism in Texas. He longed for the possibility that this might result in future recruitment of priests and nuns to Texas.

But the Baltimore venture would prove to be a great disappointment for the vicar apostolic. Throughout much of his travel he was sick with chills and fever, the first attack coming only two days into his voyage across the Gulf of Mexico to New Orleans, on March 31. Upon his arrival in New Orleans at 10:00 A.M. on the second of April, he immediately went to bed. Having recovered enough eleven days later to celebrate Mass, though he still "felt very feeble," he suffered a relapse on the March 21. The following day he departed New Orleans for Baltimore, via Natchez, Louisville, Cincinnati, and Wheeling. Odin regularly recorded in his daily journal that he suffered from fever along the route. Arriving in Baltimore in time for the opening of the preliminary session on May 13, three days later Odin relapsed into a fever that lasted four days and deprived him of being able to attend most of the council sessions.[17]

After being present at the final session of the council on May 21, Odin took a tour, visiting Philadelphia and New York and then back to Philadelphia to commence his return trip to Texas. Most of the time on his return venture to Texas he continued to suffer from fever. Spending a week journeying west from Philadelphia to Pittsburgh, Cincinnati, and finally Louisville, Odin had become so ill that by the time he reached the latter city he was compelled to turn himself over to the care of the Sisters of Charity.[18] In all, the Frenchman would endure five months more on the road making his way back to Texas, stopping en route at St. Louis, St. Mary of the Barrens Seminary, St. Genevieve, Cape Girardeau, Donaldsonville, and New Orleans. Despite his prolonged bouts with fever and the ever-present threat of debilitating migraine headaches that plagued him throughout his entire venture, the vicar apostolic labored enthusiastically as a priest and bishop in each of those locales that he visited.

Before leaving New Orleans for Galveston, on December 1, 1843, Odin met once again with Father Timon, who had come to New Orleans following his recent return from Europe. The visitor informed his friend of the death of Bishop Rosati, who had passed away in Rome on September 25 of that year. Odin was much saddened. During his visit with Father Timon the Texas vicar apostolic brought up a topic that the two Vincentians had discussed earlier in regards to priests for Texas: the possible dispatching of an Irish member of the Congregation of the Mission, Father Michael Collins, to serve with Odin at Galveston. Timon seems to have hesitatingly—and perhaps misleadingly for Odin—agreed to assign Collins to Texas. But as the months passed by after the two Vincentians' visit Timon never followed through on sending Father Collins to Texas, leaving Odin dismayed.[19]

At New Orleans on his journey back to Texas, Odin acquired the services of a Vincentian lay brother originally from Naples, Italy, Salvator Vicari. The twenty-five-year-old brother had volunteered to accompany Bishop Odin to Galveston and serve there as the cook in the vicar apostolic's small residence. But the Neapolitan's irascible personality, mixed with his lack of commitment to missionary life on the frontier, soon proved to be an irritating embarrassment to Odin. In a long letter to Father Timon dated December 30, 1843, Odin detailed the difficulties that he was having with Brother Vicari. The vicar apostolic explained that while Vicari was a good cook and carpenter, he neglected his religious duties, demanded monthly wages (violating his Vincentian vow of poverty), often was in bad humor, and frequently stated that he wanted to return to Italy. A follow-up missive from Odin to Timon dated January 26, 1844, revealed also that Brother Vicari was drinking heavily, was developing a temper, and had turned to preparing the residence's food in such a manner "that no one could taste of it." Odin begged Father Timon to recall Vicari. But no reply to the two letters arrived from Timon. Not long thereafter, a communication from Odin to Timon written on April 16, 1844, simply announced that "Br. Vicari is no longer with me; I hope you received the letters I sent you when he left this place."[20]

Upon his return to Galveston, Odin happily greeted two Alsatian priests whom he had been expecting to join him in Texas, Father Jean Pierre Oge and a Father Schneider. It may have been that these two clerics migrated to Texas as a result of the Alsatian identity of many of the Castro colonies' immigrants; though this is not certain. Both priests spoke French and German, and at first Bishop Odin was delighted to have them in Texas. However, his initial euphoria soon evaporated, and it was not long until the two priests had departed the Lone Star Republic. Father Schneider, an excellent preacher in Odin's view, possessed such an unpleasant personality that he simply could not get along with the Catholics he was supposed to serve. In April 1844, he left the vicariate apostolate.

Eventually Odin began to suspect that something was amiss with Father Oge also. Popular with his German parishioners, Oge nonetheless seemed too fond of money and appeared to lack a true missionary spirit. In his response to a query from Odin, the bishop of Strasbourg, France, Oge's former ordinary, wrote that "I have nothing good to say about him; he conducted himself wretchedly in my diocese." The French prelate went on to aver that he had never given Father Oge an *exeat* (letter of perpetual release from his former bishop for assignment elsewhere), and therefore the one that Oge had presented to Odin upon his arrival in Texas was false.[21] Bishop Odin was in a dilemma. Father Oge had endeared himself to his German parishioners, but he had lied about his past to the vicar apostolic. The resolution soon became clear in Odin's mind, and within a short time Oge was dismissed from the vicariate apostolic.

Just when Bishop Odin's discouragement must have begun to show itself, matters improved dramatically. In April 1844, Father Timon notified Father Etienne that he was sending two veteran English-speaking Vincentian priests to aid Odin in Texas, Fathers Joseph Paquín and John Brands. Both were in their mid-forties and had worked with Odin in the past. The vicar apostolic knew them especially well and was elated when they arrived at Galveston on May 11 of that year. In a letter sent to Bishop Blanc in which Odin addressed the possibility of Ursuline sisters coming to Texas, he also wrote of his reaction to the sudden appearance of Paquín and Brands in Texas, commenting that "it is useless to tell you how happy the arrival of these two old colleagues made me, and how much my spirit was uplifted."[22]

Sadly, that joyfulness too was to be short-lived. Odin had named Father Paquín his vicar general and had stationed him at Galveston, hoping to build a Congregation of the Mission community life akin to what was being established in San Antonio. Father Brands was sent to Houston. Odin then at last was able to make his long-hoped-for trek to San Antonio. While in the Bexar City, on September 14, Odin received news that Father Paquín had died. Yellow Fever had broken out in Houston, and on August 1 Father Paquín had hurried to the city to help Father Brands in ministering to the people there. Within less than a week both Paquín and Brands contracted the fever. On the morning of August 13 Father Paquín died. Father Brands barely survived.[23] What a shock it was to so many: Odin, Brands, Dr. Labadie (who was called too late to save Father Paquín), Timon and the Vincentian community in Missouri, and Blanc over in New Orleans.

What now? Bishop Odin had labored devotedly to build Roman Catholic life in Texas, but clearly he needed more priests and some nuns. In late 1844, he had with him in Texas only the original Vincentians, Fathers Calvo and Estany as well as Brother Sala, Father Brands, Father Clarke, and Father Oge who was soon to leave. He could count among his laborers no sisters. Odin had discussed at length with Bishop Blanc the possibility of Ursuline Sisters from New Orleans coming to Texas, and Odin had great hopes about the prospect. By then it was becoming clear that the time had come for Odin to make his long-anticipated journey to Europe to seek out priests, nuns, seminarians, brothers, and others. Moreover, Odin stood in great need of financial help for the missioning of Texas, the kind of support that such a venture to Europe might bring. At the same time, the missionary from France felt that he needed once again to visit his *mere,* who was in the latter years of her earthly life, and other family members and friends as well back in the little village of his birth. Thus it was that in the spring of 1845 he departed from Texas for Liverpool, England, from where he would begin his lengthy European recruiting trip.

A Long Trek in Europe

On the morning of February 26, 1845, the ship *J. McCune* cleared the port of Galveston bound for New Orleans. Bishop Odin was on board, having begun the first leg of a long and demanding journey that was to carry him to the eastern shore of the United States, across the Atlantic Ocean to Ireland and England, and then throughout much of western and central continental Europe, including Italy, and then eventually back to America and his beloved Texas. That adventure would keep Odin away from his vicariate apostolic for more than sixteen months.

Unfortunately, during Odin's absence serious disturbances erupted in Texas, ones that had surged forth as aspects of an intense historical confrontation between the United States and Mexico over the possession of Texas. The former country had been for some time in a national mood of manifest destiny, which would include the annexation of Texas while Odin was experiencing the early months of his European journey. Mexico, on the other hand, strongly assumed that Texas was part of its national parameters. The ultimate result was that the United States invaded Mexico in 1846, and war ensued.

While more will be said of that situation later, it is important to understand that Odin, whether being apprised of those developments while away from his vicariate apostolic on his European journey, or learning of them upon his return, remained firm in his conviction that amidst the tensions in Texas the Catholic Church's main calling was to strengthen the faith. Odin was convinced that no matter what chaos the political, military, and demographic disturbances then raging might bring upon the people of Texas, he and his clergy—with the support of many lay people—must continue to work toward laying a base for the future of Catholicism in the region.

On the first of April, accompanied by Bishop Francis Patrick Kenrick of Philadelphia, Odin boarded the packet *J.R. Kiddy* bound for Liverpool, England. Bishop Kenrick, a longtime friend of Odin and bishop of Philadelphia since April 22, 1842, had made his decision to travel across the Atlantic Ocean with the Texas vicar apostolic at the last moment. Disembarking from the *J.R. Kiddy* following the ship's docking at Liverpool, after a voyage of slightly less than three weeks, Odin immediately turned to Ireland. On April 22, 1845, he recorded in his daily journal, "I arrived at Cork." Staying only one day in that historic city on Ireland's southern coast, Odin then set out for Dublin, arriving there on the twenty-fourth. The Texas vicar apostolic was especially determined to visit Maynooth's Royal College of St. Patrick in the vicinity of Dublin for the purpose of recruiting priests and seminarians.[24]

Established in 1795, St. Patrick's had grown as Catholic Ireland's most productive center for training priests. One author wrote of the institution that "it was to have a profound influence on the character of the Irish clergy, and on Roman Catholicism throughout the English-speaking world."[25]

Visiting Ireland just as the potato famine was breaking out, Odin liked what he saw regarding the religious temperament visible among the Irish people, in their seminaries as well as in their religious houses, which, in addition to St. Patrick's, included others such as All Hallows near Dublin. Almost a year later, when he returned to the Emerald Isle for a brief visit following his continental journey and was preparing to set out for Liverpool and his voyage back to Texas, Odin penned a letter to Father Etienne from Castleknock, Ireland, and exclaimed, "During my stay in Ireland I was truly edified by the spirit of our colleagues. I have found here the same peace as in our house in Paris. All the young men that have been trained by us seem to preserve the fervor and peaceful contemplation of their novitiate. Their missions produce the most abundant and consoling fruits. I went to visit them last Sunday at Black Rock, where they worked all during Lent; and I was touched by the spirit of pious meditations of the people who filled the church, in spite of the most terrible weather. They have been called to do a great deal of good in their country, and I hope that one day they will come to the help of our missions in America."[26]

Odin's initial 1845 stay in Ireland was brief. The day following his visit to St. Patrick's College, on April 28, he headed for London. A few days later the missionary from France crossed the English Channel, to set foot once again on the soil of his beloved mother country. Arriving at Paris on the fourth of May, he remained there until June 11, spending a full five weeks in the ancient French capital and largest city on the European continent. At that time Paris's population had just topped one million.[27]

Jean-Marie Odin's lengthy stay in Paris was filled with activity. He celebrated Mass at the Cathedral of Notre Dame on one occasion, administered the sacrament of confirmation twice, participated in religious processions on at least two occasions, and generally involved himself with priestly duties throughout the days of his residence in Paris. At the same time he met with his Vincentian superiors at the *maison mere* (motherhouse), going over matters related to the status of the Texas vicariate apostolic, by then an episcopal entity outside the missioning purview of the Congregation of the Mission.

Two additional concerns attracted Odin's attention during his time spent in Paris. He met with officials at the Paris offices of the Society for the Propagation of the Faith and discussed with them his financial needs for Texas. Those meetings convinced him that his previously scheduled trip to the Propagation's headquarters at Lyon for the purpose of presenting his requests for support to the administrators there was absolutely necessary. Further, Bishop Odin was called upon to dispel doubts that had arisen at the *maison mere* regarding how Father Timon and other Vincentian leaders at St. Mary's of the Barrens had been overseeing affairs. This was necessary in response to several members of the Congregation of the Mission in America over the past few years having written letters of complaint to the motherhouse. In reference to this situation, Odin wrote to Father Timon on May 30, 1845, "Our Superior General left here on Tuesday after Pentecost to visit the various houses of Sisters of Charity in the south of France. When I first came [here], I perceived that the many letters written by some of our thoughtless or over busy *confreres* had created some perplexity in the minds of our superiors, but I soon removed every anxiety of mind. They have every confidence in and the greatest esteem for you and for most of our American brethren, but they apprehended that there was a want of union and kind feelings among us on account of so many complaints or so many censures conveyed by some letters. Knowing the persons who had written, I endeavored to make them known as well as I could, and they seemed to be perfectly satisfied."[28]

While in Paris, and with the Catholic newspapers, in particular *L'Univers,* having given his return to France much publicity, Jean-Marie Odin received several letters from Ambierle. Those missives increased anticipation of his long-awaited reunion with family and friends at Hauteville and in the Ambierle parish. But, he was also caught up with a sense of sadness, because his younger brother, the one who had passed away a couple of years earlier, would be missed terribly. Jean-Marie also realized that since his last visit home a decade earlier, some of his neighbors whom he had known as a young man would also no longer be alive.

Bearing up under these feelings as well as he could have been expected to, Odin set out from Paris early in the morning on that June 11 day, anxious to embrace once again his family, especially his mother. Now would surely surface deep emotions accompanied by certain nostalgia for the happy days of his youth. Traveling southeast toward the Bourbonnais, he reached the city of Moulin within two days. After celebrating Mass there he continued on to the Lyonnais, arriving at his home on the seventeenth.

Jean-Marie spent the next two weeks in Hauteville, Ambierle, and the surrounding vicinity. While the Frenchman wrote nothing about the substance of his visit with his family and friends there, certain conclusions can be drawn confidently. Undoubtedly he spent much affectionate time with his mother and siblings, cherishing his being with them and discussing family matters. It can be assumed that he visited the gravesites of his father, younger brother, and other family members, remembering them with love and praying for the repose of their souls. It also must have been a joy once again to be in the home where he was born and raised. We know that he celebrated Mass and made visits to the tabernacle of St. Martin D'Ambierle, where he had grown up, received the sacraments of first communion and confirmation, served as an altar boy, and first met Father Antoine Blanc. Finally, Jean-Marie Odin would have presented himself in Hauteville and Ambierle, seeing once again acquaintances of past years and reliving memories of his youth.[29]

His sojourn to Hauteville-Ambierle left Jean-Marie with other impressions too. From Paris on January 11, 1846, the Texas vicar apostolic wrote to Bishop Blanc back at New Orleans: "My stay at Ambierle was very short. This poor region has become very sad. There remains hardly any bourgeois famil[ies], with the exception of the youngest son of Mr. Deschaux, who had the misfortune of losing, a month ago, a young and excellent wife. Rev. Thevenard is very feeble. Rev. Camille Depany appears very old. Rev. Charles holds up rather well except for his eyes, which are becoming very weak. He also gave me a letter for you. Rev. Cahngy is still of the world and even rather vigorous. All the other priests of the vicinity are probably unknown to you. The only daughter left by Mr. August Deschaux became a Sister of Charity; she is here in Paris."[30]

On July 2, in the middle of that 1845 summer, Jean-Marie bid his family farewell and departed Hauteville bound for the city of Roanne en route ultimately to Lyon. The following day he celebrated Mass and preached at St. Stephen's Church in Roanne. On the fifth of the month the Texas vicar apostolic took his leave from Roanne and headed for Lyon, a short trek that found him in the ancient city of St. Irenaeus within a few hours. There he would stay for most of the remainder of July.[31]

After completing his mission to Lyon, Odin would follow an itinerary that called for him to venture on to Italy, where at Rome he had meetings with officials at the Holy See, including three audiences with Pope Gregory XVI. In addition, he was to engage in discussions with various Italian prelates, heads of religious orders, and other churchmen as well as members of the Italian aristocracy, seeking their help for his Texas mission. Odin then planned to return to France, with recruiting visits in Austria and the Germanies as well as a meeting with the bishop of Strasbourg scheduled along the way.

The missionary bishop from France enjoyed much greater success in Lyon than he expected he would. At the headquarters of the Society for the Propagation of the Faith he successfully argued for the separation of Texas from the Vincentian missions regarding receiving grants of financial support. From that point on the Vicariate Apostolic of Texas would be listed as a distinct ecclesiastical entity destined for help. To his great satisfaction Odin was then awarded forty thousand francs to aid in building the faith in Texas. He could anticipate similar amounts in the future. As a matter of fact, between 1846 and 1901, the area that matured from the Vicariate Apostolic of Texas into the Diocese of Galveston would emerge the greatest single beneficiary in the history of the society, being awarded a total amount of $249,370.[32]

Expecting little cooperation from the archbishop of Lyon, Cardinal Louis de Bonald, in his attempts to recruit priests, seminarians, brothers, and nuns from the archdiocese, Odin was surprised when the cardinal actually agreed to release several clerics for the Texas mission. But the missionary from France apparently had to exert considerable pressure on Cardinal de Bonald to convince him to give up those churchmen. Odin verified such in a letter to Bishop Blanc in January 1846, wherein he wrote, "What measures I had to take to extract from him [Cardinal de Bonald] an approval that he took little pleasure in granting."[33]

It seems that during this, his first visit at Lyon, Odin was able to attract five or six seminarians—all deacons or subdeacons—for Texas. He also sought, with little immediate success, Sisters of Charity.[34] The Texas vicar apostolic's tour of Italy, which took up most of August and all of September and October as well as a few days of November 1845, was profitable in terms of garnering spiritual support for the vicariate apostolic and obtaining an English-speaking priest from the Roman province of the Congregation of the Mission, Father Richard Hennesy.

Turning back to France from Italy for a brief second visit at Lyon and Paris as well as another visit with his family at Hauteville-Ambierle, on November 11 Odin arrived at Vienna. Continuing on from the Austrian capital, his route carried him to Munich, Augsburg, and several other cities, and finally on to Strasbourg for an appointment with that diocese's ordinary. There Odin arrived on the nineteenth of the month. The encounter with the bishop of Strasbourg, a meeting that had been on Odin's mind ever since he left Galveston back in February of that year, promised to be unpleasant. In the vicar apostolic's view the Strasbourg prelate needed to be held to account for his having released for service in Texas several priests who were unworthy. Most noted among them were Fathers Oge, whom we saw Odin dismiss from the Texas vicariate back in the spring of 1844, and Schneider.

Odin's own account of his confrontation with the Bishop of Strasbourg was contained in a January 1846 letter to Bishop Blanc back at New Orleans, wherein Odin exclaimed, "I spent two weeks in Vienna, three days in Munich, and I returned to France by way of Strasbourg. The need to rebuke Monseigneur, the bishop of that city, who indeed deserved to be rebuked, directed me there. I shudder again thinking about the great harm that the vicars of that diocese did to the poor mission of Texas. The five priests to whom they gave such favorable and false leaves were corrupted in every respect and of whom they wanted to rid themselves at any cost. The poor bishop signed without reading the papers that were submitted to him."[35]

Reassured that the bishop of Strasbourg would not release any such priests again to his Texas vicariate apostolic, Odin then spent the winter of 1845–46 in and around Lyon, Hauteville-Ambierle, and Paris, spending more time with his family and finalizing recruiting efforts. Toward the end of his long sojourn to Europe, on March 20, 1846, he recorded in his daily journal that "fifteen missionaries left [for America] on board the *Elizabeth Allen*." In that group was the future second bishop of Galveston and close colleague of Odin for many years, Father Claude Marie Dubuis.[36]

Before returning to Texas, as already noted, Odin went back to Ireland for a brief visit. At Castleknock, the Congregation of the Mission headquarters for Ireland, he attained the services for Texas of a young Vincentian priest (he was born on February 6, 1816), Father John Lynch.[37] On April 11 of 1846, Bishop Odin, Father Lynch, and some others sailed for New York aboard the ship *Great Western*. The missionary vicar apostolic was to return to a Texas just recently annexed by the United States, a land about to enter into a war with Mexico.

13

Back from Europe

AFTER AN UNEVENTFUL OCEAN VOYAGE of slightly more than two weeks, the *Great Western* docked in New York on April 27. Jean-Marie Odin had arrived back in the United States fatigued from his many months of travel and recruiting but content with the promising results of his trip. Soon he would be back in his beloved Texas. Since 1840 Odin had been laboring to revitalize Catholic life in the vicariate apostolic. But now, he realized, it was time to start building for the future, to lay a foundation for the deepening of Catholicism in Texas for the next several decades, well into the forthcoming twentieth century. That vision of reinvigorating Catholic life in the Lone Star Republic and then subsequently laying an ecclesiastical base throughout the land for the coming decades would mature as the main legacy that Bishop Odin would leave to Catholic Texas.

Odin understood only too well that the two goals of rebuilding while developing for the years that lay ahead were interrelated, the latter emerging from the former. His labors in Texas as well as those of others up to the time of his return from Europe had served as stepping stones from the earlier missionary efforts in Texas. From that 1846 arrival back in Texas onward, Jean-Marie Odin would be seen as not only the architect of a restored Catholic Church in the land in the 1840s but as the architect of Catholic life in Texas for the next several decades.

Anxious to see Texas once again, Odin, upon disembarking the *Great Western,* immediately turned southward to visit Philadelphia, Washington, DC, and Baltimore. In the Maryland city he attended the Sixth Provincial Council of Baltimore. Following the close of the council Odin headed west to the Mississippi River, with his final destination being downriver at New Orleans, his usual port of departure for Texas. En route, while passing through Missouri, the Texas vicar apostolic visited several locales so very familiar to him: St. Louis, St. Mary's of the Barrens at Perryville, St. Genevieve, and Cape Girardeau.

Two months later, on June 28, having arrived in New Orleans the night before, Odin wrote to Father Etienne, reporting to the Vincentian superior general about his return to America. In his letter Odin also commented about other matters of concern that he felt were bound to impact the Vincentian establishment in the United States and the growth of the church on the American frontier, especially in Texas. The vicar apostolic expressed himself openly to Etienne regarding such matters as the situation of the Congregation of the Mission in the United States, the results of his recruitment efforts in Europe, and his fears about the US-Mexican War that had erupted a few months earlier in the wake of the US annexation of Texas in December 1845.

With respect to the Vincentians in the United States, as he visited their establishments in those previously mentioned sites on his way home from Baltimore, Odin had made it a point to observe carefully the environments existing in those establishments he visited on his return trip to Texas. He seemed to be especially anxious about the clergy's interaction with each other and the religious life they were bringing to the people of their areas. Upon the completion of his inspection, Odin judged that the complaints made against Timon and others regarding conditions existing within the American Vincentian community were "exaggerated."

Consequently, in his June 28 letter, he was able to inform Etienne about what he witnessed, writing that "I tried to examine the conditions at our different houses with care. The various letters of which I was apprised in Paris had truly distressed me, and thanks to God, I found that all the complaints that reached you are filled with exaggeration."[1]

Odin was not suggesting to Etienne that disagreements within the US Vincentian community, from Philadelphia through Missouri and down into Louisiana, were nonexistent. On the contrary, he realized only too well that internecine squabbling had been going on since the mid-1830s.[2] Rather, he came to the conclusion that the complainers focused on the negative—poor living conditions, the personal behavior of some of the confreres, and so forth—while ignoring the dedicated missioning labors that the Congregation of the Mission had carried out in America for almost three decades. In Odin's own words to Etienne, "they write to you in order to complain, but they refrain from speaking to you of the good which is brought about through the ministry of our colleagues."[3]

However, notwithstanding Odin's encouraging words, problems were to be evidenced in the Congregation of the Mission in America for years to come. Etienne himself, in a circular letter dated November 1, 1852, was to scold the Vincentians of the American province for suffering "unfortunate ups and downs, aborted projects, sterile arrangements, failed undertakings, [and] deceived hopes that had caused so much work and sacrifice to be without fruit."[4]

In his June letter Odin let Etienne know that the young clerics whom he had recruited from Europe had arrived safely at New Orleans on May 25, a month before his own appearance in the bayou city. He confirmed to the superior general that six of those soon-to-be missionaries were dispatched immediately to St. Mary's of the Barrens Seminary at Perryville to study English, while four others were presently in St. Louis as theology students. The vicar apostolic noted further to Etienne that two other recruits, ones destined for service in Mexico, were detoured to Louisiana's Assumption Seminary because the US-Mexican War then raging prevented them from entering Mexico after their arrival at New Orleans. In apprising Etienne of this development, Odin had once again to address the subject of war, which caused him considerable dismay.

The issue of the US annexation of Texas had surfaced as a central topic of debate during the 1844 US presidential election campaign as well as a serious point of contention between the United States and Mexico. When James K. Polk, the Democratic Party candidate from Tennessee and an avowed expansionist, defeated the Whig anti-expansionist Henry Clay of Kentucky in the election, the US Congress reconvened in early 1845 and approved annexation. The actual date of annexation was December 29, 1845, while Odin was still in Europe. As a consequence of this action, all land in Texas to the Rio Grande was taken. Mexico rejected the US action and broke off diplomatic relations with the United States.

President Polk then sent John Slidell to Mexico City as his emissary for negotiations about the annexation of Texas, as well as discussions over US designs on other lands making up Mexico's far northern frontier. This region included territory that eventually would be divided into the US states of New Mexico, Arizona, California, Nevada, Utah, and Colorado. The Mexican government, however, refused to formally receive Slidell.

At about the same time, in January 1846, Polk dispatched Gen. Zachary Taylor, commander of the US Army of the Southwest, to lead a contingent of his troops south from the Nueces River to the Rio Grande near Matamoros. By April Taylor had his forces in place. Viewing this action as an invasion of their nation, on April 24 several hundred Mexican soldiers crossed the river and the following day attacked the Americans. Even before the United States declared war on May 13, the US government, featuring the leadership of such historical figures as John C, Fremont, Comm. John D. Sloat, and Comm. Robert F. Stockton, was moving to take California. At the same time, on August 18, 1846, Col. Stephen Kearney and his forces occupied Santa Fe, New Mexico. Kearney then, with three hundred of his men, headed west toward California.

This was the situation as Jean-Marie Odin returned home to Texas from Europe. He realized from the beginning that the battlefield of the war would be Mexico rather than Texas. But he understood also that US troops would be transported along coastal Texas. Thus, he feared for the Texans as well as the people of Mexico. Moreover, he and the Mexicans had a common bridge, their Roman Catholic faith.[5] Remember, as we have already observed, that Odin appreciated that the roots of the Hispanic Catholic heritage of Texas were deeply cemented in Mexican soil. And Odin admired the spiritual and cultural essence of that legacy.

In his letter to Etienne the vicar apostolic expressed his concern about the war: "This war we hope will not last long unless England incites Mexico into prolonging it. The population of Texas increased considerably during my absence. People go there from all parts of the United States, and new events will not stop this emigration, for the theatre of war is already a great distance away from Texas establishments. The American army is already in possession of the right bank of the Rio Grande. I greatly regret to see that the Mexicans did not want to come to an agreement amicably and that the United States has profited from this circumstance to push the boundaries of their country farther away, because they will have a lot of difficulty in determining their conquests."[6]

Just a few days later, on July 8, Odin expressed himself more forthrightly to the Propagation of the Faith in Lyon, lamenting that "Here we are again at war with Mexico. After the annexation, the American government placed troops on the border of the country. The Mexicans had the temerity to attack them and soon hostilities began. The United States army had already seized several small cities situated on the banks of the Rio Grande. . . . They speak of seizing California and all of the departments of the Northeast. This issue distresses me very much for poor Mexico."[7]

Wishing that the war could have been avoided, Odin at the same time distrusted US expansionism and the manifest destiny ideology that fueled it. The vicar apostolic's way of viewing matters regarding armed conflict and its destructive impact on the population and land proved consistent throughout the twenty-five-year period of his life when troubles between Texas—and then the United States—and Mexico, followed by the US Civil War, dominated the times for him. When the region in which he was serving fell prey to the plunders of war, Odin's response was to pray for peace and carry forward his ministering to the people and taking the lead in striving to strengthen the Catholic presence in the area. Simply stated, his reaction to the tensions was that of a missionary priest and bishop.

As the military and diplomatic activities associated with the US-Mexican War intensified and US forces penetrated farther into the territories of Mexico, Odin continued his efforts to build Catholic life in Texas. During latter 1846, and into 1847, he would welcome to the vicariate apostolic several of the priests whom he had recruited from Europe. Augmenting the small band of missionaries already on location in Texas, these fresh new evangelists were to increase considerably the number of laborers in the vineyard available to Odin.

As those churchmen began arriving, Odin thought carefully about where each should be stationed. Two considerations loomed paramount in his mind. First, he wanted them assigned to various locales according to where their individual nationalities and cultures—especially languages—would best serve the host Mexicans and increasing numbers of immigrant Catholics coming into Texas. The vicar apostolic hoped that the new clergy would be able to hear confessions, preach, teach, and otherwise catechize in the vernacular of the different peoples they would be serving.[8] The languages initially were to include Spanish, German, English, and French. Later Polish, Italian, and some others would be added to the list. Odin himself served as an inspirational example of what was needed. Fluent in his native French and knowledgeable in Latin when he arrived at the Barrens Seminary in Perryville, Missouri, as a young twenty-two-year-old, he had struggled to learn English. Then after coming to Texas in 1840, he took it upon himself to study Spanish.

Beyond his concern for fitting the right priests with different nationalities and cultures, Odin was determined to create Vincentian communities wherever feasible. Though it needed firming up somewhat, a Vincentian house existed at San Fernando Church in San Antonio, with Fathers Calvo and Estany (when Estany actually was residing there and not riding the circuit or serving the Catholic soldiers of General Taylor's army) as well as Brother Sala. By the end of the summer of 1846, Odin had living with him at Galveston three fellow Vincentians: Fathers John Brands, Richard Hennesy, and Bartholomew Rollando. The vicar apostolic envisioned a Congregation of the Missions house maturing from this group.

Houston, however, proved to be a more difficult situation. Odin was able to assign two of his recently recruited priests there for St. Vincent's Church, clerics that Father Dowley had sent from Castleknock College in Ireland. One of them, Father John Joseph Lynch, was a Vincentian; but the other one, Father James Fitzgerald, was a secular. Thus, establishing a Vincentian house at that time in Houston proved impossible. Beyond that, a few months later Father Timon visited Galveston at Odin's invitation to help officiate at the March 14, 1847, laying of the cornerstone ceremonies for the new St. Mary's Church planned for that city.[9] During the course of Timon's stay, he and Odin engaged in serious discussions about the vicar apostolic needing to be sensitive to both the interests of the Vincentians as well as the needs of the vicariate apostolic. Both Odin and Timon were aware that some understanding regarding property titles had to be worked out. The two Vincentians sensed that Texas was maturing toward becoming a diocese, and they knew that distinctions would have to be made in the future between what would be considered diocesan properties as opposed to those claimed by the Vincentians. Eventually, with some intense negotiations, the two Vincentian friends came to agree upon mutually acceptable decisions.

Meanwhile, still convinced that laying any permanent base for Catholicism's future in Texas would require the presence of female religious, Odin, in January 1847, brought to a successful conclusion his five-year search for nuns by escorting to Galveston a band of eight Ursulines and a lay sister from New Orleans. The importance of Catholic sisters, especially in the fields of education for girls, running orphanages and hospitals, and generally raising the cultural and spiritual levels of the locales whereat they were established, was well known to the vicar apostolic. Odin's own native France had matured over the centuries as a nation in which the influence of religious orders of nuns had become indispensable to society. The trauma and destruction female religious suffered during the devastating French Revolution only made them more appreciated.

The Daughters of Charity, which St. Vincent de Paul and St. Louise de Marillac had established together in early seventeenth-century France, bore the Vincentian mark of Odin's own Congregation of the Mission. He would have loved to have been able to bring them to Texas, but they would not appear in the Lone Star State until 1869. But, returning to the Ursulines, Sister Monica LaFleur of the Congregation of the Sisters of Charity of the Incarnate Word in Houston, Texas, reminded us that as a result of Odin's entreaties over a period of several years, "On 16 January 1847, four months before the erection of the Diocese of Galveston, eight Ursuline Sisters left New Orleans for the island city. Three of them, Sisters Augustine Metton, Angela Noyer, and Ursula Renaud, had come from France specifically for the new Galveston foundation and had made their novitiate and their religious profession in New Orleans. The religious superior of the group, Sister Arsene Blin, had come from France thirty years earlier to enter the Ursuline Order in New Orleans. The other four, Sisters Stanislaus Truchet, St. Bruno Boyle, Ambrose Benett, and Agnes had also been members of the New Orleans community."[10]

Odin himself, in an April 9, 1847, letter to the Propagation of the Faith at Lyon, happily reported that "A work which is to contribute greatly to the progress of faith and good principles in the region has been accomplished. On the 18th of January five professed Ursuline Nuns with three novices and a lay sister arrived at Galveston to take up the administration of the establishment of their order with which the community of New Orleans has so generously endowed my poor mission." Having moved into their house, which Odin described as being "the largest in the region," the Ursulines opened their academy on February 8. Within a short period of time it was filled to capacity with both Catholic and Protestant students.[11] Their labors had begun.

Bishop of Galveston

"IAM POSITIVELY GOING TO BEGIN THE NEW CHURCH which we so greatly need." This promise Odin penned to Bishop Blanc from Galveston on April 18, 1847, affirming his determination to start construction on the new St. Mary's Church in the Texas bay city. A French émigré architect, Theodore E. Giraud, developed the design of St. Mary's and would oversee its being built.[1] But, as the story was to unfold, the new edifice would be dedicated a year and a half later as more than a parish church. It would be the cathedral of a newly established diocese, the Diocese of Galveston.

Three weeks after Odin's letter to Bishop Blanc, on May 4, Pope Pius IX responded to the urgings of the Catholic bishops of the Sixth Provincial Council of Baltimore the previous year and raised Texas to the hierarchical status of a diocese. The Pontiff followed that action seventeen days later, on May 21, by naming Jean-Marie Odin Galveston's first bishop. Those developments were hardly unexpected, given the widely recognized need at the time to begin forming the church's future ecclesiastical structure for Texas. Moreover, as the reigning pope in 1846 when the process of erecting the Diocese of Galveston commenced, Gregory XVI knew Odin well and greatly appreciated the Frenchman's dedication to rebuilding the church in the Lone Star State. To Pope Gregory XVI such an appointment only seemed natural. The death of Pope Gregory XVI on June 1, 1846, and the election of Pope Pius IX fifteen days later, however, delayed movement on the creation of the Galveston diocese for a while.[2]

Unquestionably, in planning St. Mary's Church Odin anticipated it becoming the mother church, cathedral, of the expected new diocese when such was established. St. Mary's Church was Odin's pride and joy, wrote the distinguished historian of Catholic Texas, Carlos Eduardo Castaneda. Castaneda quoted Odin as describing St. Mary's Church as "a solid, adequate building of Gothic style, with inside measurements of 120 feet by 60 feet and a transept of 80 feet." A noted scholar of the architecture of houses of worship in Texas, the late Willard B. Robinson, bragged that St. Mary's Church was "a twin-towered work on the traditional cruciform plan, aesthetically worthy of the seat of the bishop."[3]

While the sequence of events was evolving that eventually would bring him the news of the erection of the Diocese of Galveston and his appointment as the diocese's first ordinary, Odin carried on with his labors in Texas. Among his most cherished responsibilities was that of giving encouragement and support to the Ursulines and their developing girls' academy in Galveston. On April 11, 1847, he happily wrote to Father Rousselon in New Orleans that "our religious sisters are all in good health and already have 54 pupils in their classes." That communication was just one of many that the soon-to-be bishop of Galveston was to make throughout 1847 and early 1848 about the Ursulines and their Galveston academy.[4]

In September 1847, Odin finally learned officially of his and Catholic Texas' changed status. On September 21 he acknowledged to Bishop Blanc at New Orleans that "the letter you had forwarded to me on the part of the archbishop [Archbishop Samuel Eccleston of Baltimore] contained the bull of the establishment of the See of Galveston."[5]

That same mailing from Blanc included additional information that was to dramatically impact Odin's working intimacy with his friend and confrere Father Timon. On the very day five months earlier that Timon boarded a stagecoach headed eastward from San Antonio to Houston, commencing the first leg of his return jaunt to Missouri following his several weeks' stay in Texas after the laying of the cornerstone for St. Mary's Church, Pope Pius IX established the new Diocese of Buffalo, New York, and named Timon as that diocese's first bishop. The date was April 23.[6]

Odin and Timon's friendship would now have to endure in circumstances wherein, except for rare occasions, they would be separated by great distances. Odin in Texas and Timon as the bishop of a diocese on the shores of Lake Erie, hundreds of miles northeastward from their common Vincentian working ground in Missouri, would now have to concentrate on their respective dioceses. They would be serving the church in regions almost two thousand miles distant from one another. Moreover, Timon, who had served for twelve years as visitor of the American Vincentians, was relieved of those duties upon his being named bishop of Buffalo, further altering his relationship with Odin. But they remained close friends for the rest of their lives.

By the latter days of October 1847, Odin had ceased using the hierarchical title "bishop of Claudiopolis and vicar apostolic of Texas" and appropriately adopted instead the appendage "bishop of Galveston." At the same time, rarely did he employ use of the academic designation of doctor of divinity, D.D., an identity to which he was entitled as far back as 1842 when he was consecrated a bishop.[7] So, as the US-Mexican War pressed on into its final stages, the need to form the Diocese of Galveston became the center of Bishop Odin's enthusiastic focus. Central to that effort at the time was completing and consecrating the cathedral.

St. Mary's Cathedral Consecrated as Part of Building the Faith

The situation for the Catholics of Texas had visibly improved over the recent years as the result of the work of Odin, his clergy, and most recently the Ursuline nuns. Yet new challenges loomed on the horizon. The war with Mexico, which led US troops to be occasionally stationed in San Antonio, dragged on into the spring of 1848.[8] It was only on February 2 of that year that the US diplomat Nicholas P. Trist signed the Treaty of Guadalupe Hidalgo with the Mexican government, which ended the conflict and granted to the United States vast regions of Mexican land that were to become known to history as the Mexican Cession. Clearly Bishop Odin's previously voiced fear that the Americans would prove to be greedy in their expansionist designs was accurate.

The US victory in the war failed to relieve the confusion that surrounded the boundary question regarding the Diocese of Galveston. For three more years Bishop Odin remained uncertain as to just how extensive were the limits of his diocesan jurisdiction. The papal bull establishing the Diocese of Galveston, *Apostolicae Sedis fastigio,* called for the new diocese to encompass "all of Texas such as its limits may be after the difficulties with Mexico have been settled."[9] Such a description had left the matter of boundaries in question when the diocese was erected in 1847.

Beyond this, Bishop Odin worried about the increasingly aggressive proselytization going on among Catholics of his diocese from Texas' burgeoning Protestant population.[10] Further frustrating the new bishop was Texas' continuing shortage of priests. To be sure, the situation regarding priests and nuns laboring in the Lone Star State had improved, but illnesses, deaths, or reassignments of personnel tended to undermine the positive impact of increases among male and female missionaries gained through recruitment.

The fall of 1847 saw the deaths of two priests: Fathers Matthew Chazelle at Castroville and Bartholomew Rollando at Galveston. Of Father Chazelle's passing away, Odin, in December of that year lamented to the Society for the Propagation of the Faith at Lyon that "Heaven has just made me pass through some rough trials. . . . On the first of September I had the sorrow of losing Rev. Chazelle, a young priest upon whom I had based the finest hopes." In that same December letter, in writing of Father Rollando, Odin sorrowfully exclaimed that "On the eleventh of October Heaven demanded of me another sacrifice in the person of Rev. Rollando, dead of Yellow Fever, in the prime of life, after 14 years of ministry in America."[11]

In addition, when Odin was named bishop of Galveston, the Vincentians removed Texas from their mission field and began withdrawing their priests and brothers from the diocese for assignments elsewhere. This action of his own congregation, which was only completed five years later, in 1852, dismayed Odin. Finally, the new prelate would once again need to deal with the institution of slavery and for the first time in a serious vein confront nativism.

However, in 1847–48, finishing and consecrating St. Mary's Cathedral stood out as a primary goal for Bishop Odin. He felt that the completion was essential to the forging of an ecclesiastical configuration for the new diocese. Ten days before laying the cornerstone for St. Mary's, on March 4, 1847, he had written to Father Rousselon at New Orleans that "the wood for our church is being unloaded at this time. The laborers are working to make the bricks, and I hope that we shall begin our building around the first days of May."[12]

When he was in Europe a year earlier making plans to send his recruits to America, Odin had been promised a donation of five hundred thousand bricks for the construction of St. Mary's by a Belgian brick merchant. Those bricks, however, never arrived. The new ordinary was then forced to contract for others bricks locally at what was for his budget an exorbitant price of eight dollars per thousand. He trembled at the thought of that unexpected heavy expense.[13]

Notwithstanding that setback, progress on the construction of the cathedral progressed from May 1847 through the spring and summer months of 1848 under the watchful eye of architect Giraud. Even though a hurricane demolished a good part of the tin covering of the roof of St. Mary's on August 17 and 18, 1848, adding three hundred dollars more in unwanted costs to the project, the edifice was completed by the fall of that year.[14]

As early as June, Odin had begun to finalize plans for the consecration of the cathedral. A major consideration in fixing the exact date was the availability of Bishop Timon to make the long trip south from Buffalo to Galveston.[15] After some delays, in August Timon confirmed to Odin that he would be able to travel to Galveston in latter November for what would turn out to be his last reunion with Odin in Texas. The date for the consecration was then set for August 25.

At nine o'clock that Sunday morning "in procession, choristers, sanctuary boys, clergy, and prelates marched the quarter-mile distance from the episcopal residence to the Cathedral." Bishop Blanc celebrated the Mass, and Bishop Timon preached the sermon. Among the many clergy assisting were Fathers Napoleon Perche and Edward D'Hauw from New Orleans and Texas priests Edward Clarke, James A. Miller, Richard Hennesy, James Giraudon, James Fitzgerald, Charles Padey, and Joseph Anstaett.[16] Other clergy and the Ursuline sisters as well made up segments of the throng that packed into St. Mary's Cathedral on that all-important morning.

Bishop Jean-Marie Odin, not far from his fiftieth birthday, was buoyant throughout the entire consecration. The Diocese of Galveston had its cathedral! A few days later, having bid farewell to both Bishops Blanc and Timon, Odin wrote to Father Rousselon at New Orleans: "You have been told about the ceremony; it was a beautiful day for me and for our entire city. The solid instruction that was taught to our population left a strong and durable impression, I hope, upon all their minds. Last Sunday [the Sunday following the consecration] I believed that we would have only a small congregation, but to my great pleasure and against my expectations, our new church was sufficiently full. This building, which gave me so much anxiety, will, I hope, contribute to the strengthening and the propagation of the Faith."[17]

Odin Brings in Oblates and More Ursulines

Late April 1849 found Odin in Montreal, Canada, seeking priests and nuns for his diocese. He made the long and demanding journey from Texas to the Canadian city as part of an excursion of several months' duration that he had undertaken to attend the Seventh Provincial Council of Baltimore scheduled to convene on May 5 of that year. Even before departing Galveston Odin had determined that while traveling he would reach out for support in terms of both personnel and finances for his Texas diocese.[18]

In Montreal, while attending a dinner given in his honor at the major seminary of the Sulpicians, Odin met Father Pierre Telmon, an Oblate of Mary Immaculate priest seeking a missionary assignment. Telmon had previously labored in Canada as well as Pittsburgh and responded enthusiastically to the bishop of Galveston's plea for help. He pledged to accompany Odin to Texas to serve in the lower Rio Grande region of the Galveston diocese. Father Telmon even promised to bring with him other Oblates of Mary Immaculate.[19]

Agreeing to return to Canada following the Baltimore council, Odin then hurried back to the Maryland city, as the meeting of bishops was about to convene. Among the numerous issues on their agenda, the synod fathers wanted to take a careful look at the growth of the church in America's West and Southwest, including the Diocese of Galveston and New Mexico. Most important, upon hearing Bishop Odin's report on how expansive his diocese had become with the end of the US-Mexican War, the bishops concurred that further hierarchical development was needed for the lands beyond the Mississippi River. Thus, on May 15, they wrote to the Holy See urging that in addition to new archdioceses being established at Cincinnati and New York, New Orleans should also be raised to such an ecclesiastical dignity. When New Orleans was given that status (summer 1850) the Diocese of Galveston was attached to it as a suffragan see.

Further, with regards to the Southwest, the prelates entreated Pope Pius IX to elevate the Indian Territory and New Mexico to the ranks of vicariate apostolics. When this was done, Galveston was now hierarchically sandwiched in between the Archdiocese of New Orleans and the Vicariate apostolic of New Mexico. This situation became a key to Catholicism's growth in that part of the United States. In retrospect, it can be seen that Odin's influence among the Catholic episcopacy certainly was ever-increasing (though he personally would have ignored any such claim).

Meanwhile, Bishop Odin's labors on behalf of his beloved Texas were continuing to show results. On September 14, 1849, a few weeks before he started out on his jaunt back to Texas from Baltimore, but following his second visit to Canada, he wrote to Bishop Blanc, who was by then back in New Orleans, reporting that, "I arrived Saturday evening at Philadelphia after a trip of several days in Canada. The good Ursuline nuns of Quebec have given me two of their Sisters for our house at Galveston. I have also found two postulants in Boston. Upon returning to Montreal I met the Oblate Fathers, who offered to provide me with four of their colleagues for the Rio Grande Valley."[20]

Setting out from New York in late October, Odin and his entourage made their way to the Mississippi River. Enjoying only a brief stay in Missouri, the group then headed downriver to New Orleans, a trip so familiar to Odin. Following a week's rest in the bayou city, they ventured into the Gulf of Mexico southwestward-bound for Galveston. A short though rough voyage brought their vessel to the Texas port in late November. The Oblates of Mary Immaculate included Fathers Telmon, Alexander Soulerin, and Augustine Gaudet as well as Brother Paul Celot and lay brother Joseph Mensche.[21]

With his new missionaries, male and female, having finally arrived on Texas soil, Bishop Odin dispatched Fathers Telmon and Soulerin, as well as Brother Mensche, to Brownsville in deep southeast Texas on the northern bank of the Rio Grande across from Matamoros. Sailing south along the Texas coast, the Oblates' ship reached Port Isabél on December 3. Two days later the three were in Brownsville. Not long after that Odin was able to write to soon-to-be Archbishop Blanc that "the two priests whom I sent to the Rio Grande have arrived at their destination and have been very well received by the inhabitants of the country." Father Gaudet and Brother Celot remained at the side of Odin in the see city.[22] The Ursuline nuns and postulants were assigned to the convent of their order in Galveston.

At Brownsville the Oblates found many of the populace living their lives religiously and morally in such a lax manner as to affirm the need for priests to come among them. Yet, discouragingly, within less than a year Bishop Charles Joseph Eugene de Mazenod withdrew his men from the Diocese of Galveston. Understandably, Mazenod's action dismayed Bishop Odin. It seems that Mazenod had been unenthusiastic about the Texas project from its very beginning. Mazenod had been especially wary of Father Telmon's role in leading the adventure. And when neither Odin nor Telmon kept the Oblates superior informed well enough about the progress of his priests and brothers missioning in the Lone Star State, in particular the good work being accomplished at Brownsville, Mazenod pulled out his men.[23]

The main reason for Odin's failure to write regularly to Bishop Mazenod about the successful efforts of his Oblates in Texas was that on April 22, 1850, the Texas bishop set out on a seven-months-long pastoral and missioning trek that carried him throughout the southern half of his diocese, and at one point he even crossed the Rio Grande into Mexico. During that lengthy trip the saintly bishop had to endure a fifteen-day siege of fever while at the same time being constantly under the threat of attack from Comanches. Yet on the trip he confirmed thousands of Catholics, celebrated Mass regularly, heard confessions, preached, and otherwise evangelized.[24]

It was only when he returned to Galveston on December 3 of that year that Odin learned of the recall of the Oblates. Sadly for him, on that same day Bishop Odin discovered that his own Congregation of the Mission had partly vacated Texas. While Odin was making his pastoral visits just mentioned, the US Vincentian visitor, Father Mariano Maller, had reassigned the Vincentians stationed at Galveston. Further, Father Maller had also ordered closed San Fernando Church in San Antonio, a church that at the time the Vincentians manned. Returning to an empty bishop's residence at Galveston, Odin was angered at such a turn of events. Regarding the continued removal of the Vincentians, two days before Christmas he penned a strongly worded letter of protest to Father Etienne at Paris.[25] It is important to understand that Father Maller, worried about his Vincentians being overextended, had nonetheless never even so much as set foot in Texas. Thus, he had been unable to observe firsthand the work of his Vincentians and see how much Bishop Odin needed them there.

Meanwhile, more than fifteen hundred miles northeast, an historic drama had unfolded on the floor of the US Senate in Washington, DC, that finally resolved the Texas boundaries question: the promulgation of the Compromise of 1850. With the final bills of the legislation passed in early September 1850, US president Millard Fillmore signed them on the twentieth. The confusion over the Texas boundaries question had confounded Odin ever since his arrival in the land a decade earlier. Such political stalwarts as seventy-three-year-old Henry Clay, the "Great Compromiser"; John C. Calhoun (seriously ill with tuberculosis and not far from death); Daniel Webster; Thomas Hart Benton; William H. Seward; Stephen A. Douglas; and Jefferson Davis emerged as leading personages in the notable debate.

As mentioned already, for years the Lone Star State—and earlier the

Republic of Texas—had claimed that its boundaries followed the extent of the Rio Grande from its source to its emptying into the Gulf of Mexico. But one of Clay's solutions embedded in the final draft of the compromise denied Texas' "extreme claim to the Rio Grande boundary up to its source." The Texas boundary decision was described under the title "The Texas and New Mexico Act," dated September 9, 1850. It stated: "Texas will agree that her boundary on the north shall commence at the point at which the meridian of one hundred degrees west from Greenwich is intersected by the parallel of thirty-six degrees thirty minutes north latitude, and shall run from said point due west to the meridian of one hundred and three degrees west from Greenwich; hence her boundary shall run due south to the thirty-second degree of north latitude to the Rio Bravo del Norte, and thence with the channel of the said river to the Gulf of Mexico."[26]

Advice to Bishop Lamy and Then More Recruitment in Europe

The withdrawal of the Oblates and Vincentians from Texas meant that Odin would one more time have to seek out priests and brothers. Yet the Frenchman dreaded another strenuous journey to Europe. He was getting older and his health remained a concern. Still, realizing that for the sake of the Texas mission such a trip likely would be demanded of him, he wrote to Archbishop Blanc on March 19, 1851. In wording his letter to his longtime friend Odin was careful to outline the needs of his diocese following the departure of the two religious communities, while at the same time voicing his reluctance to venture back to Europe. He wrote: "I am coming to consult you on a measure that is very repugnant to me but nevertheless seems indispensable to me. At this moment I would need at least ten more missionaries to fill the various posts where a priest would be usefully employed. . . . Perhaps in person I could succeed in finding some devoted men. However, I am extremely reluctant to return to Europe; I am tired of seeking and begging. I really do not know how to decide. Please help me with your advice."[27]

Meanwhile, in the summer of 1850, Pope Pius IX named New Mexico a vicariate apostolic. A few months later, on November 24, in Cincinnati's Cathedral of Saint Peter in Chains, in an inspiring ceremony over which Bishop Martin John Spalding of Louisville presided, the French priest Jean Baptiste Lamy was consecrated titular bishop of Agathonica *in partibus infidelium* and vicar apostolic of New Mexico.[28] Shortly afterwards Odin wrote to Lamy offering the new vicar apostolic advice about how to travel to Santa Fe. Odin was aware that he and Lamy were two of several French-born priests who had become bishops over territories long boasting of Catholic heritages. Odin was convinced that it was therefore important for those bishops to mature as prelates sensitive to the religious and worship traditions—even popular ones—of all ethnic groups As such was true for him in Texas, so too would it be for Lamy in New Mexico.

Reflecting his missioning zeal, Odin showed concern for the entire American Southwest. In that spirit he was anxious to offer Bishop Lamy suggestions aimed at easing the way for the new vicar apostolic into his area of ecclesiastical jurisdictional responsibility. In a December 30, 1850, letter to Archbishop Blanc, Odin included detailed recommendations for Lamy (who was at the time in New Orleans) regarding what Odin saw as the best modes of travel through Texas to Santa Fe. Likely, though, Lamy never received that communication, because eight days later, on January 7, 1851, he arrived at Galveston en route to New Mexico. Staying at Bishop Odin's residence only a few hours, Lamy then departed for Santa Fe.[29]

In their conversations Odin was careful about not presuming to advise Lamy, perhaps only making suggestions to him. Drawing from his own experience in Texas, Odin urged the new vicar apostolic to travel to Europe in search of priests and nuns before actually going on to Santa Fe. Looking back at his own confrontations at San Antonio with Fathers de la Garza and Valdéz ten years earlier, Odin feared that Bishop Lamy might encounter similar problems in New Mexico. Odin predicted to Lamy that he would find in his new vicariate apostolic a few "scandalous men."[30] If Lamy first went to Europe, Odin reasoned, he could then bring back to New Mexico with him several clerics and nuns to help in the event that, as Odin expected would be the case, the vicar apostolic would be forced to undertake clerical reform.

At the same time, Odin recommended that while in Europe Lamy could continue to study his Spanish, a language that the New Mexico bishop was already attempting to learn. In spite of these urgings, Lamy, apparently even before he visited Odin at Galveston, had decided to travel on to Santa Fe through San Antonio and west Texas. It does seem, however, that Lamy also felt that if he deemed it necessary he would eventually go on to Europe for recruiting purposes. As a result of the Galveston visiting, both prelates agreed that the views of Archbishop Blanc on this and other matters should be sought.[31]

Following his visit with Lamy, Odin crystalized in his mind his own intent to embark on the recruiting trip to Europe. "I plan to leave here by the first boat that leaves port after the twenty-ninth of this month," he wrote to Archbishop Blanc from Galveston on May 23, 1851. Voyaging by sea along the Texas coast to New Orleans and then heading north by land to New York, Odin departed the latter city for Liverpool, England, on the fifth of July. Ten days later his ship, the *Arctic*, docked at Liverpool.[32] Though shorter in duration than his last trip to Europe six years earlier, this current venture nonetheless consumed about a year's time.

Venturing first to Ireland for a ten-day sojourn, in Dublin Odin received a promise of help in finding priests and brothers from Father Dowling. The Texas prelate then acquired for Galveston two Ursuline nuns from that community's convent at Waterford, a port town from which many Irish emigrants sailed for America during the famine years. In addition, he found two young female postulants anxious to serve in the missions. He anticipated leaving the postulants at the Ursuline convent in New Orleans for further formation before bringing them to Galveston.

Returning to England, Odin assisted at the consecration of two Roman Catholic bishops at Westminster Cathedral in London on July 27. That ceremony, which came in the wake of the recent restoration of the Roman Catholic hierarchy in England, was presided over by English cardinal Nicholas P. Wiseman, archbishop of Westminster. Commenting on the event, Odin lamented the historical suppression that Catholics had suffered in England ever since the time of King Henry VIII. Odin cited in particular the prejudices against Catholics (strongly anti-papal in character) of the current Whig party leader and prime minister from 1846 to 1852, Lord John Russell.[33]

After crossing the English Channel to the European continent, Odin spent several months recruiting in Paris, Lyon, Marseilles, and Rome, where he enjoyed at the Vatican a visit with Pope Pius IX. He also stayed for a short time with his family at Hauteville.[34] On this trip the Frenchman had determined that he would seek only priests, nuns, seminarians, brothers, and postulants and avoided asking for any financial help for his diocese.

The most important aspect of his recruiting may have been his meeting with Bishop Mazenod of the Oblates of Mary Immaculate at the bishop's Diocese of Marseilles. As a consequence of Odin's discussion with him, Mazenod tempered his negative views of the Texas mission and agreed to once again assign his priests and brothers to the Diocese of Galveston. Father P. F. Parisot, a priest of the Oblates of Mary Immaculate, wrote of the recruits that Bishop Odin gained and of their departure from France for the American mission field: "In the month of March, 1852, six Oblate Fathers and one lay brother, accompanied by four nuns of the Incarnate Word, two Ursuline Sisters, four Brothers of Mary, and eighteen seminarians, bade adieu to 'la belle France' and went aboard the sailing vessel '*La Belle Assise*,' at [La] Havre, en route for Texas. 'My native land adieu! I cannot always stay with you.' The wharf is crowded, thousands are there, in expectation of an unwonted spectacle. The saintly Bishop Odin, in his episcopal robes, blesses the band of missionaries from the pier and then goes back to Paris, in the interest of his diocese." Father Parisot, who was to himself emerge as one of Catholic Texas' outstanding missionaries, further captured the spirit of the mood of the clerics and nuns on that occasion when he wrote: "I saw tears trickling down the cheeks of a tender-hearted seminarian, as he cast a last glimpse on the coast of France disappearing on the horizon, 'Adieu mother.'"[35]

Back in Texas Continuing to Build a Catholic Foundation

Fifty-two days after sailing from France *La Belle Assise* docked at New Orleans. Upon disembarkation, the seminarians headed up the Mississippi River for St. Mary's of the Barrens Seminary. There they would finish their studies and formation in preparation for ordination and assignment in Texas. The rest of the group journeyed on to Galveston. Meanwhile, on March 28, following his return to Paris, Odin composed a letter to the Propagation of the Faith at Lyon, happily reporting that most of the 340 passengers aboard the *La Belle Assise* were Alsatians bound for Texas.[36]

Odin was delighted with the success of his recruitment trip to Europe. He believed that because of that trek, which brought to Texas more clergy and nuns at one time than ever before, efforts to reinvigorate the church in the Lone Star State had rebounded from its recent setback of the loss of the Oblates of Mary Immaculate and the Vincentians. By mid-July Odin himself had returned to Galveston and begun assigning his newly arrived priests, brothers, and nuns where they were most needed. The previous year he had stationed Ursulines in San Antonio to found a convent and school. Now the four Sisters of the Incarnate Word and Blessed Sacrament who had formed part of the contingent aboard the *La Belle Assise*—Sisters St. Ange Barre, Dominique Ravier, Ephrem Satin, and Claire Valentine—augmented the small but growing complement of women religious in Texas. Odin initially placed those nuns in the Ursuline convent at Galveston, affording them several months' training before assigning them to service at Brownsville in January 1853.[37]

Meanwhile, Odin began to feel content that he finally could count enough clergy and sisters, at least for the time being, to handle the needs of the Catholics throughout the diocese. As the year 1852 gave way to 1853, twenty priests were laboring in the Diocese of Galveston: the nine Odin had left in Texas during his European tour, five Irish priests obtained through the help of Father Dowling, and the six Oblates of Mary Immaculate. In addition, the Oblate lay brother and the four Brothers of Mary who also made up part of Bishop Odin's *La Belle Assise* band were now available. And still more clergy and religious were to come: in particular from the Germanies and the Polish-speaking world.

As soon as the Brothers of Mary appeared on the scene in Texas, Odin urged them on to San Antonio de Bexar, with instructions to found a school. Their school opened on August 30, 1852, and by November it boasted an enrollment of eighty young boys. Keeping a couple of the Oblates of Mary Immaculate with him in Galveston, Odin dispatched the rest to the lower Rio Grande Valley to serve from Brownsville to as far west as Laredo. Following up on agreements that Odin had made with Bishop Mazenod, the Oblates established a parish church at Brownsville, constructed under the architectural supervision of Father Pierre Keralum and completed in 1859: Immaculate Conception Church. Additionally, the Oblates housed at Galveston assumed direction of the small diocesan seminary that Odin established at his residence there.[38]

As these initiatives developed, Odin reaffirmed his commitment to having his priests laboring in predominantly Mexican-populated areas learn Spanish. Throughout the lower Rio Grande Valley Bishop Odin insisted that the clergy use Spanish instead of Latin when making entries in the various parish records. As the ordinary bishop, he himself taught Spanish classes daily at the diocesan seminary to the Oblate professors and students alike.[39] In the meantime, he transferred Father Claude Marie Dubuis from Castroville and its environs—where Dubuis had often been ill and frustrated, even to the point at one time of asking for permission to leave Texas and join the Jesuits—to the pastorate of San Antonio de Bexar's San Fernando Church. Notwithstanding Father Dubuis's difficulties at Castroville, Odin maintained a great confidence in his fellow Lyonnaise missionary and considered him to be one of the best priests in the diocese.

During that same September of 1852, Bishop Odin welcomed to Texas four Franciscans to serve the German-speaking Catholics in the western reaches of the diocese: from New Braunfels north to beyond Fredericksburg and southward to Kerrville, Comfort, and the area surrounding Castro's colonies of Castroville, D'Hanis, and Quihi. Those Sons of Saint Francis included Fathers Leopold Moczygemba (Polish) and Bonaventure Keller (German), both of whom Odin had recruited for the diocese during his European journey, and two other priests. It was during that time that the dedicated bishop began ordaining priests for his diocese on a regular basis.

On July 1, 1853, in another of his letters to the Propagation of the Faith at Lyon, Odin was able to report: "The two years that have just passed have been for me years of great solicitude but also of great importance, I hope, for the future of religion in the land. The scarcity of evangelical workers which forced me to recross the seas has produced happy results. I have had the consolation of acquiring fifty-four new co-workers within the last eighteen months, priests, seminarians, brothers, and nuns."[40]

September of 1853, however, brought to the diocese a devastating outbreak of yellow fever, one that decimated the body of Catholic clergy in Texas. Odin reported that particularly hard hit were Galveston, Houston, Richmond, Indianola, Port Lavaca, Victoria, and Brownsville. Fourteen priests were stricken with the disease, and six of them died. This setback caused Odin to go ahead and ordain to the priesthood seven of the seminarians whom he had recruited from Europe a year and a half earlier.[41]

On a happier note, in December 1854, Odin gratifyingly blessed the efforts of Father Moczygemba to establish the first permanent Polish-American colony in the United States, Panna Maria (Polish for Virgin Mary). The settlement was located approximately sixty miles southeast of San Antonio de Bexar, where the San Antonio River and Cibolo Creek came together. There, on Christmas Eve, the Polish priest celebrated Holy Mass, giving thanks to God for the safe arrival of a group of Catholic settlers from Upper Silesia for whom he had been preparing for several months.[42]

Bishop Odin Continues to Build during the Turbulent Latter 1850s

Jean-Marie Odin was destined to lead the Diocese of Galveston only a few more short years before being named to head the Archdiocese of New Orleans, his final assignment before returning home to Hauteville for the final days of his life. Just ten days before celebrating his sixty-first birthday, and eight days after the constitution of the Confederate States of America had been drawn up at Montgomery, Alabama, on February 15, 1861, Odin would succeed his close friend and confidant of more than four decades, Antoine Blanc, as Archbishop of New Orleans. Blanc had died the previous June 20. During the span of time left to him in Texas the French-born prelate continued his dedication to laying the foundation for the future of the Catholic Church there. The capstone of those labors would be reflected in his calling of Galveston's first diocesan synod in 1858.

Building the Diocese of Galveston during the latter 1850s would demand much resolve from Odin and his clergy, nuns, and laypeople. With the 1860s approaching, the missionary bishop saw little relief from his continued shortage of funds, a situation he usually referred to as "embarrassments." Financial support from the Propagation of the Faith at Lyon, France, to the Texas mission consisted of about twenty-five thousand francs. But that amount was never enough to meet even the minimal needs of a growing frontier diocese. The reality of Bishop Odin's consistent financial stress unfolded clearly in his letters in the second half of the decade of the 1850s.[43]

Throughout his by then almost two decades of laboring in Texas, right up to his departure for New Orleans in the spring of 1861, Odin lamented the inability—or sometimes just unwillingness—of many Catholics of the Galveston diocese to help meet the costs of building the faith in their land. To be sure, there were examples of the Catholic faithful heroically rising to the occasion in giving to their church. Such was certainly the case when in the mid-1850s the Mexican people of San Antonio de Bexar rallied behind then Vicar General Father Claude Marie Dubuis in his efforts to renovate San Fernando Church.[44] But for the most part, Texas Catholics were simply too poor to contribute much financially.

Beyond the economic pressures that characterized the diocese, Odin and his co-workers were forced to confront serious national antagonisms that were being played out in Texas. By the mid-nineteenth century, in certain ways US society was in turmoil. People often were pitted against one another according to where they were born and raised and in particular in reference to what attitudes they exhibited regarding slavery. Were they "Northerners" or "Southerners"? Thus was maturing a sectional crisis that about the time of Odin's appointment to New Orleans erupted into civil war. While various forces were fomenting the crisis, at its heart existed the slavery-abolitionist-free soil debate that had aggravated national polemics for years.

Along with this national divisiveness another sad aspect of the American story was coming to the forefront—nativism. That human blight on society had been nurtured in certain segments of the US Protestant population since the 1830s. With Roman Catholic immigration to America increasing noticeably along the upper Atlantic seaboard and inland into the interior of the continent as well as southwestward to Texas, where as discussed previously, it buttressed the Catholic Mexican presence, a growing Catholic visibility was surfacing throughout much of the nation. Nativists viewed this demographic metamorphosis as threatening to their own perception of the ethnic-religious purview of US society, a vision that excluded non-Protestant and generally non-Anglo immigrants. Common targets of this view were Catholics, especially the Irish. Nativists desired that in the United States there would be as few "papists" (a negative term originally coined in sixteenth-century England referring to Catholics and their loyalty to the pope) as possible. In the United States during the nineteenth century a severe anti-Catholic nativist crusade dramatically intensified. Both the slavery versus anti-slavery and the nativist movements erupted in Texas.[45]

How did Odin respond to this social, economic, and political environment in which slavery, abolitionism, and nativism all co-existed? Odin, as has been shown, was a consistent critic of slavery beginning with his earlier-mentioned denunciation of the harsh treatment of slaves, as he observed upon his arrival for the first time in New Orleans in 1822, and then again a few weeks later as he witnessed the peculiar institution in operation on the property of his own Vincentian community at Perryville, Missouri. Odin believed that as human beings with souls, slaves were not to be treated as chattel property. Serving for decades as a missionary in regions of the nation where slavery existed, his approach was to insist that slaves were to be treated humanely.[46]

A nagging question remains to this day, though, regarding whether Odin influenced Timon's views on slavery. In January 1847, Odin had received from Father Timon a slave family—Clement, his wife, Emily, and their three children—to work at his (Bishop Odin's) residence in Galveston. They had been slaves at the Vincentian school at Cape Girardeau, Missouri. Odin, however, had not sought them. Rather, Father Timon, feeling that Odin needed the help of a cook and caretaker at Galveston, and he being unable to dispatch to Odin's residence any Vincentian lay brothers, simply sent Clement, Emily, and their children. Father Louis Derbes, of the Vincentian Archives at Perryville, has suggested that in fact Odin may have influenced his friend Father Timon to assume an anti-slavery posture. This consideration seems especially important since as the first bishop of Buffalo, New York, Timon emerged as a noted opponent of the peculiar institution.[47]

Regarding abolitionism, Bishop Odin did not fear the movement because it called for the manumission of the slaves. Instead, Odin grew increasingly alarmed that the abolitionists' actions would so intensify divisions within US society that civil war might result. And as had been the case with his earlier concerns during the US-Mexican War of 1846–48, Odin most dreaded the terrible consequences of war on the people.

Looking at Odin's reaction to the nativists, in particular the Know Nothings, the bishop himself left a definite statement about that group and its attacks on Catholicism in Texas, an assessment worth reporting on in full. In a letter to the Propagation of the Faith dated February 14, 1856, Odin exclaimed:

> Our success had saddened all of the enemies of religion, who alas, are only too numerous. Two years ago in the United States a political party was formed so hostile to the Church that its animosity against Catholics scarcely differs from open persecution. Their newspapers and their speeches are but at issue of the most atrocious calumnies against the head of the Church and all the priests. At the time of the last election their defeat in Texas rendered them truly furious. We have feared of seeing our churches and institutions destroyed in several localities. At Goliad they resorted to acts of violence against the good and peaceful Abbot [Antoine] Borias and overwhelmed him with blows and bad treatment. Thank God, all their efforts against Christ and his Church have had an entirely different effect from what they intended. The wholesome part of the country was shocked by this violence so contrary to the constitution; many men who did not belong to the Church openly took our defense and refuted the absurd beliefs that were imputed to us. In the entire country there arose an insatiable curiosity to learn of our true doctrines, and many people who would have spent their life [sic] without being concerned about acquiring the least idea about our faith [now] eagerly read all the religious books they can obtain. Here, as everywhere and always, persecution turns to our profit.[48]

In the midst of all that vehemence, Bishop Odin and his co-laborers continued in their dedication to laying the base for the growth of Catholicism in Texas. Steadfast in Odin's planning by then was his calling of the first diocesan synod for Galveston.

15

Adieu, Texas

I N THE SUMMER OF 1858, Jean-Marie Odin had no way of knowing that
within just a little more than two years he would have departed his adopted
Texas to head up the Archdiocese of New Orleans, an assignment that was
to consume the remaining nine years of his earthly life. But the Frenchman's
final thirty months as bishop of Galveston marked the apex of that diocese's
early ecclesiastical development. The cornerstone of this was Odin's convening
of the see's first diocesan synod in 1858. With the calling of the synod the future
growth of the church in the Lone Star State could be envisioned more clearly.

In terms of rules, organization, and structure, the synod served as a foundation for both the immediate and future of Catholic Texas. As the Lone Star
State was growing in population and becoming ever more complex demographically, a more complex development of the institutional church would
be needed. Given the frontier character that in many ways still marked Texas,
missioning would remain an urgency for the clergy and nuns of the diocese.
The fathers of the synod fully recognized this.

The synod also would prove significant to future generations of Catholics
in their appreciation of Bishop Jean-Marie Odin as the chief architect of the
laying of a base for the Catholic Church in Texas during the mid-to-latter half
of the nineteenth century. The synod reflected that under Odin's leadership the
Catholic face of Texas had matured in a wondrous manner since his arrival in
the land eighteen years earlier. The synod of 1858 has survived to the present
day as a visible monument to this most important aspect of Odin's contribution
to the Catholic narrative of Texas.

On the third Sunday after Pentecost of 1858, several priests from throughout
the diocese gathered in Saint Mary's Cathedral for a Solemn Pontifical Mass,
with their bishop as celebrant, opening the synod. It was June 13, a warm but
comfortable day in a city known for usually being cooler than most of the rest
of Texas during the summer.[1] Odin, in his capacity as ordinary bishop, presided
as the sole lawgiver of the diocese. The synod enacted decrees and statutes

that were to help form the character and structure of the Galveston diocese for decades to come. These included prescriptions that dealt with the erection of parishes, the clarification of rules for the clergy and nuns, the setting out of budgetary principles, and the establishment of guidelines for Catholic life in general throughout the diocese, even among laypeople.

These enactments were formed in harmony with the decrees of the Council of Trent (1545–63) and the seven Provincial Councils and one Plenary Council of Baltimore, as well as those of the First Provincial Council of New Orleans. But they definitely bore the stamp of a Bishop Odin who by that time in his life had become known as a disciplined ecclesiastic. Included in the list of prescriptions appeared one "to honor the Blessed Virgin Mary, especially under the title of The Immaculate Conception."[2]

The opening session gave way the next day, Monday, June 14, to the beginning of a three-day retreat for the attending priests, one that Father Michael McDonnell conducted. On the seventeenth, the synod returned to its public and private sessions and continued through the next four days. It concluded with another Solemn Pontifical Mass and a lengthy public session on Sunday, June 20. The topics covered in the decrees of the synod were broad in scope but stated with precision. Specifically, they named diocesan consultors and vice-chancellors, established norms for the formation of parishes, set rules for diocesan and seminary funding, defined clerical dress and customs, outlined the requirements for the erection of churches and the keeping of clerical records, made recommendations for the education of youths and the administration of the sacraments, and introduced into the diocese the Society for the Propagation of the Faith and the Archconfraternity of the Immaculate Heart of the Blessed Virgin Mary. The final statute mandated that the synodal decisions were to become effective as soon as all of the diocese's missionaries had received them.[3]

The Waning of His Labors in Texas, 1858–60

With the drawing to a close of the synod, Bishop Odin began preparing for his annual pastoral visit among the Catholics of his vast diocese. On this occasion he looked southward to the Rio Grande Valley, planning to spend significant time among the mostly Mexican people of that region. How helpful it was that by that time in his life he had come to understand the Spanish language well. On July 14 the bishop departed Galveston headed for Victoria, San Patricio, and other settlements en route to his ultimate destination, the communities along the Rio Grande. These would include, among others, Roma, Laredo, and likely Eagle Pass.[4] His return to Galveston several months later followed a path north from the Rio Grande to San Antonio de Bexar, then on to his see city. Bishop Odin completed his lengthy journey of catechizing, administering the sacraments, regularizing marriages, and carefully studying what other needs the Catholics of the valley might have.

As so often had been the case in the past, it proved to be a fatiguing excursion. Odin spent many weeks traveling and laboring in the excessive heat and humidity of the Texas summer months. And, as always, he had to be concerned about the possibility of an onset of the severe migraine headaches that had regularly plagued him. And beyond these difficulties, during the fall months yellow fever rampaged communities from Point Isabel to Laredo.[5] With all of this, it must be remembered that Odin was a man not far from his sixtieth birthday.

That journey served to reinforce in him a realization that Texas was still a missionary country. In the middle of his travels he wrote to Father Anstaett from Roma, describing what he found in relation to the needs of the Catholics in the Rio Grande Valley: "The part of Texas that I travel over is highly populated; there must be nearly twenty-five thousand Catholics from the mouth of the Rio Grande to Eagle Pass [well upriver from Laredo]. The priests who administer to this population are too few in number to satisfy the demands of the holy ministry. Inevitably I shall have to give them new colleagues. I also need priests in San Antonio and in many other localities."[6]

Back in Galveston at the end of his jaunt, the missionary bishop found himself exhausted but, from a pastoral perspective, quite pleased with the results of his trip. Remaining for a time in the see city and catching up on administrative matters, he awaited anxiously the arrival in Texas of six Franciscan priests: three English, one French, one German, and an Italian. They were being sent in response to his earlier request for help from the Franciscan superior general at Rome. Those Sons of Saint Francis were destined to replace the Oblates of Mary priests in the administration of the college-seminary recently founded at Galveston. Recently the Oblates had decided to leave Galveston and join their confreres at Brownsville. At that time also, Odin anticipated finishing a convent for the Sisters of the Incarnate Word at Laredo by the following spring. With their new convent this religious community of nuns then would be established at both Brownsville and Laredo.[7]

The year 1859 opened with Odin making plans to take passage on a ship for New Orleans in answer to the urgings of Archbishop Blanc that he come for a visit. Following that January excursion the Frenchman returned to Galveston and began preparations for the upcoming seasons of Lent and Easter. However, on May 22 he received a letter from Archbishop Blanc informing him of the death of their mutual friend and fellow ordinary, Bishop Michael Portier of Mobile, Alabama.[8] Odin had already heard the news about Bishop Portier. Odin expressed his grief in a response to Blanc the next day, promising to leave for New Orleans on the third of June: "Your letter of the 18th was delivered to me last night. I had already been informed of the sad news of the death of

Msgr. Portier. That caused me a great deal of sorrow, because I was not expecting it. I believed he had already left for Europe, or was on the point of setting out, and he is no longer."[9]

The lives of Portier and Odin had been closely intertwined for many years. Portier was a French missionary only slightly more than four years older than Odin, having been born on September 7, 1795. He was a native of Montbrison, one of the cities not far from Hauteville, where, as we know, a young Jean-Marie Odin had attended seminary. Portier also had been one of the assisting prelates at the consecration of the missionary from France as vicar apostolic of Texas in New Orleans's Saint Louis Cathedral back on March 6, 1842. Beyond these, in any number of ways Odin and Portier, in concert with Blanc, had labored together to build the church in the American South.[10] From that decades-long shared missioning grew a strong priestly and personal friendship between Odin, Portier, and Blanc.

Upon his return to Galveston in the early summer following his New Orleans trip to commemorate the memory of Bishop Portier, Odin once again turned to his annual pastoral visits. These tours were briefer in duration and shorter in distance than the months-long one of several hundred miles that had been undertaken the previous year. Nevertheless, they were demanding jaunts. Odin's health suffered from various ailments, and the threat of yellow fever persisted. For example, back in Galveston following a trip to Liberty, he complained of "rheumatic pains."[11]

During those months Odin also found his attention increasingly being drawn to preparing for the forthcoming Second Provincial Council of New Orleans, a gathering that Archbishop Blanc had scheduled to commence on January 22 of the coming year, 1860. A series of letters between Odin and Blanc spread over the second half of 1859 recorded that the archbishop asked Odin, as bishop of Galveston, to offer some of the instructions to be presented at the council. Odin was requested also to suggest questions to be considered in the deliberations of the attendants and to assist in sending out invitations, in Blanc's name, to the meeting.[12]

On a cold January 22, 1860, New Orleans morning the council opened in the traditional manner with a Solemn Pontifical Mass in the cathedral. Odin and Bishops Andrew Byrne of Little Rock, Augustus Mary Martin of Natchitoches, and William Henry Elder of Natchez, joined Blanc as the members of the episcopacy in attendance. Most Reverend John Quinlan (an Irishman from Cloyne, Ireland), named Portier's successor at Mobile the previous August 19, soon arrived at New Orleans. Present too were the superiors of several religious communities, including the Benedictines, the Jesuits, Odin's own Vincentians, the Congregation of the Most Holy Redeemer, the Oblates of Mary Immaculate, and the Congregation of the Holy Cross. Witnessing to the importance of the council with their assistance at the celebration of the Mass were several representatives of female communities from throughout the archdiocese.[13]

Odin assumed a greater role at the council than perhaps had originally been planned. This in part was due to his position as bishop of Galveston and his being a trusted colleague and supporter of Blanc. But his greater role became necessary also because as the second session of the gathering commenced on January 26, Blanc became ill. Though the archbishop recovered somewhat and was able to be present at the council's closing on January 29, Bishop Odin rather than Archbishop Blanc gave the Papal Benediction, sending off those present to continue their labors of spreading the "Good News."[14]

When he returned to Galveston, Odin, by then quite concerned about Blanc's health, tried to keep in even closer contact with his friend and metropolitan than he had in the past. In one of his several letters written to Blanc during the months immediately following the council, on March 13, 1860, Jean-Marie exclaimed that "I have learned with happiness that your strength is returning. If I can help you in any way, do not spare me."[15]

The Death of Blanc and Odin's Call to New Orleans

But the aging archbishop, the rock of the church in New Orleans for a quarter of a century, failed to recover his health. Three months after Odin's March letter, on June 20, Antoine Blanc died.[16] Five days later the vicar general of the archdiocese, Monsignor Etienne Rousselon, assumed the position of administrator of the archdiocese. He was to hold that position until February 15 of the following year, when Jean-Marie Odin would be named to succeed Blanc as archbishop of New Orleans. Rousselon was a veteran French diocesan priest with whom Odin had worked for many years. The vicar general frequently had handled matters of finances and supplies for the Texas bishop and had also done countless personal favors for him. Odin had developed a great respect for Rousselon.

That Pope Pius IX would select Jean-Marie Odin to head up the vacant archbishopric came as no surprise to the US Catholic hierarchy. Members of the episcopacy throughout the country universally held Odin in high esteem. Nor did the Vincentian's election find the numerous clergy and nuns who knew him well to be disapproving of his nomination. Virtually all of the priests, brothers, and sisters with whom he had labored regarded him with great affection. Immediately following the New Orleans provincial council, in February 1860, Blanc had initiated the process of seeking a coadjutor bishop for his archdiocese with a letter to the Congregation of Propaganda Fide in Rome. Ironically, still feeling poorly from the illness that had felled him during the council, Blanc asked Odin to compose the letter on his behalf (February 14).

The story that surfaced around the search for a coadjutor for New Orleans prior to Archbishop Blanc's death highlighted several US prelates coming forth to urge the pope to appoint Odin himself. Among those churchmen writing to the Congregation of the Propaganda Fide and making such suggestions were Archbishops Francis Patrick Kenrick of Baltimore (March 17, 1860) and John Baptiste Purcell of Cincinnati (March 18, 1860). Communicating too were the aforementioned Bishops Martin of Natchitoches (March 10, 1860) and Quinlan of Mobile (April 4, 1860).[17] With Blanc's passing away, however, the quest no longer was to focus on a search for a coadjutor but to seek out a new metropolitan archbishop. Unquestionably, those ecclesiastics who favored Jean-Marie Odin for New Orleans coadjutor then would support strongly him being named archbishop.

Back in Texas and having been unable to attend Blanc's funeral, Odin mourned the loss of his friend and offered many prayers including numerous Masses for the repose of his soul. There can be little doubt also but that Odin often found himself nostalgically reflecting upon his long friendship with Blanc. As we recall, that relationship dated back to the summer of 1816, when as a teenager at home in Hauteville on vacation from his seminary studies, he first met the new priest, Father Blanc, at St. Martin d'Ambierle. It can be presumed that memories of Blanc, carrying a special meaning for the by-then sixty-year-old bishop of Galveston, would have regularly tugged at the prelate's heartstrings. Surely the meeting between Jean-Marie, Blanc, and Blanc's younger brother Jean-Baptiste, at Pointe-Coupee decades earlier in the summer of 1822, when Jean-Marie and Jean-Baptiste first arrived in Louisiana, would have fallen into this category. Another example most likely would have been Antoine Blanc's presiding at Odin's own consecration as a member of the Catholic hierarchy in March 1842.

Other matters, however, demanded the attention of Bishop Odin. He was chief pastor of a diocese which by 1860 included forty-five churches or chapels, five convents of sisters dispersed from Galveston to the Rio Grande, two large schools (including a seminary), several small parochial schools, and forty-eight clergy—sixteen regulars and thirty-two seculars—serving the growing and ever more multicultural Catholic population of Texas. Odin had even begun to envision building a hospital in Galveston.[18]

Moreover, the national sectional crisis, which with increasing intensity was matching the northern and southern states against each other in a potential deadly manner, noticeably concerned Odin. The roots of that struggle were ingrained in a broad panorama of causes. These, in the view of noted Civil War historian James M. McPherson, pitted the southern agrarian planters against the northern industrialists in their different perceptions of what were the characteristics of the ideal society. In addition, a general posture evidenced in the South that imaged northerners as challengers of the southern way of life had been growing for decades. The slavery versus anti-slavery contest remained at the heart of this crisis. Surfacing as a potential threat to national unity even before the 1830s and fomenting vehemently during the forties and fifties, this trial of societal wills by 1860 deeply cemented in sectionalism had assumed an increasingly threatening character.[19]

It was difficult, under such circumstances, for Odin to keep abreast of speculations about who would be named the new archbishop of New Orleans. Naturally the issue concerned him greatly. His own preference for the ecclesiastical post was Bishop Elder of Natchez.[20] Odin himself avoided seeking the appointment. Not only did he consider such an office to be above his capabilities, but he longed to spend the remaining years of his life in his beloved Texas.

The Frenchman wrote of these sentiments in several missives written to Vicar General Rousselon in the fall of 1860. In one, dated November 28, Odin stated that while he had "received several letters from Rome, none alluded to the vacant see of New Orleans." Three and a half weeks later he once again wrote from Galveston, exclaiming, "I have not received any letters from Rome since the last time I wrote you." Finally, in a note from December 29 he commented to Rousselon that "I have not yet received from Rome any communication on the successor of our dear deceased."[21]

But regarding the vacancy in the archdiocese of New Orleans and as well the deepening national sectional tensions, April 1861 brought great drama. In the third week of that month, from Rome through the office of Archbishop Kenrick of Baltimore, came to Odin at Galveston the papal bulls naming him the new archbishop of New Orleans. Jean-Marie was dumbfounded! Making matters more challenging for him, a few days prior to his receiving the notification of his new assignment the Texas ordinary had learned of the outbreak of the US Civil War. That conflict had erupted at 4:30 A.M. on Friday, April 12, when a group of Confederate soldiers under the command of Brig. Gen. Pierre Gustave Toutant Beauregard, of an old-line French Catholic family of Saint Bernard Parish, New Orleans, began shelling Union-held Fort Sumter on an island in the middle of Charleston Harbor, South Carolina.

Taken aback by his nomination as the new archbishop, on April 24 Jean-Marie poured out his heart to Rousselon in an emotional lamentation at the turn of events. "I have been unable to eat or sleep." "For three days I have vainly tried to submit and to resign myself. Impossible," he wrote. Odin further indicated to Rousselon that he had written to Archbishop Kenrick seeking his advice. The Frenchman would await Kenrick's reply before deciding whether or not to accept the nomination.[22] Jean-Marie was in anguish, overwhelmed by the weight of the appointment and not wanting to leave his adopted Texas.

Rousselon offered Odin encouragement as his friend struggled with his conscience to make the correct decision. Meanwhile, Archbishop Kenrick responded to Jean-Marie's letter, urging him to take the New Orleans assignment. After finally deciding to accept, on May 15, in what may have been his last letter as bishop of Galveston, Odin wrote to Rousselon: "I was hoping to leave for New Orleans on board the boat that leaves our port this morning, but a matter of rather great importance will not be able to be concluded until tomorrow. I am therefore obliged to postpone the voyage, and I shall not arrive until Sunday morning or Monday evening. Your letter of the tenth of this month encouraged me; I thank you very sincerely. Monsignor of Baltimore also answered me, and I must resign myself. How much I shall need your generous cooperation! I count on your charity. Pray for me.[23]

❧

New Orleans, the Civil War and Reconstruction, Then Home

ON PENTECOST SUNDAY OF 1861 (May 19) Jean-Marie Odin arrived in New Orleans to take up the hierarchical reigns of the archdiocese as chief pastor. He, however, already longed for his beloved Texas. As he lamented in a letter mailed back to Father Anstaett in the Lone Star State just a few days after his disembarkation at the bayou city, on May 23, "I wanted to write you a short letter, but since my arrival in New Orleans I have not had a moment to myself. From Mass until sunset visits follow each other without interruption. How I miss my poor Texas and the good friends I have left there."[1]

Upon his arrival at New Orleans, Odin immediately published a pastoral letter to the clergy of the archdiocese in which he expressed further his love for the Texas he had left behind. He exclaimed, "Yes, D.B.B. everything contributed to render the ties that bound us to Texas, both dear and sacred, and to see them torn asunder without pang, would prove us devoid of that heart of a Father and Pastor, which every Bishop, who is the Vicar of the tenderness of God for man, must necessarily possess towards the people entrusted to him. You will, I trust, pardon this tribute of affection to the past, which is replete with so many sweet memories, nor will you reprove the tears we shed over a wound that is still bleeding."[2]

For quite some time following his departure for New Orleans, Jean-Marie Odin received letters from Catholics in his former diocese of Galveston, and he made an effort to answer each of them. Doing so, however, often proved to be difficult, because soon after the Civil War broke out the US Navy blockaded the Texas coastline. While written communications between Texas and New Orleans continued throughout Jean-Marie Odin's years as archbishop, they were particularly frequent up until the time that a successor to him as bishop of Galveston was named in the fall of 1862. That regular exchange of correspondence reflected Odin's continuing dedication to buoying the religious life of Catholic Texans he had left and those Catholics' affection for their departed bishop. Apart from his knowing them so well and their remaining close to his

Jean-Marie Odin, archbishop of New Orleans. Courtesy Archives of the
University of Notre Dame.

heart, the diocese of Galveston, it must be recalled, existed as a suffragan see to the archdiocese of New Orleans. Odin therefore carried a hierarchical responsibility for his former Texas diocese.

The new archbishop was especially concerned about communicating with Father Louis Chambodut, vicar general of the Diocese of Galveston during the Civil War and one of the three priests whom Odin had recommended as a possible successor as bishop of Galveston. The other two priests that Odin listed as a potential successor were Fathers Claude Marie Dubuis and Pierre F. Parisot. Among the missives sent to Odin were some from individual sisters as well as female religious communities in Texas and other Catholics, clerical and lay. For example, Father Augustin d'Asti, stationed in Houston, sent Odin letters at least twice in late 1861 assessing the health of Catholic life in his neighborhood and in so doing reporting on the labors of priests, brothers, and sisters in and near that Texas port city.[3]

Turning to the New Orleans archdiocese, Odin realized only too well that his new assignment would demand much from him. He had been named at the age of sixty-one to lead one of Catholic America's major archdioceses and an ecclesiastical entity headquartered in the South's largest city. Odin's age might arguably be considered more advanced in those days than it would be viewed today. In addition, the migraine headaches from which he suffered for years continued to plague him.

He now faced the pastoral challenges of ministry and ecclesiastical administration over a heavily Catholic populated area that could be perceived as a unique segment of southern society. Many of the residents of that region of Louisiana were Catholics. Thus they were not part of the Protestant Bible Belt, a religious demographic area that in Louisiana could be seen maturing farther north around Shreveport, but existed instead as a populace that Protestants, especially southerners, usually disliked. In such a religious-societal environment it must be remembered that the United States was experiencing in many locales the pinnacle of the anti-Catholic nativism crusade that had reached its high point just a few years earlier during the 1850s. Furthermore, southern Louisiana Catholics were mainly French or of another continental Latin-based European heritage, Irish, Creole (of mixed European and Negro ethnicity), or pure Negro—slave or free. These ethnic conditions simply made more complex the base of prejudices toward Catholics from Anglo Protestants.[4]

Within the overall ecclesiastical purview of the universal church as set in the particular conditions of the Catholic Church in the Archdiocese of New Orleans, Odin's challenges were clear. He saw an immediate need to strengthen the financial condition of the archdiocesan see. He also observed that the religious life of New Orleans's Catholics needed to be regularized more along proper ecclesiastical lines. This was particularly obvious concerning marriages, funerals, and times scheduled for celebrating Masses in parishes.

Regarding the see's finances, Odin quickly focused his attention on the problem of the lack of economic support for the archdiocese from the cathedral as well as several parish churches. These funds were needed desperately to meet the archbishopric's expenses.[5] Looking at the issue of parish boundaries and sacramental life, Odin would become insistent that the sacraments be administered for the Catholics in each individual's or family's parish church. In other words, each Catholic was urged to live his or her sacramental life in his or her own parish. Beyond this, the French-born new archbishop discovered that sometimes archdiocesan guidelines for celebrating Mass were in various ways ignored. All of these inconsistencies Odin determined to correct. At the same time, it must be remembered that his efforts to improve matters in the archdiocese initially had to be undertaken while New Orleans as well as much of the rest of Louisiana was bearing up under Civil War conditions. This included in the late spring of 1862 military occupation by Union forces. Following the Civil War, social, economic, and political changes would come to New Orleans as part of Reconstruction.

Feeling overwhelmed at the prospective heavy responsibilities his new office as archbishop promised and harboring anxieties over the outbreak of the Civil War as a conflagration on the nation and its citizens, Odin wrote to Archbishop Kenrick of Baltimore a month after his May 21, 1861, letter to Father Anstaett, commenting that "I avail myself of as private conveyance to send you this letter, as we have no communication by mail with the North. My last letter to your Grace has no doubt been lost. On the receipt of your favor of April 9th [referring to Kenrick's earlier letter urging Odin to accept the New Orleans post], I resigned myself to obey. Alas, since my arrival here I discover more and more every day that an awful responsibility has been laid on me. I stand in great need of your prayer. In consequence of the disturbed state of the country, it has been difficult to correspond not only with the Most Rev. [Reverend] Archbishops, but even with Rt. [Right] Rev. Bps [Bishops] of the province."[6]

Turning first to the problem of archdiocesan income, back in the sixteenth century the Council of Trent (1545–63) had decreed that cathedral and parish churches must contribute toward defraying archdiocesan or diocesan expenses. This tradition had grown as a universally accepted standard throughout the Catholic world. However, there had developed areas where such was resisted, one of these being the Archdiocese of New Orleans. In part as a legacy of lay-trustee clashes with previous bishops and Archbishop Blanc, there had existed in New Orleans for some time a body of opposition to fiscal support for the archdiocese from the cathedral and some parish churches.

The late Archbishop Blanc had been working on plans to systematize a fair sharing approach of about 5 percent of cathedral and parish church incomes with the office of the archbishop. With Blanc's death in 1860 and Odin's 1861 succession, it would be Odin who would put into operation the plans. By the end of December 1861, the archdiocesan financial difficulties had been addressed with some success. Regarding the parish boundaries issue, in a Lenten pastoral letter in 1862, Archbishop Odin informed the clergy, religious, and laity that such demarcations had been finalized. To them he wrote, "We take this opportunity . . . to inform you that, agreeably to the decrees of the Holy Council of Trent, we have divided our Archiepiscopal city of New Orleans into distinct parishes. Your pastors will make known to you the respective limits of each parish. The duties imposed by that division of parishes shall begin to be strictly obligatory from Easter-day next. The necessity of such a division of parishes had been felt for a long time."[7]

These developments focused attention on Jean-Marie Odin as an archbishop intent upon establishing more discipline in the Roman Catholic life of the archdiocese. Previous ordinaries, including Archbishop Blanc, had been known as builders of churches, schools, academies, hospitals, seminaries, and other institutions vital to the mission of the church. Back in Texas Odin also was a dedicated builder. But at the same time he had earned a reputation as a disciplined ecclesiastic. In Louisiana Odin was to distinguish himself in that same way.

Meanwhile, as the chief shepherd of the archdiocese, Odin for virtually four years strove to minister to the Catholics of New Orleans while the archdiocese suffered the devastating four-year impact of the Civil War. Describing some aspects of that effort by clergy and religious—male and female—to serve the needs of the people in a letter he wrote to the headquarters of the Propagation of the Faith at Lyon, France, on January 28, 1862, he pointed out that many of the soldiers departing New Orleans to engage in battle against federal forces had asked for chaplains. Odin indicated that he had provided seven and that all of the bishops of the New Orleans province, including Galveston, furnished some. Amplifying his comments about the demands that the war situation made on the archdiocese, Odin indicated that the Daughters of Charity and the Irish Sisters of Mercy stationed in the New Orleans metropolitan see "are in charge of almost all of the ambulances and military hospitals, and conversions on the deathbed are numerous."[8]

There is little doubt but that Odin favored the Confederacy in the Civil War. He sometimes voiced his support for the Southern forces, but in so doing often the priest in him showed forth. One clear example of that feeling of Odin's was reflected in a letter that he wrote to Father Anstaett from New Orleans on April 14, 1862. Referring to the April 6 Battle of Shiloh, where the Confederate Army under Gen. Albert Sidney Johnston—who in the fighting died from a wound to his leg—and General Beauregard—having assumed command—surprised the federal army of Gen. Ulysses Simpson Grant, Odin wrote, "Doubtless you have heard of the brilliant victory that the south won on April sixth. On the seventh the battle still continued; our advantages were very great [sic] but upon the appearance of reinforcements that the enemy was receiving, General Beauregard retreated toward Corinthe [*sic*], in order not to expose too much his troops so wearied from a two-day battle." In his next few remarks in that same letter to Father Anstaett the priestly feelings of the missionary from France continued: "Abbot Pont, chaplain in chief, wrote me on the eighth that our troops fought in an admirable manner. Mourning is great among our inhabitants."[9]

By mid-April 1862, Union forces were gathering for a move against New Orleans. By the twenty-fourth of that month, a Union fleet under the command of sixty-year-old Vice Adm. David Glasgow Farragut had passed the forts in the delta of the Mississippi River. The following day the fleet anchored at New Orleans. Shortly afterward the Union Army of Maj. Gen. Benjamin Franklin Butler occupied Archbishop Jean-Marie Odin's metropolitan see city.[10]

Though supporting the South in the war, Odin's own view of the struggle between the Union and the Confederacy appears to have been like that of many foreign-born Catholic clerics and nuns serving in the United States during that period of history. Although he had spent much time, almost four decades, missioning mainly in southern or border slave states (Missouri, Arkansas, Texas, and Louisiana), where many Catholics—including his own Vincentian community back at Perryville, Missouri—owned slaves, Odin lamented the lot of the slaves and abhorred the institution of slavery.

Possibly coming to the point where he hesitatingly adjusted to social attitudes dominating the southern populations' views regarding such matters as slavery, Odin himself never personally accepted such positions. It is true that in Galveston he at one time had a slave and his family working for him in his episcopal residence, but he had never sought them. Instead, Father Timon, himself an opponent of slavery—a posture he maintained faithfully as the first bishop of Buffalo (1847–67)—had sent the slave and his family unsolicited from Perryville to Odin. Father Timon at the time felt that his confrere would need help in keeping up the bishop's residence and property at Galveston. Moreover, as was common among Catholic clergy and nuns during that era, slaves were considered more as servants than chattel slaves.[11]

Although he opposed the election of Abraham Lincoln as the sixteenth president of the United States, Odin did so because, as did many people in both the North and the South, he mistakenly judged Lincoln to be an abolitionist. Already by early 1861 the soon-to-be new archbishop of New Orleans fearfully considered the abolitionist crusade as threatening a social, civil, and economic upheaval as well as a promised war that would result in deaths and maiming of countless thousands of human beings. Of his concern about the election of Lincoln, from Galveston on January 26, 1861, Odin wrote to the Propaganda of the Faith back at Lyon, exclaiming, "Finally, the election of

Lincoln, abolitionist candidate, to the presidency, has put all the states of the South in a state of anxiety. Six have separated from the Union and it is probable that others will have proclaimed their independence before the end of February. What will be the result of this revolution? Impossible to foresee. Trade is almost ruined, bankruptcies are the order of the day and thousands of laborers find themselves out of work. Civil War is expected."[12]

Some Catholic churchmen in the South did emerge as supporters of Confederate views. Among this group were Fathers Abram Joseph Ryan and Napoleon Joseph Perche. Ryan was a noted poet and journalist and former Vincentian priest who at one time had resided at the Barrens Seminary after Jean-Marie Odin had departed for Texas. During the years 1872–75, residing in Mobile, Alabama, Ryan served as an editor for the New Orleans archdiocesan newspaper that Odin—who by that time had passed away—had established following the Civil War, the *Morning Star and Catholic Messenger*. Father Perche acted as vicar general of the archdiocese of New Orleans under Odin and was named coadjutor archbishop of New Orleans on May 1, 1870. He succeeded the French Vincentian as the third archbishop of New Orleans twenty-four days later, on May 25, 1870, immediately following Jean-Marie Odin's death on that date.[13]

In addition, any number of Catholic laypersons were supporters of the Confederate cause. Already mentioned as just one of many noted examples of this was the military commander who led the Confederate Army that fired on Fort Sumter to start the Civil War, Brigadier General Beauregard. Historians have viewed Beauregard, of French heritage, as a prominent member of the southern Catholic elite, who was more southern than French.

Obviously, then, in his early years as archbishop of New Orleans Jean-Marie Odin sometimes found himself in the company of churchmen and churchwomen who supported the Confederacy and its worldviews. But Odin was first and foremost a French-born Catholic archbishop, and it was that identity more than his Southern sympathies that remained the formative influence on him. In that context, as he had earlier during the US invasion of Mexico during the years 1846–48, Odin daily prayed for an end to the hostilities. In addition to his concerns for the people, central to his thinking was that the mission of the church must go on uninterrupted as much as possible.

In the meantime, Odin grew increasingly anxious about the hierarchical vacancy existing in his former diocese of Galveston. Even though appointments from the Vatican regarding successor ordinaries (diocesan bishops) almost always took some time, Odin felt uneasy with his former flock in Texas being left without a chief pastor. This was a situation especially worrisome during wartime, when the operations of the church could be expected to be hampered. Odin hoped that the priest from Coutouvre, France, whom Odin himself had recruited to labor for souls in Texas a decade-and-a-half earlier,

Father Claude Marie Dubuis, would be named Bishop of Galveston. That is exactly what occurred.

Father Dubuis, hoping to improve his health, had accompanied Odin to New Orleans when the new archbishop arrived at the bayou city to take up his residence there. Dubuis had remained in or near New Orleans as the Union forces of Admiral Farragut and General Butler blockaded and occupied the city in the spring of 1862. His health improved somewhat, but he was unable to return to Galveston because of the naval blockade of the Texas coastline. Dubuis therefore decided to journey to Europe in hopes of seeking out priests, brothers, seminarians, and nuns for Texas. Odin traveled with Dubuis, hoping that while making his *ad limina* visit (the meeting with the pope required of all archbishops and bishops every five years to report on the conditions of their archdioceses or dioceses) he might urge Pope Pius IX to make the appointment of a new bishop of Galveston.

Once in France, Odin and Dubuis learned that indeed the priest from Coutouvre, France, had been named the second bishop of Galveston. On October 15, 1862, Pope Pius IX issued the necessary documents to this effect. How providential it was that Archbishop Jean-Marie Odin himself, assisted by Bishop Emeritus of Toronto Armand de Charbonnel and Bishop of Valence Jean-Paul Lyonnet, consecrated Father Dubuis in Lyon's *grand seminaire,* the great seminary so prominent in Odin's own earlier formation. The ordination and consecration took place on November 23, 1862.[14]

Odin and Dubuis both soon returned to the United States. Dubuis departed France bound for New Orleans from the port of Le Havre on February 4, 1863, in the company of a group consisting of fifty-nine priests, nuns, and seminarians. His ship arrived at New Orleans on April 4 of that year. Because of the US Navy's blockade of the coastline of Texas at that time Bishop Dubuis left his seminarians and sisters in New Orleans and sailed on alone to Matamoros, Mexico. From that Mexican city Dubuis re-entered Texas by crossing the Rio Grande at Brownsville, where he had arrived on April 24.[15] Archbishop Odin, meanwhile, returned to New Orleans determined to lead the archdiocese through the remaining years of the Civil War as peacefully as could be possible.

For the return to his metropolitan see city of New Orleans Archbishop Odin, after having completed his *ad limina* visit to Pope Pius IX, having ordained Bishop Dubuis for the Galveston diocese, and having also finished a recruiting tour of Europe wherein he sought priests, brothers, sisters, and seminarians, chartered in France the passenger ship *Sainte Genevieve.* The US Navy blockade of New Orleans having just been lifted, Odin's ship docked at the bayou city on Good Friday, April 3, 1863. It is believed that the *Sainte Genevieve* was the first ship to enter the port of New Orleans after the blockade was ended.[16]

Following his return to New Orleans Odin made it known that the Sacred

Congregation at Rome had approved the various ecclesiastical reforms that he, as the new archbishop, had implemented earlier. In a pastoral letter dated April 15, 1863, Odin notified his clergy "that he had noted with uneasiness the following of practices in the archdiocese, but that he had preferred to consult Propaganda about them first and having consulted the Holy See, he was now decided to reform them. Among these, he ordered every parish church to have a baptismal font in the church; he forbade baptisms in the sacristy; he ordered baptismal fonts be installed before the following Pentecost Sunday; he abolished so-called "carpet Masses" and demanded finally strict compliance with the ritual in funeral services." Archbishop Odin in a sense culminated his reform three years later, when on August 15, 1866, he had the archdiocesan see "incorporated under the legal title of "The Roman Catholic Church of the Diocese of New Orleans."[17]

Enduring the War to its End

Archbishop Odin made it clear throughout his archdiocese that he was committed during the war to maintaining as much as possible a peaceful environment among the people. This meant that he opposed any fermenting of societal attitudes based on racialism, views promoting the confrontation of the South versus the North, and so forth. He did not want the Catholics of New Orleans, nor throughout the archdiocese, to stir up dangerous situations in which arguments and violence might erupt. Odin was especially concerned about such possibilities given the Union Army's occupation of the city.

But a serious obstacle to Odin's hopes had surfaced during the latter months of 1862 and early 1863 in the person of Father Claude Pascal Maistre, pastor of the new Church of St. Rose of Lima "on the Bayou Road, New Orleans." Because of his history of acting independently regarding obedience to his ecclesiastical superiors, Father Maistre previously had been asked to leave two Catholic dioceses before coming to Louisiana. Some students of this period of history have argued that Maistre was a Unionist abolitionist who inspired Negroes against whites.[18] This may have very well been true, but whatever his motives, in the eyes of Odin, Maistre was acting from the pulpit, especially in his preaching, in such a manner as to create a perilous environment threatening the very concerns that Odin feared. Maistre appeared to be inciting racial antagonisms pitting Negroes against whites and encouraging Union versus Confederacy enmities, among other things. Thus, in the spring of 1863, the archbishop ordered Father Maistre to desist from this kind of conduct. When Father Maistre continued his preaching, Odin, for a second time, commanded the St. Rose of Lima pastor to halt his activities. Once again Father Maistre ignored his archbishop. Odin then interdicted the parish and, on May 16, 1863, "imposed ecclesiastical censure upon Father Maistre."[19]

But still the pastor disregarded his archbishop's authority and persisted in carrying out his priestly duties at the parish. At the same time, Father Maistre refused to cease his fomenting discord among the parishioners. Odin then closed the Church of St. Rose of Lima, and it did not reopen until February 14 of the following year, with the Abbe J. Ferec then named pastor.[20] To make matters worse, on October 12, 1863, and without hierarchical authorization, Father Maistre opened a new church in New Orleans on Ursuline and North Claiborne streets. That schismatic church remained in operation into 1871, whereupon Father Maistre finally made his peace with his ecclesiastical head, by then Archbishop of New Orleans Napoleon Joseph Perche, and then continued for a while longer serving in southern Louisiana.[21]

In looking at the life of Jean-Marie Odin, the struggle with Father Maistre can be seen as a notable example of his consistent dedication to laboring as a priest even during the most difficult times. Various students of the Catholic story in New Orleans, and even historians of the overall narrative of Catholics in the South during the US Civil War period generally, have offered interpretations of why Odin so determinedly pursued the issue with Father Maistre. It is clear that regarding Father Maistre, Odin mirrored a purview consistent with the temperament and character that had molded his life from his earliest days as a shepherd and altar boy back home in France, through his decades as a missionary from Missouri to Texas, into his years as archbishop of New Orleans, which was that a Catholic view of the world and the church's presence in that vision was uppermost in his heart and mind.

As Prof. Timothy Matovina, noted scholar of Catholic Texas and director of the Cushwa Center for the Study of American Catholicism at the University of Notre Dame, recently wrote, "The interdict of St. Rose of Lima parish and the suspension of Father Maistre was a move to keep the Church united; pastors publicly supporting the Union may have attracted a small following, but ultimately they would have divided the archdiocese. Above all, the appeals for prayers for peace [Odin's urgings to the Catholics of his archdiocese] were a direct response to the pope's request, a sure sign that no matter what Odin's personal views on the matter, his first allegiance was to the Church." Matovina went on to make the point: "It is significant that Odin never once mentioned the Civil War after his Lenten pastoral letter of 1865, except to remind people that they should put the pope's needs ahead of any financial straits that the war might have caused them. The intensity of conviction in Odin's pro-South stance pales by comparison. Odin's priority was clearly the affairs of the Church. The affairs of the state had values only to the extent that they promoted or deterred the interests of the Church."[22]

Odin concerned himself and the archdiocese with other important matters that he considered essential to the mission of the church. One such issue was education for the Negroes, especially after President Lincoln's Emancipation Proclamation freeing all slaves in areas where the Union Army came into control went into effect on January 1, 1863. The Catholic bishops of America, particularly in the South, would then begin to feel a need to develop educational opportunities for the countless former slaves being freed as the war progressed. E. B. Long and Barbara Long, in their masterful 1971 publication entitled *The Civil War Day by Day: An Almanac, 1861–1865,* wrote the following:

"I do order and declare that all persons held as slaves within said designated States, and parts of States, are and henceforward shall be free." Thus read the final Emancipation Proclamation of Jan. 1, putting into effect President Lincoln's preliminary proclamation of Sept. 22. Even that very morning discussion had continued, but shortly after noon the President signed the document that opened the door to the end of slavery in the United States.[23]

For more than three years Archbishop Odin tried to persuade clergy and religious to focus more on building schools or admitting former slaves, especially children, into their schools. Odin's effort would meet stiff resistance from the clergy and religious—male and female—because they felt that giving attention to Negroes would hurt their work among Anglo Catholics. But the problem would be addressed by the US hierarchy at their Second Plenary Council of Baltimore in 1866, and Archbishop Odin would play a major role in an attempt to provide education for the freedmen in New Orleans.[24] Much of the growth of Catholic education among the free Negroes grew after Archbishop Odin had passed away, but certainly his early dedication to such, in spite of the resistance coming from religious communities and many lay Catholics, helped to lay a base for future work among the Negro population that matured in the latter nineteenth century.

As the Civil War was winding down, the female religious orders of New Orleans labored gallantly to take care of the people, including soldiers from both the Confederacy and the Union, in their convent hospitals and other sites. On April 9, 1865, Palm Sunday, Gen. Robert E. Lee surrendered the Army of Northern Virginia to Gen. Ulysses S. Grant at Appomattox Court House. Three days later, on April 12, the last major city of the Confederacy, Mobile, Alabama, fell to Union forces. Then at 10 P.M. on Good Friday, April 14, at Ford's Theatre, actor John Wilkes Booth shot President Lincoln as he attended with his wife and a very small party the comedy *Our American Cousin.* General Grant and his wife had been invited, but they had turned down the invitation. Lincoln died the next morning. Throughout the nation a new era had begun, and in the South that meant Reconstruction.

Reconstruction

As the Civil War came to an end and Louisiana began to experience Reconstruction, one prominent historian's view of Jean-Marie Odin appears accurate regarding history's assessment of that missionary from France as archbishop of New Orleans during both of those eras in New Orleans's narrative. In his 1888 book *Lives of the Deceased Bishops of the Catholic Church in the United States*, the distinguished scholar Richard H. Clarke wrote: "There was something providential in the appointment of so saintly a prelate for New Orleans at the trying period of the history of that city at the time of his arrival there. His childlike simplicity, straightforwardness of purpose and conduct, his openness, sincerity, and benevolence, challenged the respect of the world and its followers, [*sic*] and elevated him above the breath of censure or suspicion, amid the shifting fortunes of war. 'We witnessed,' writes his successor, 'the unrepining patience with which he bore the excruciating pains to which he fell victim, shortly after his arrival in this city. This patience, this meekness, this calm unruffled resignation, accompanied him to the last.'"[25]

These high qualities in the person of Jean-Marie Odin would certainly be needed as he led the archdiocese through those days. The Civil War had almost impoverished many families in the South, and Louisiana was no exception. Those economic realities continued during Reconstruction. Of this Roger Baudier wrote: "If there was want while the conflict [the Civil War] lasted there was still more of it during the Reconstruction period which came with a turmoil and confusion that brought activities almost to a complete standstill. The Church suffered severely, not only in loss of revenue, but also in loss of property and damage to many of its properties. Archbishop Odin unquestionably faced one of the most dire situations in the history of the Church in the state."[26]

Then, given his position as archbishop, Odin continued to focus on strengthening Catholic life in New Orleans. Such culminated in his convening the Fifth Diocesan Synod on January 29, 1869, a synod which so solidly built up ecclesiastical reforms that another diocesan synod was not called until almost two decades later, in 1888. Odin continued to serve the Catholics of New Orleans in a dedicated manner, regularly celebrating Mass, administering the sacrament of confirmation, and much more in spite of his often being fatigued or ill.[27]

Of great importance, Archbishop Odin oversaw the establishment of New Orleans's first English-speaking Catholic newspaper, *The Morning Star and Catholic Messenger*. An announcement describing the foundation of the newspaper appeared in its first volume. The publication was created within the structure of a joint stock company composed of stock in the total amount of $100,000 under the laws of the state of Louisiana. It was to be administered by a committee of seven people, four clergy that the archbishop would name and three laypersons. Heading up the committee was the Most Reverend Napoleon Joseph Perche, vicar general and future successor to Odin as archbishop.[28]

While he served as archbishop following the Civil War, Odin created three new parishes: St. Francis de Sales, St. Michael for the Irish Catholics, and St. Boniface for German Catholic immigrants. He also turned his attention to caring for the elderly. According to Baudier, elderly Negro women were, when needed, already under the care of the Sisters of the Holy Family in New Orleans. In 1868 Odin brought a group of Little Sisters of the Poor to New Orleans to operate homes for the elderly non-Negro population, both female and male. The first such residence was called the St. Joseph Home for the Aged.[29]

The Death of Jean-Marie Odin and His Legacy

As he continued in several ways to bolster his parishioners in their faith religiously, educationally, economically, and more, Odin also had to look at matters of the universal church, particularly with trips to Rome. He had already journeyed to Europe twice in the 1860s, but a third such venture became necessary when Pope Pius IX called for a General Council (Vatican Council I) to convene in Rome beginning on the feast of the Immaculate Conception 1869. Some one thousand bishops and archbishops were eligible to attend the council, but never more than eight hundred were present. Odin arrived at Rome on November 19, 1869, accompanied by Bishop Dubuis, his close friend and successor as bishop of Galveston. On December 14 of that year, Dubuis had written a letter to his family at Coutouvre, France, with whom he had visited on his way to Rome, stating that "Upon leaving you I remained close to Msgr. Odin; his weakened condition did not permit him to travel alone."[30]

By early January 1870, as the council fathers were debating serious questions, one being papal infallibility in matters of faith and morals, Odin's health had deteriorated enough that he, again in the company of Bishop Dubuis, returned to the home of his birth at Hauteville, Ambierle, France.[31] There, on May 25, 1870, after slightly more than four months of continued declining health, in the very house in which he was born more than seventy years earlier, he died. It is unlikely that Bishop Dubuis was with him at the time of his death, as Dubuis was most assuredly back at the council for the discussions and votes on the issues that surfaced at Rome. For example, Dubuis was a strong supporter of papal infallibility. But Dubuis was heartbroken that his longtime friend had died.

Odin had suffered much pain in his last days. On the morning of his death he received the Viaticum. It was reported that he had lifted his eyes to heaven and had a smile on his face at the instance of his passing away. Almost immediately upon the news of his death being made public, people not only from Hauteville-Ambierle but the surrounding neighborhoods as well began to proceed to the Odin home. The *Propagateur* (local paper) reported those activities. The publication also wrote that people viewed Odin's body from Wednesday through Saturday and that when his body was laid in the coffin his legs, arms, and fingers were flexible. At the chamber where the Odin body was exposed the mayors of both Ambierle and Roanne gave "handsome discourses." At the insistence of the people the funeral procession included carrying Odin's body around the village before depositing it in the church. Two little boys, one a grand-nephew and the other a near relative, carried Odin's cross and miter. The archbishop was buried in the same Church of St. Martin d'Ambierle where he attended Mass and was an altar boy as a youth.[32]

Back in New Orleans the Catholics of the see city received the word of their archbishop's death with grieving and sorrow. Vicar General Most Reverend Napoleon Joseph Perche, who had been named coadjutor archbishop just three weeks before Odin's death, published a pastoral letter, he by then having become the third archbishop of New Orleans, in the July 19, 1870, issue of *The Morning Star and Catholic Messenger,* in which he sadly reported the news of Odin's death and praised his predecessor. Among other words, he wrote, "With sentiments of profound grief, which you will certainly partake with us, we perform the melancholy duty of announcing the heavy loss which the [Arch] Diocese of New Orleans has just sustained in the death of its first Pastor. Archbishop John Mary [Jean-Marie] Odin Archbishop Odin was eminently what St. Paul terms *a man of God.*"[33]

By direction of Archbishop Perche each parish of the Archdiocese of New Orleans was to celebrate a funeral Mass for the repose of Jean-Marie Odin's soul. A solemn Requiem Mass was scheduled for the Cathedral of St. Louis. In addition, Archbishop Perche urged that each year in the future around the date of May 25 masses be celebrated remembering the deceased second archbishop of the archdiocese. The Catholic Archives of Texas in Austin has a copy of Odin's will and probate.[34] That document is also filed with the county of Galveston, the state of Texas, by Deputy Clerk William T. Austin, dated August 11, 1879.

As history looks back at the legacy of Jean-Marie Odin, as he labored in the regions of Missouri, Illinois, and Arkansas, worked as a vice-prefect apostolic and then vicar apostolic of Texas, became the first bishop of Galveston, and ended his earthly life as the second archbishop of New Orleans, it will record that more than anything else he was always a missionary.

Notes

Chapter 1. From France He Came

1. On the history of the priory church of St. Martin d'Ambierle see *Cette brochure est editee sous la patronage de Syndicat d'Initiative d'Ambierle, a la occasion du L'Eglise, 1450–1950 et des ceremonies commemoratives de 17 septembre 1950*, 13–14, De Andreis-Rosati Memorial Archives.

2. Bony, *Vie de Mgr. Jean-Marie Odin*, 15.

3. Odin's birth certificate, *Extrait du Registere des Actas de Bapteme*, St. Martine d'Ambierle Parish, Diocese de Lyon (Loire), 12 juillet, 1949.

4. Bony, *Vie de Mgr. Jean-Marie Odin*, 16.

5. Ibid., 17. On Odin's consecration as the second archbishop of New Orleans see Bransom, *Ordinations of U.S. Catholic Bishops*, 18.

6. Bony, *Vie de Mgr. Jean-Marie Odin*, 10, 17.

7. Bertier de Sauvigny and Pinkney, *History of France*, 62.

8. Ibid., 214.

9. Ibid., 215.

10. Ibid., 214. On the depth and breadth of negative impact of the Civil Constitution of the Clergy against the church in France see Warren H. Carroll, *The Guillotine and the Cross*, 29–30.

11. Andre Latrielle, "The Church and the Counterrevolution," in *The Shaping of Modern France: Writings on French History Since 1715*, ed. James Friguglietti and Emmet Kennedy, intro. Crane Brinton (New York: MacMillan, 1969), 142, 143.

12. Bertier de Sauvigny and Pinkney, *History of France*, 223.

13. Ibid., 245–50.

14. Dom Jean-Baptiste Chautard, O.C.S.O., *The Soul of the Apostolate* (Trappist, Ky.: Abbey of Gethsemani, 1946).

15. J. Edgard Brunes, "Antoine Blanc: Louisiana's Joshua in the Land of Promise He Opened," in *Cross, Crozier and Crucible*, ed. Conrad, 120–21. Father Jean-Marie Jammes, a French American scholar in Louisiana, holds similar positive views of Cardinal Fesch. See his "The Early Years of the French Catholics in Texas," a paper read at the annual conference of the Texas Catholic Historical Society, 3 March 1988, Austin, Texas.

16. *L'Ami de la religion* (n.p.: LeClere, 1816), 8.

17. Jacques Gadille, ed., *Le Diocese de Lyon*, vol. 16 of *Histoire des Dioceses de France* (Paris: Beauchesne, 1983), 213.

18. Brunes, "Antoine Blanc," 120–34. For this period in the life of Father Antoine Blanc, fourth bishop and first archbishop of New Orleans, see Baudier, *Catholic Church in Louisiana*, 326–28.

19. Bony, *Vie de Mgr. Jean-Marie Odin,* chap. 2, p. 3.

20. Christopher J. Kauffman, *Tradition and Transformation in Catholic Culture: The Priests of Saint Sulpice in the United States from 1791 to the Present* (New York: MacMillan, 1988), xiii.

21. On Father Angelo Inglesi, whose personal reputation at the time he commenced recruitment for Bishop DuBourg in Europe was unraveling due to reported romantic and financial improprieties. See Melville, *Louis William DuBourg,* vol. 2: 572–601.

22. For examples of other missionaries (both priests and nuns) who suffered similar struggles regarding leaving home for the foreign mission field see Horgan, *Lamy of Santa Fe,* 18–21, and Costa, trans., *Letters of Marie Madelein Hachard.* The author wishes to thank Marlene and Tom Loughran, formerly of St. Thomas the Apostle Catholic Church in Fort Worth, Texas, for this book. The Archives of the Archdiocese of St. Louis (hereafter referred to as AASL) houses a copy of the April 22, 1822, letter from the vicar general of the Archdiocese of Lyon releasing Jean-Marie Odin from that metropolitan see's ecclesiastical jurisdiction. The author is indebted to the late Martin G. Towey for a copy of this letter.

23. Bony, *Vie de Mgr. Jean-Marie Odin,* chap. 4, p. 4.

24. Ibid., chap. 5, 1. It was common at that period in history for nonindigenous people from Europe and America to use the word "savages" when referring to the indigenous people of America. See Ray Allen Billington, *Land of Savagery, Land of Promise: The European Image of the American Frontier in the Nineteenth Century* (New York: Norton, 1980).

25. Patrick Foley, "Jean-Marie Odin, C.M., Missionary Bishop Extraordinaire of Texas," *Journal of Texas Catholic History and Culture* 1 (1990): 48. The name of the ship on which Odin booked passage is identified in Rieder and Rieder, *New Orleans Ship Lists,* 38. For confirmation of the date of Odin's departure from Le Havre see letter to Patrick Foley from Father John Rybolt, C.M., noted Vincentian historian and then president and rector of Saint Thomas Theological Seminary, Denver, Colorado, 13 April 1987.

Chapter 2. At the Barrens

1. Bony, *Vie de Mgr. Jean-Marie Odin,* chap. 5, p. 1; Melville, *Louis William DuBourg,* vol. 2: 588, 976.

2. Bony, *Vie de Mgr. Jean-Marie Odin,* chap. 5, p. 45.

3. Regarding French settlers in America—including clergy and sisters or nuns—and their reaction to slavery see Blumenthal, *American and French Culture,* 20, 87–89.

4. For a discussion about slavery existing at the Barrens Seminary see Rybolt, ed., *American Vincentians,* 25, 34, 36–38; Poole and Slawson, *Church and Slave,* 148–49.

5. Bony, *Vie de Mgr. Jean-Marie Odin,* chap. 5, p. 45.

6. Ibid. This letter contains no date in Bony's citation.

7. According to Vincentians Father Louis Derbes of the De Andreis-Rosati Memorial Archives (hereafter cited as DRMA) at Saint Mary's of the Barrens Seminary, Perryville, Missouri, the *mason mere* (motherhouse) of the Congregation of the Mission at Paris in the early 1800s informed the US Vincentians that slavery existed as a contradiction to Vincentian ideals. The mason mere reminded the Vincentians in the United States that their founder, St. Vincent de Paul, himself had once been a slave. Phone conversation between Father Derbes and Patrick Foley on May 25, 1994. On the views of Vincentians who saw no moral difficulty with slavery see James Hitchcock, "Race, Religion, and Rebellion: Hilary Tucker and the Civil War," *The Catholic Historical Review* 80, no. 3 (July 1994), 497–517. Father Hilary Tucker was a member of the Missouri Tucker clan from whom the name "Tucker Settlement" would come, the locale that later became known as the Barrens Colony.

8. Bagen, *St. Mary's of the Barrens Parish,* 1.

9. Patrick Foley, "The Sons of St. Vincent from the Mississippi River to the Rio Grande," *Catholic Social Science Review* 1 (1996): 147–55.

10. Bagen, *St. Mary's of the Barrens Parish*, 1.

11. *Saint Mary's of the Barrens, 1818–1993*, 3.

12. Bagen, *St. Mary's of the Barrens Parish*, 4; Rybolt, *American Vincentians*, 231. Archival records provide no first name for Father Maxwell.

13. Bagen, *St. Mary's of the Barrens Parish*, 5, states that Father Dunand visited the Barrens Colony "three or four times a year." Rybolt in his *American Vincentians*, 23, reports that Dunand made monthly trips from Florissant to the Barrens Colony.

14. Bagen, *St. Mary's of the Barrens Parish*, 9.

15. Ibid., 19.

16. Ibid.

17. Ibid.

18. Ibid.

19. DuBourg to Rosati, 2 August 1818, DRMA.

20. Bagen, *St. Mary's of the Barrens Parish*, 16.

21. Rybolt, *American Vincentians*, 26; Odin to Father Jean Cholleton, 10 March 1823, *Annales de L'Association de la Foi* (Lyon, 1827) 1:65, DRMA; "Odin, Jean-Marie, Rev. 1800 Febr. 25 Natus in Ambierle Dioc. Lyons in France," AASL. The author wishes to thank Professor Martin Towey, archivist of the AASL, for this source. Odin to Cholleton, 21 October 1822, *Annales* (Lyon, 1827), DRMA.

22. Bony, *Vie de Mgr. Jean-Marie Odin*, chap. 6, p. 3. Regarding the date of Odin's ordination see also Bransom, *Ordinations of U.S. Catholic Bishops*, 18; "Odin, Jean-Marie, C.M.," AASL.

23. "Odin, Joannes Marie, C.M.," AASL; "Advice Given on the Departure of Missionaries for Distant Countries," Luis Abelly, Bishop, *La Vie du Venerable Serviteur de Dieu, Vincent de Paul* (1664), bk. III, 12, DRMA.

24. Bony, *Vie de Mgr. Jean-Marie Odin*, chap. 8, p. 2.

25. E. A. Livingstone, *The Concise Dictionary of the Christian Church* (Oxford: Oxford University Press, 1977), 311.

26. John Hardon, *Modern Catholic Dictionary* (New York: Doubleday, 1980), 562; Pierre Coste, C.M., ed. "Conferences on Conformity with the Will of God, 7 March 1659," vol. 12 of *Saint Vincent de Paul Correspondence, Entretienes, Documents*, DRMA.

27. Rybolt, *American Vincentians*, 98.

28. Bayard, *Lone-Star Vanguard*, 3–6.

29. Ibid., 8.

30. Ibid., 8–9.

31. John Timon, "Barrens Memoir," 12–13, DRMA.

Chapter 3. Missouri and Arkansas

1. "Odin, Jean-Marie, C.M.," AASL.

2. Timon, "Barrens Memoir," 5, DRMA.

3. Ibid.

4. Ibid.

5. Ibid.

6. Odin to Cholleton, 1824 [day and month not recorded], DRMA.

7. On Arkansas Post being established as a northern settlement of New Spain see Carlos M. Fernández-Shaw, *Preséncia española en los Estados Unidos* (Madrid: Ediciones Cultura Hispanica, 1972), 661. Timon, "Barrens Memoir," 5, DRMA.

8. On the Adams-Onis Treaty see George Lockhart-Rives, *The United States and Mexico, 1821–1848*, vol. 1 (New York: Scribner's, 1913), 18–19; Philip C. Brooks, "The Pacific Coast's First International Boundary Delineation," *The Pacific Historical Review* 3, no. 1: 62–79. Ashmore, *Arkansas*, 3–6; *Souvenir of a Silver Jubilee*, 1–4, DRMA.

9. *The De Andrein* 19, no. 3 (December 1948): 1, 3, DRMA. Ashmore, *Arkansas*, x.

10. For a brief description of Jesuit Father Jacques Marquette's missionary visit to the Quapaw lands see Raphael N. Hamilton, S.J., *Marquette's Explorations: The Narrative Reexamined* (Madison: University of Wisconsin Press, 1970), 178–79.

11. Timon, "Barrens Memoir," 5, DRMA

12. Ashmore, *Arkansas*, xiv; *The De Andrein* 19, no 3 (December 1948): 3, DRMA.

13. Timon, "Barrens Memoir," 9, DRMA. In a letter to Father Cholleton back at Lyon, written sometime after October 31, 1824, following the two Vincentians' return to the Barrens Seminary from Arkansas, Odin developed in detail the facts of the trip. (That correspondence material for the later *Souvenir of a Silver Jubilee*, Timon's "Barrens Memoir," and issue of *The De Andrein*.) See Odin to Cholleton, *Annales de L'Association de la Propagation de la Foi* 2, no. 12 (November 1827): 374–89. See also *Souvenir of a Silver Jubilee*, 3, DRMA; Timon, "Barrens Memoir," 6, DRMA; *The De Andrein* 19, no. 3 (December 1948): 3, DRMA.

14. Clarke, *Lives of the Deceased Bishops*, vol. 2: 203.

15. *Annales*, vol. 3: 533.

16. Ibid. Pauline Jaricot founded the Propagation de la Foi at Lyon in 1822 to aid Catholic missionaries throughout the world with prayers and financial support.

17. Bransom, *Ordinations of U.S. Catholic Bishops*, 20.

18. Bayard Collection, Box 22, "Seminary History," DRMA.

19. Earl F. Niehaus, "Catholic Ethnics in Nineteenth-Century Louisiana," in *Cross, Crozier, and Crucible*, ed. Conrad, 52.

20. Odin to Timon, 20 November 1826, "Vincentian Papers," Archives of the University of Notre Dame (hereafter cited as AUND).

21. The term "culture" is used here in the sense that James V. Schall, S.J., defines it in his article "Culture, Multiculturalism, Cultural Wars, and the Universal Culture," *Journal of Texas Catholic History and Culture* 5 (1994): 11–24.

22. Odin to Cholleton, 2 August 1823, *Annales* 1 (1823), DRMA.

23. Odin to Timon, 20 November 1826, "Vincentian Papers," AUND.

24. Ibid.

CHAPTER 4. ODIN AND THE EMERGING AMERICAN VINCENTIAN PRESENCE

1. Bagen, *St. Mary's of the Barrens Parish*, 38.

2. Ibid.

3. For a discussion of these issues see Rybolt, *American Vincentians*, 33–34.

4. Bransom, *Ordinations of U.S. Catholic Bishops*, 15.

5. *United States Catholic Miscellany* 9, no. 49 (5 June 1830): 390.

6. Odin to Timon, 10 April 1828, DRMA.

7. Bransom, *Ordinations of U.S. Catholic Bishops*, 14.

8. Bony, *Vie de Mgr. Jean-Marie Odin*, chap. 9, p. 4.

9. Ibid.

10. Shea, *Hierarchy of the Catholic Church*, 125.

11. Timon, "Barrens Memoir," 20.

12. Bayard Collection, Box 22, "Seminary History," DRMA.

13. LaVeille, *Life of Father de Smet*, 62.

14. Odin to Timon, 20 October 1833, AUND. A copy of this letter is located in the "Odin Letters," Catholic Archives of Texas (CAT).

15. Ibid.

16. Ibid.

17. Ibid.

18. Odin to Timon, 31 December, AUND. The main apparitions of the Virgin Mary to which Odin referred were those reported to have occurred beginning on July 18, 1830, to Catherine Laboure, a twenty-four-year-old postulant at the motherhouse of the Daughters of Charity at 140 Rue de Bac (Street of the Ferryboat) in Paris. On these apparitions see Catherine M. Odell, *Those Who Saw Her: The Apparitions of Mary,* intro. John Joseph, Cardinal Carberry (Huntington, Ind.: Our Sunday Visitor, 1986), 47–61.

19. Bony, *Vie de Mgr. Jean-Marie Odin,* chap. 10, p. 1, CAT.

20. Ibid., chap. 10, p. 3, CAT, AUND.

21. Odin to Timon, 24 December 1834, AUND.

22. Clarke, *Lives of the Deceased Bishops,* 6.

Chapter 5. The Call to Texas

1. Rybolt, *American Vincentians,* 235.

2. Donald E. Chipman, *Spanish Texas, 1519–1821* (Austin: University of Texas Press, 1992); Habig, *San Antonio's Mission San José.*

3. Habig, *San Antonio's Mission San José,* 2. See also Bishop David Arias, *Spanish Cross in Georgia* (New York: University Press of America, 1994).

4. Habig, *San Antonio's Mission San José,* 3.

5. Habig, *Alamo Mission,* 12.

6. On Fray Antonio Margil de Jesus see Habig, *San Antonio's Mission San José;* Oberste, *Restless Friar.*

7. Almaráz, *Tragic Cavalier,* 8.

8. In a recent article in which he addressed the topic of the Hispanic legacy of Texas, Bishop Ricardo Ramirez of Las Cruces, New Mexico, referred to this ethnic-religious metamorphosis by identifying the Hispanics as being persons not only of Spanish or Latin American heritage but also as descendants of immigrants or immigrants themselves from Spanish-speaking nations who possess a common language and enjoy a mutual shared history and cultural development whose roots go back to Spain. See Bishop Ricardo Ramirez, C.S.B., "The Hispanic Peoples of the United States and the Church from 1865–1985," *U.S. Catholic Historian* 9, nos. 1–2 (winter/spring 1990): 163.

9. Robert Wright, O.M.I., "The Catholic Church and Mexican Americans in Texas, 1840–1880," a paper read at the CEHILA conference, Las Cruces, New Mexico, 15 January 1989. Robert Wright, O.M.I., "Local Church Emergence and Mission Decline: The Historiography of the Catholic Church in the Southwest during the Spanish and Mexican Periods," *U.S. Catholic Historian* 9, nos. 1–2 (winter/spring 1990): 27–48.

10. On the cult of the Virgin of Guadalupe see Timothy M. Matovina, *Guadalupe and Her Faithful: Latino Catholics in San Antonio, From Colonial Origins to the Present* (Baltimore: John Hopkins University Press, 2005); Warren H. Carroll, *Our Lady of Guadalupe and the Conquest of Darkness* (Front Royal, Va.: Christendom Publications, 1983); Francis Johnston, *The Wonder of Guadalupe: The Origin and Cult of the Miraculous Image of the Blessed Virgin in Mexico* (Rockford, Ill.: Tan Books, 1981). For a discussion of the December 1841 celebration of the Feast of Our Lady of Guadalupe in San Antonio see Matovina, *Tejano Religion and Ethnicity,* 43–45.

11. Chipman, *Spanish Texas,* 61. See also Marilyn H. Fedewa, *Maria of Agreda: Mystical Lady in Blue* (Albuquerque: University of New Mexico Press, 2009).

12. On the quotation regarding the "Lady in Blue," see Seymour V. Conner, *Texas: A History* (New York: Crowell, 1971), 15–16.

13. Chipman, *Spanish Texas*, 61.

14. Ibid. 105.

15. On the issue of the indeterminate boundaries of Texas see Barker, *French Legation in Texas,* vol. 1: *Recognition, Rupture, and Reconciliation,* 193–206; *Mission Miscarried,* 676–77; Robert Wright, "Popular and Official Religiosity: A Theological Analysis and a Case Study of Laredo-Nuevo Laredo, 1755–1857," PhD diss., Graduate Theological Union, Berkeley, California, 1992, 183–84; Horgan, *Lamy of Santa Fe,* 65, 69.

16. Patrick Foley, "From Linares to Galveston: Texas in the Diocesan Scheme of the Roman Catholic Church to the Mid-Nineteenth Century," *Catholic Southwest: A Journal of History and Culture* 8 (1997): 25–27.

17. Foley, "From Linares to Galveston," 25–27.

18. Margaret Swett Henson, *Lorenzo de Zavala: The Pragmatic Idealist* (Fort Worth: Texas Christian University Press, 1996), 28–33.

19. Foley, "From Linares to Galveston," 32–33; see also Bishop Francisco José Maria de Jesús Belaunzarán y Ureña to Bishop Antoine Blanc, 21 February 1839, "Texas Letters," AUND.

20. Linn, *Reminiscences,* 48–49.

21. The best study available on the colony of San Patricio de Hibernia is Rachel Bluntzer Hébert's *The Forgotten Colony, San Patricio de Hibernia* (Burnet, Tex.: Eakin Press, 1981). See 15–24.

22. Ibid., 340.

23. Bagen, *St. Mary's of the Barrens,* 43–49.

24. John Rybolt, C.M., "Vincentian Seminaries in Louisiana," *Vincentian Heritage* 15, no. 2 (1994): 163–90.

25. Blanc to Purcell, 29 August 1838, "Vincentian Collection," AUND; Purcell to Blanc, 12 February 1839, "Vincentian Collection," AUND.

26. Eccleston to Blanc, 8 April 1839, "Vincentian Collection," AUND; Timon to Nozo, 15 June 1839, "Vincentian Collection," AUND, cited in Bayard, *Lone-Star Vanguard,* 86.

CHAPTER 6. SEND US SOME PRIESTS

1. John Joseph Linn and others to Archbishop Samuel Eccleston and the Bishops in Counsel [*sic*] at Baltimore, 20 March 1837, AUND. The other signers of the letter were (for San Patricio) John McMullen, William R. C. Hayes, R. O'Boyle, and Andrew A. Boyle; (for Mission de Refugio) Robert P. Hearn; (for Our Lady of Guadalupe at Victoria) John Linn (John Joseph Linn's son).

2. Jean-Marie Odin, "Daily Journal," 17 July 1840, C.A.T; Linn, *Reminiscences,* 9–10. The full title of Odin's journal is "Daily Journal for the year 1840–2–3 & of the Vy Rev. J. M. Odin V[ice] [Prefect] A[postolic] of Texas." The journal includes 113 pages, and after the year 1843 its entries contain significant voids. The journal continues through 1852, but those from 1849 through 1852 are sketchy.

3. Linn, *Reminiscences,* 15–16.

4. Linn and others to Eccleston, 20 March 1837, AUND.

5. Bayard, *Lone-Star Vanguard,* 18.

6. Bayard Collection, Box 22, "Seminary History," DRMA. This collection contains a brief reference to a Mr. Linn. The source is undated, but the materials with which it is stored are all from the mid-1830s.

7. *The French Legation in Texas,* vol. 1: 44n. For a detailed account of Farnese's role in attracting the Holy See to the needs of Catholics in Texas see Bayard, *Lone-Star Vanguard,* 20.

8. Odin to Timon, 18 September 1837, DRMA.

9. Ibid.

10. Moore, *Through Fire and Flood*, 12.

11. Odin to Timon, 22 March 1838, DRMA.

12. Odin to Timon, 1 May 1839, DRMA.

13. Bayard, *Lone-Star Vanguard*, 23.

14. Jean-Baptiste Etienne, C.M., to Blanc, 9 August 1838, AUND; Etienne to Blanc, 15 March 1839, AUND.

CHAPTER 7. ON THE SHOULDERS OF ODIN

1. Odin to Mrs. Simonin, 15 September 1838, DRMA; Timon, "Barrens Memoir," 26–27, DRMA.

2. Odin to Etienne, 25 September 1838, DRMA.

3. For a discussion of the substance of this trip see Bayard, *Lone-Star Vanguard*, 51–53; and Moore, *Through Fire and Flood*, 14–22.

4. Bayard, *Lone-Star Vanguard*, 52.

5. Foley, "From Linares to Galveston"; Belaunzarán y Ureña to Blanc, 21 February 1839, "Vincentian Collection," AUND.

6. Teja, ed., *Revolution Remembered*, 172.

7. Ibid.

8. Bayard, *Lone-Star Vanguard*, 54.

9. Ibid., 54–63.

10. Timon to Blanc, 12 March 1839, "Vincentian Collection," AUND.

11. Blanc to Belaunzarán y Ureña, 15 January 1839, "Vincentian Collection," AUND.

12. Belaunzarán y Ureña to Blanc, 21 February 1839, "Vincentian Collection," AUND.

13. Nozo to Propaganda Fide, 25 April 1839, Fols. 572 rv and 573 rv, "Oeuvre de la Prop. De la Foi," AUND; Anduze to Blanc, 20 February 1839, "Vincentian Collection," AUND; Anduze to Blanc, 21 April 1839, "Vincentian Collection," AUND. For coverage of Abbe Anduze's discussion about French-Mexican relations and Catholicism in Texas see Barker, *French Legation in Texas*, vol. 1: 82, 83.

14. Timon, "Barrens Memoir," 28, DRMA.

15. Ibid.

16. Rosati to Propaganda Fide, 12 April 1840, Fols. 847 rv and 848 rv, AUND.

17. Ibid., both letters.

18. Jean-Marie Odin, "Daily Journal," 2 May 1840, CAT.

19. Odin, "Daily Journal," 2 May 1840, CAT.

20. Ibid.

21. Ibid. Since the Vincentians in America commonly used the title "Mr." for their clerics, both Mr. Paris and Mr. O'Neill possibly were Vincentians, but their names do not appear in the indexes of major studies of the American Vincentians for that period of history. Odin paid their ship passages as well as that of the three nuns, and Mr. O'Neill was scheduled to join Doutreluinue at Natchitoches.

22. On the struggle between the Catholic Church in Spain and that nation's liberals during the early to mid-nineteenth-century era see Stanley Payne, *Spanish Catholicism: An Historical Overview* (Madison: University of Wisconsin Press, 1984), 71–96; Alexandra Wilhelmsen, *La formación del pensamiento politico del carlismo (1810–1875)* (Madrid: Actas, 1995), 11–410; and Charles Patrick Foley, "The Catholic-Liberal Struggle and the Church in Spain: 1834–1876," PhD diss., University of New Mexico, 1983.

23. Odin, "Daily Journal," 7 May 1840, CAT.

24. Odin to Rosati, 27 August1840, "Vincentian Collection," AUND.

25. Odin to Timon, 14 May 1840, "Vincentian Collection, AUND.

26. Ibid.

27. Odin to Timon, 20 June 1840, "Vincentian Collection," AUND; Odin, "Daily Journal," 2 July 1840, CAT.

CHAPTER 8. A VICE PREFECT APOSTOLIC ARRIVES

1. Odin, "Daily Journal," 13 July 1840, CAT; Odin to Blanc, 14 July 1840, "Odin Letters," CAT; Odin, "Daily Journal," 12 July 1840.

2. Linn, *Reminiscences,* 13–14, 247; Odin, "Daily Journal," 13 July 1840, CAT. Regarding the estimated population of Linnville in 1840, see June Rayfield Welch, *Riding Fences* (Dallas: GLA Press, 1983), 71.

3. Odin to Blanc, 14 July 1840, "Odin Letters," CAT.

4. Odin, "Daily Journal," 13 July 1840, CAT.

5. Odin to Blanc, 14 July 1840, "Odin Letters," CAT; *Texas Almanac, 1996–1997* (Dallas: *Dallas Morning News,* 1995), 272.

6. Odin, "Daily Journal," 16 July 1840, CAT.

7. On the Irish of Victoria see Flannery, *Irish Texans,* 91–96. On the Mexican settlers in the area see Hebert, *Forgotten Colony,* 358–61.

8. Odin to Blanc, 24 August 1840, "Odin Letters," CAT; Hebert, *Forgotten Colony,* 112–22.

9. Odin to Blanc, 23 August 1840, "Odin Letters," CAT; Odin, "Daily Journal," 21 July 1840, CAT.

10. Linn, *Reminiscences,* 67.

11. Pool, *Historical Atlas of Texas,* 106–107; Odin, "Daily Journal," 21 July 1840, CAT.

12. Odin, "Daily Journal," 21 July 1840 and 22 July 1840, CAT.

13. Ibid., 23 July 1840.

14. Ibid., 24 July 1840; Odin to Blanc, 24 August 1840, "Odin Letters," CAT.

15. Odin, "Daily Journal," 25 July 1840, CAT. In his daily journal, Odin recorded that there were twenty-eight ranches. Carlos Eduardo Castañeda wrote that Odin visited fourteen to sixteen of them, *Our Catholic Heritage in Texas,* vol. 7:46.

16. Odin, "Daily Journal," 28 July 1840, CAT.

17. On Juan José Maria Erasmo Seguin see Teja, *Revolution Remembered,* 1–17.

18. Odin to Etienne, 28 August 1840, "Odin Letters," CAT; Pool, *Historical Atlas,* 47.

19. Teja, *Revolution Remembered,* 172. Father de la Garza's failure to make entries into the San Fernando parish church records from 1836 into 1840 was confirmed to Patrick Foley by Brother Edward Loch, S.M., archivist of the Archives of the Archdiocese of San Antonio, in a phone conversation on 5 June 1996.

20. Odin, "Daily Journal," 30 July 1840, CAT; Castañeda, *Our Catholic Heritage in Texas,* vol. 7:50.

21. Odin to Rosati, 27 August 1840, "Odin Letters," CAT; Castañeda, *Our Catholic Heritage in Texas,* vol. 7:26.

22. Some scholars argue that as social and political rivals of Father de la Garza, Seguín and Navarro focused on the priest's weaknesses. See for example Castañeda, *Our Catholic Heritage in Texas,* vol. 7:26. In his *Through Fire and Flood,* Father James Talmadge Moore wrote that "Perhaps Odin was too ready to believe what rumor, rather than justice, laid at the aged priest's door" (39). Both Castañeda and Moore seemed to be concerned about whether or not Fathers de la Garza and Valdéz were treated justly. Gilberto Miguel Hinojosa criticized Father Odin, saying in *Mexican Americans and the Catholic Church, 1900–1965* (South Bend, Ind.: University of Notre Dame Press, 1994), which Hinojosa edited with Jay P. Dolan, and in which Hinojosa wrote the initial

section on the Southwest, that "in Texas, Bishop Jean-Marie Odin made a cursory investigation of the work of the native-born Refugio de la Garza and his Mexican compatriot José Antonio Valdéz, and then evicted them, alleging neglect and scandal" (19). Hinojosa's study was heavily documented but focused little on archival research. Also the work failed to convey a deep understanding of the life of Odin. Perhaps that is why Hinojosa referred to Odin as a bishop, when in fact the Frenchman did not become a bishop until nineteen months after his confrontation with Fathers de la Garza and Valdéz.

23. Odin to Etienne, 28 August 1840, "Odin Letters," CAT.

24. Odin to Blanc, 24 August 1840, "Odin Letters," CAT.

25. Odin to Rosati, 27 August 1840, "Odin Letters," CAT.

26. Ibid.; Odin, "Daily Journal," 3 August 1840, CAT.

27. Odin to Rosati, 27 August 1840, "Odin Letters," CAT.

28. Ibid.; Odin, "Daily Journal," 5, 6, 7, 8, 9 August 1840, CAT.

29. Odin to Rosati, 27 August 1840, "Odin letters," CAT.

30. Linn, *Reminiscences,* 338–43.

31. Odin, "Daily Journal," 13 August 1840, CAT.

32. Odin to Rosati, 27 August 1840, "Odin Letters," CAT.

33. Odin, "Daily Journal," 15 August 1840, CAT; Odin to Blanc, 24 August 1840, "Odin Letters," CAT.

34. Odin, "Daily Journal," 16, 17 August 1840, CAT; Odin to Blanc, 24 August 1840; Odin to Rosati, 27 August 1840; Odin to Etienne, 28 August 1840, "Odin Letters," CAT.

35. Robert E. Wright, O.M.I., treats this topic thoroughly in his "Popular and Official Religiosity: A Theoretical Analysis and A Case Study of Laredo-Nuevo Laredo, 1755–1857," PhD diss., Graduate Theological Union, Berkeley, California, 1992, 183–331.

36. Odin to Blanc, 24 August 1840, "Odin Letters," CAT.

37. Ibid.

38. Urged on by Mayor Smith, the agitators against Odin had their complaints published on August 26, 1840, in the newly established Austin newspaper, the *Texas Sentinel.* Odin was left with no choice but to refute them. His answer to the claims of those false witnesses, a clear and incisive defense of Catholic Church teaching and tradition, was sent to the *Texas Sentinel* on September 5 of that year and published shortly thereafter. See Odin, "Daily Journal," 5 September 1840, CAT. Editors George W. Bonnell and Jacob Cruger had only founded the *Texas Sentinel* in Austin on January 15, 1840. See also Sibley, *Lone Stars and State Gazettes,* 122.

CHAPTER 9. THE MISSION BEYOND SAN ANTONIO

1. Odin, "Daily Journal," 11 August 1840, CAT.

2. Odin to Etienne, 13 December 1840; Odin to James Cardinal Fransoni, 15 December 1840, "Odin Letters," CAT. Father Jean Baptiste Etienne, C.M., in 1840 held the position of procurator general of the Congregation of the Mission. Cardinal Fransoni at the time served as cardinal prefect of the Sacred Congregation de Propaganda Fide.

3. Bayard, *Lone-Star Vanguard,* 138. For a further discussion of Odin's September inspection of the missions see Habig, *San Antonio's Mission San José,* 141–43.

4. Odin, "Daily Journal," 9 November 1840, CAT.

5. Ibid., 9, 13 November 1840.

6. Ibid.

7. Odin to Etienne, 13 December 1840, "Odin Letters," CAT; Moore, *Through Fire and Flood,* 28; Bayard, *Lone-Star Vanguard,* 72

8. Haydon to Blanc, 13 March 1840, cited in Moore, *Through Fire and Flood,* 244, n. 52.

9. Moore, *Through Fire and Flood,* 30.

10. Odin to Etienne, 13 December 1840, "Odin Letters," CAT.

11. Bayard, *Lone-Star Vanguard,* 161.

12. Odin to Fransoni, 15 December 1840, "Odin Letters," CAT.

13. Odin, "Daily Journal," 26, 28 November 1840, CAT; Pool, *Historical Atlas of Texas,* 65.

14. Odin, "Daily Journal," 30 November, 1 December 1840, CAT.

15. For coverage of the negative side of Saligny see Barker, *French Legation,* vols. 1, 2. See also Kenneth Hafertepe, *The French Legation in Texas: Alphonse Dubois de Saligny and His House* (Austin: Texas State Historical Association, 2010), 1–12.

16. Odin to Fransoni, 15 December 1840, "Odin Letters," CAT.

17. Odin, "Daily Journal," 14 December 1840, and finished a couple of days later, CAT.

18. Joe B. Frantz, *Texas: A Bicentennial History* (New York: Norton, 1976), 79–80; Robert A. Calvert and Arnoldo De León, *The History of Texas* (Arlington Heights, Ill.: Davidson, 1990), 77–78.

19. On this aspect of Timon's trip to Texas see Castañeda, *Our Catholic Heritage in Texas,* vol. 7: 53–54; Bayard, *Lone-Star Vanguard,* 141–43; and Timon, "Barrens Memoir," 29–31. Odin, "Daily Journal," 1–21 December 1840, CAT.

20. Odin, "Daily Journal," 6–8 December 1840; Bayard, *Lone-State Vanguard,* 159. At that time several members of the Texas Congress asked Odin to serve temporarily as their chaplain.

21. Bayard, *Lone-Star Vanguard,* 159; Odin, "Daily Journal," 15, 16 December 1840, CAT.

22. Bayard, *Lone-Star Vanguard,* 162; Odin to Fransoni, 15 December 1840, "Odin Letters," CAT.

23. Habig, *San Antonio's Mission San Jose,* 141–42.

24. Moore, *Through Fire and Flood,* 52.

25. Timon, "Barrens Memoir," 33; Odin, "Daily Journal," 31 December 1840, CAT.

26. Odin, "Daily Journal," 31 December 1840, through 7 February 1841, CAT.

27. For a discussion on nativism and its impact in Texas commencing in the 1840s, see Moore, *Through Fire and Flood,* 113–20; Weaver, *Castro's Colony,* 129–30. Odin, "Daily Journal," 4 January 1841, CAT.

28. Odin, "Daily Journal," 31 December 1840, through 8 January 1841, 10 January 1841, CAT.

29. Bayard, *Lone-Star Vanguard,* 43, 188.

30. Ibid.

31. Odin, "Daily Journal," 12 January 1841, CAT; Timon to Blanc, 29 April 1841, "Vincentian Collection," AUND.

CHAPTER 10. HE IS TO BE VICAR APOSTOLIC

1. Odin, "Daily Journal," 8 February 1841, CAT. Here Odin was referring to Donald McDonald, whom the two Vincentians had met at San Augustine (San Agustin), and who had been appointed to a committee of three men to head up an effort to erect a church at the locale. See Bayard, *Lone-Star Vanguard,* 205.

2. Odin to Cardinal Alessandro Barnabo, 18 September 1851, "Odin Letters," CAT. On that date Odin summarized his dilemma of 1841 to Cardinal Barnabo in a letter responding to the churchman's inquiry about the diocesan boundaries of Texas. The office Propaganda Fide is the executive department of the Roman Curia of the Catholic Church that oversees the foreign missions.

3. Pool, *Historical Atlas,* 61.

4. Gilbert Ralph Cruz, "The Vicariate Apostolic of Brownsville, 1874–1912: An Overview of Its Origins and Development," a paper read at the annual conference of the Texas Catholic Historical Society, Austin, Texas, March 1978.

5. Timon, "Barrens Memoir," 34.

6. Odin, "Daily Journal," 30 March 1841, CAT; Bayard, *Lone-Star Vanguard,* 395.

7. Odin, "Daily Journal," 16 April 1841, CAT.

8. Hardon, *Modern Catholic Dictionary,* 122. Confirmation is "the sacrament in which, through the laying on of the hands, anointing with chrism, and prayer, those already baptized are strengthened by the Holy Spirit in order that they may steadfastly profess the faith and faithfully live up to their profession." Timon to Blanc, 29 April 1841, "Vincentian Collection," AUND.

9. Timon to Blanc, 29 April 1841, "Vincentian Collection," AUND.

10. Odin, "Daily Journal," 1 May 1841–8 June 1841, CAT.

11. Timon, "Barrens Memoir," 34–35.

12. Castañeda, *Our Catholic Heritage in Texas,* vol. 7: 70; Odin to Blanc, 9 May 1841, "Odin Letters," CAT.

13. Odin to Etienne, 7 February 1842, "Odin Letters," CAT.

14. Odin, "Daily Journal," 8 July 1841, 29 June 1841, CAT.

15. Odin to Blanc, 8 July 1841, "Odin Letters," CAT.

16. Odin, "Daily Journal," 5, 19 July 1841, CAT.

17. Carlton J. H. Hayes and Marshall Whithed Baldwin, *History of Europe,* vol. 1, to 1648 (New York: Macmillan, 1949), 153. The origins of the Lorraine are traceable back to the ninth-century Carolingians, when it emerged as an identifiable demographical, cultural, religious, and political entity through the Treaty of Mersen in 870. It was a region running west from the Rhine River that was contested by the Germans and the French.

18. Nicholas Stehle to Timon, 12 April 1842, "Vincentian Collection," AUND; Bayard, *Lone-Star Vanguard,* 232.

19. Odin to Timon, 16 July 1841, "Odin Letters," CAT.

20. Timon, "Barrens Memoir," 35.

21. Hardon, *Modern Catholic Dictionary,* 561. A vicariate apostolic is an ecclesiastical territory under the hierarchical authority of a vicar apostolic, the latter usually being named a delegate to a titular see *in partibus infidelium* ("in the region of the infidel") and having episcopal consecration. Thus, Jean-Marie Odin was to be consecrated a bishop.

22. Bayard, *Lone-Star Vanguard,* 239.

23. Fr. James Boullier, C.M., to Blanc, 27 July 1841, "Vincentian Collection," AUND.

Chapter 11. A Missionary Still

1. Cardinal James Philip Fransonito to Odin, 31 July 1841, "Vincentian Collection," AUND. John A. Hardon, S.J., defines the phrase *inpartibus infidelium* as "In the region of the infidels." "A technical expression designating territories in which there are not now any residential episcopal sees. It was used at one time to identify bishops who were not local ordinaries but to whom would be assigned a titular see in non-Christian lands." *Modern Catholic Dictionary,* 279–80.

2. Odin, "Daily Journal," 8–25 August 1841, CAT.

3. Timothy M. Matovina, *Tejano Religion and Ethnicity: San Antonio, 1821–1860* (Austin: University of Texas Press, 1995), 43.

4. Bony, *Vie de Mgr. Jean-Marie Odin,* chap. 14, p. 1; Conrad, ed., *Cross, Crozier and Crucible,* xxiii.

5. Odin, "Daily Journal," 6–9 February1842, CAT.

6. Odin to Etienne, 28 March 1842, "Odin Letters," CAT. See also Bony, *Vie de Mgr. Jean-Marie Odin,* chap. 14, p. 1.

7. Conrad, ed., *Cross, Crozier and Crucible,* 206, 207.

8. Odin, "Daily Journal," 5 March 1842, CAT; Timon to Bishop John Baptiste Purcell, 16 February 1842, "Vincentian Collection," AUND.

9. Bransom, *Ordinations of U.S. Catholic Bishops,* 18.

10. Bony, *Vie de Mgr. Jean-Marie Odin,* chap. 14, p. 1.

11. This ordination-consecration sequence follows closely that for Bishop Jean Baptiste Lamy of Santa Fe, which Paul Horgan describes vividly in his *Lamy of Santa Fe,* 75–81.

12. Letter to Odin's mother in Bony, *Vie de Mgr. Jean-Marie Odin,* chap. 14, p. 2.

13. Hardon, *Modern Catholic Dictionary,* 122.

14. For an excellent discussion of Seguín's difficulties in this area see Teja, *Revolution Remembered,* 40–50.

15. Odin, "Daily Journal," 9–14 March 1842, CAT.

16. Moore, *Through Fire and Flood,* 66; Odin, "Daily Journal," 15 March 1842, CAT; Odin to Etienne, 28 March 1842, "Odin Letters," CAT.

17. Odin to Blanc, 16 May 1842, "Odin Letters," CAT.

18. For an in-depth discussion of these issues see Castañeda, *Our Catholic Heritage in Texas,* vol. 7: 76–77.

19. Odin to Etienne, 28 March 1842, "Odin Letters," CAT.

20. Odin to Blanc, 22 May 1842, "Odin Letters," CAT. See also Castañeda, *Our Catholic Heritage in Texas,* vol. 7: 83.

21. Odin to Blanc, 22 May 1842, "Odin Letters," CAT.

22. For an unbiased and historical view of the US invasion of Mexico in 1846 and the ensuing war see "The U.S.-Mexican War (1846–1848) Part 1: "The Borderlands," KERA Channel 13, 8:00–10:00 P.M.; 13 September 1998; Part 2: "The Hour of Sacrifice: The Fate of Nations," 8:00–10:00 P.M., 14 September 1998.

23. Odin, "Daily Journal," 12, 19 June 1842, CAT.

CHAPTER 12. THE SEARCH FOR PRIESTS AND NUNS

1. For an in-depth discussion of the history behind the establishment of the Diocese of Galveston and Bishop Odin's place in that process see Patrick Foley, "From Linares to Galveston: Texas in the Diocesan Scheme of the Roman Catholic Church to the Mid-Nineteenth Century," *Catholic Southwest: A Journal of History and Culture* 8 (1997): 25–44.

2. Claude Jaillet, "Sketches of Catholicity," a paper read at a Catholic society on 17 January 1888 by Francis X. Reuss (no further identification provided), 2, "Dubuis Papers," CAT.

3. Weaver, *Castro's Colony,* 10.

4. Ibid., inside cover; Odin to Timon, 20 August 1842, "Odin Letters," CAT. See also Weaver, *Castro's Colony,* 42, 43; Odin to Etienne, 13 January 1843, "Odin Letters," CAT. See also Weaver, *Castro's Colony,* 43. Weaver cites the amount that Castro repaid to Odin on behalf of the Castro colonists as 1,000 francs. The actual receipt revealed in correspondence between Odin and Etienne was 1,063 francs.

5. Weaver, *Castro's Colony,* 50; Odin, "Daily Journal," 12 September 1844, CAT; Weaver, *Castro's Colony,* 73–108.

6. One of the most thorough treatments of nineteenth-century German settlement in Texas is Biesele's *History of the German Settlements in Texas.* Another important study is Benjamin J. Blied, *Austrian Aid to American Catholics, 1830–1860* (Milwaukee: self-published, 1944).

7. Biesele, *History of the German Settlements in Texas,* 2, n. 1; Blied, *Austrian Aid,* 145.

8. Blied, *Austrian Aid,* 146.

9. In correspondence with the author dated August 27, 1987, Theresa Gold, a scholar of German settlement in Texas, stated that her research indicated that Father Menzel was not in New Braunfels in 1846. Bayard, *Lone-Star Vanguard,* 355, n. 12; Father James Talmadge Moore in his *Through Fire and Flood* indicated that Father Menzel (spelled Menzl) appeared in Texas in 1846 and served the "area around Fredericksburg and New Braunfels before returning to his homeland in 1856" (103). The story of Father Menzel in Texas remains somewhat of a mystery.

10. In his *Lone-Star Vanguard* (376–77) Ralph Bayard reported that in 1846 "ten priests, dispersed through the Vicariate, were functioning apostolically. In addition to Timon's six appointees—John Brands, Bartholomew Rolando, Richard Hennesy, John Lynch, Eudald Estany, and Michael Calvo—four non-Vincentians served the faithful: Edward Clarke, Anthony Lienhart, James Miller, and James Fitzgerald. And a fifty percent increase was about to reinforce the band: Claude Dubuis, James Girandon, Louis Chambodut, Matthew Chazelle, and Anthony Chanrion."

11. Sister Monica LaFleur, CCVI, "They Ventured to Texas: The European Heritage of Women Religious in the Nineteenth Century," *Catholic Southwest: A Journal of History and Culture* 8 (1997): 45.

12. Odin to Etienne, 17 June 1842, "Odin Letters," CAT; Odin to Timon, 20 June 1842, "Odin Letters," CAT.

13. Bony, *Vie de Mgr. Jean-Marie Odin,* chap. 15, p. 2. This letter printed in Bony's study repeats the quotation from Odin's letter to his *mere* verbatim but gives no date other than December 1842. Moreover, this letter is not located in the "Odin Letters" collection at the CAT.

14. In his daily journal dated December 14, 1842, Odin recorded that "I have received a letter from Rev. Mr. Botton announcing to me the death of my poor brother, who died on the 15th of October last." Odin, "Daily Journal," 14 December 1842, CAT; Bony, *Vie de Mgr. Jean-Marie Odin,* chap. 15, p. 1.

15. Odin to Rousselon, 17 December 1842, "Odin Letters," CAT.

16. Odin, "Daily Journal," 29 March 1843, CAT.

17. Ibid., 31 March 1843; 13 April 1843; 21 April 1843; 22 April–20 May 1843.

18. Ibid. 21 May–5 June 1843, 12 June 1843.

19. Bayard, *Lone-Star Vanguard,* 311; Odin to Timon 31 December 1843; Odin to Blanc, 8 January 1844; Odin to Timon, 16 January 1844, "Odin Letters," CAT.

20. Bayard, *Lone-Star Vanguard,* 312; Odin to Timon, 30 December 1843, 26 January 1844, 16 April 1844, "Odin Letters," CAT.

21. Odin to Blanc, 10 December 1844, "Odin Letters," CAT.

22. Ibid., 18 May 1844.

23. Odin, "Daily Journal," 14 September 1844, CAT; Bayard, *Lone-Star Vanguard,* 329–30.

24. Odin, "Daily Journal," 1 April 1845, CAT. See also Odin to Blanc, 1 April 1845, "Odin Letters," CAT; Odin, "Daily Journal," 22 April 1845, 23–24 April 1845.

25. Beckett, *Making of Modern Ireland,* 257.

26. Odin to Etienne, 8 April 1846, "Odin Letters," CAT.

27. Bertier de Sauvigny and Pinkney, *History of Modern France,* 264.

28. Odin to Timon, 30 May 1845, "Odin Letters," CAT. The tensions centered on the seminary and the college at Perryville, though the college was transferred to Cape Girardeau, Missouri, in 1844. The roots of the tensions dated back to the 1830s and involved such topics as resentments growing among the Vincentians over the Congregation of the Mission's working slaves on their property at Perryville, bad feelings over the somewhat primitive living conditions that the Vincentians had to tolerate at Perryville, and a general resentment regarding the administrative tempiments of some of the leaders of the Vincentian establishments in America. Especially mentioned was Father John Tornatore, Vincentian head in Missouri from 1830 to 1835. See Rybolt, *American Vincentians,* 34–35.

29. Odin, "Daily Journal," 17 June 1845–2 July 1845, CAT.

30. Odin to Blanc, 11 January 1846, "Odin Letters," CAT.

31. Odin, "Daily Journal," 2 July 1845–27 July 1845, CAT.

32. Edward J. Hickey, *The Society for the Propagation of the Faith, 1822–1922* (Washington, DC: Catholic University of America, 1922), 188. Cited in Bayard, *Lone-Star Vanguard,* 356.

33. Odin to Blanc, 11 January 1846, "Odin Letters," CAT.

34. Odin to Timon, 2 August 1845, "Odin Letters," CAT.

35. Odin to Blanc, 11 January 1846, "Odin Letters," CAT.

36. Odin, "Daily Journal," 20 March 1846, CAT. For a brief treatment of the life of Bishop Claude Marie Dubuis see Williams, *Lone Star Bishops,* 238–45. For a notation on Claude Marie Dubuis's birth at Coutouvre (Loire), France, in 1817, his volunteering for the Texas mission, and his death in 1895 back in his native country see Yannick Essertel, "Lyon et les missions a l'epoque contemporaine, 1815–1962: Prosopographie du personnel missionaire du Diocese de Lyon," PhD diss., Universite Jean-Moulin Lyon III, 1994, 541.

37. Odin to Etienne, 8 April 1846, "Odin Letters," CAT. See also Bayard, *Lone-Star Vanguard,* 370.

CHAPTER 13. BACK FROM EUROPE

1. Odin to Etienne, 28 June 1846, "Odin Letters," CAT.

2. The most vocal Vincentians in their complaints were Fathers John Tornatore, Francis Barbier, Bartholomew Rollando, and John Escoffier. Each of them had their own personal weaknesses of character that, when reflected in their behavior, caused irritation among their confreres. Tornatore, an Italian, proved to be a strict superior, focusing on many minute issues wherein he commonly saw infractions of the Vincentian spirit among his confreres and often reacted to them with irritation. This caused resentment toward him from those with whom he worked. In the latter 1830s he served as superior of the community at the Barrens. Barbier, a French priest who answered Father Timon's beckoning to the American mission field in late 1841, soon emerged as one of Timon's most severe critics. Rollando, who was to die on October 11, 1847, was referred to by Bayard in *Lone-Star Vanguard* (368) as a "habitually dissatisfied irregular." Apparently Rollando was jealous of Timon and behaved in such a manner as to reflect that negative feeling. John Escoffier was simply a constant complainer. On the correspondence of those annoying Vincentians see the "Vincentians" file and reels at the AUND, "Correspondence: General Curia and U.S.A.," 1–598.

3. Odin to Etienne, 28 June 1846, "Odin Letters," CAT.

4. Rybolt, *American Vincentians,* 46.

5. This common bridge was more visible to devout Catholics in Texas than often is realized. Perhaps the most noted example of that in the US-Mexican War is the quixotic narrative of the San Patricio Batallion. See "Renegades and Rebel Heroes?" *Fort Worth Star Telegram,* 21 September 1997, 10; "A Day to Remember, Irish-Mexican Connection," *Houston Chronicle,* 17 March 1997, A21.

6. Odin to Etienne, 28 June 1846, "Odin Letters," CAT.

7. Odin to Propaganda of the Faith, Lyon, 8 July 1846, "Odin Letters," CAT.

8. On the matter of languages and culture see Sister Mary Generosa Callahan, C.D.P., *The History of the Sisters of Divine Providence, San Antonio, Texas* (Milwaukee: Bruce Press, 1955), 5. She wrote, "Several nationalities, as soon as they were permitted to enter, sought here economic and political betterment. The Irish, brought in by Irish impresarios in the 1820s and 1830s, settled between the Lavaca and Nueces Rivers; but since they were English-speaking, they created no great problem either for the Vincentians or the French priests. But, when the Germans, with an entirely different language, came to settle areas which they made distinctly German in culture, a tremendous problem faced the French bishop; he needed priests who could speak German and understood German people."

9. On the date of the laying of the cornerstone there is some confusion. In his *Lone-State Vanguard,* 379–80, Ralph Bayard used the March 14 date. But Odin himself wrote to Propagation of the Faith, Lyon, on April 9, 1847, reporting that the date was March 18 ("Odin Letters," CAT).

Yet all other available sources, including Sister Mary Angela Fitzmorris's *Four Decades of Catholicism in Texas, 1829–1860* (Washington, DC: Catholic University of America Press, 1926), 67, use the March 14 date.

10. Hannefin, *Daughters of the Church*, 177; Sister Monica LaFleur, CCVI, "They Ventured to Texas: The European Heritage of Women Religious in the Nineteenth Century," *Catholic Southwest: A Journal of History and Culture* 8 (1997):47–48.

11. Odin to Propagation of the Faith, Lyon, 9 April 1847, "Odin Letters," CAT.

CHAPTER 14. BISHOP OF GALVESTON

1. Odin to Blanc, 18 April 1847, "Odin Letters," CAT; Robinson, *Reflections of Faith*, 56.

2. The title of the papal bull establishing the Diocese of Galveston was *Apostolica Sedes fastigio*. See Bayard, *Lone-Star Vanguard*, 380; Castañeda, *Our Catholic Heritage in Texas*, vol. 7, 109. Bransom, *Ordinations of U.S. Catholic Bishops*, 18; see also chap. 12, n. 1, of this book. J.N.D. Kelly, *The Oxford Dictionary of Popes*, 308–309.

3. On the life of Carlos Eduardo Castañeda, see Félix D. Almaréz, Jr.'s 1999 biography that has become the classic work on Castañeda, *Knight without Armor: Carlos Eduardo Castañeda, 1896–1958*. Castañeda, *Our Catholic Heritage in Texas*, vol. 7, 116; Robinson, *Reflections of Faith*, 56.

4. Odin to Rousselon, 11 April 1847, "Odin Letters," CAT; Odin to Blanc, 18 April 1847, "Odin Letters," CAT.

5. Castañeda, *Our Catholic Heritage in Texas*, vol. 7, 110; Odin to Blanc, 21 September 1847, "Odin Letters," CAT.

6. Bransom, *Ordinations of U.S. Catholic Bishops*, 20. See also Bayard. *Lone-Star Vanguard*, 404–405.

7. Odin to Blanc, 21 October 1847, "Odin Letters," CAT; information received from Reverend Louis Derbes, C.M., of St. Mary of the Barrens Seminary at Perryville, Missouri, in a phone conversation with the author on June 15, 1994. Odin never studied at a pontifical university.

8. Odin to Propagation of the Faith, 9 April 1847, "Odin Letters," CAT. He placed the number of US soldiers garrisoned at San Antonio at four thousand. Odin further made the point of how his priests served the soldiers' religious needs: Holy Mass, confessions, and such.

9. Odin to Propagation of the Faith, 18 September 1851, "Odin Letters," CAT.

10. For an excellent discussion of this phenomenon see Robert E. Wright, O.M.I., "Popular and Official Religiosity: A Theological Analysis and a Case Study of Laredo-Nuevo Laredo, 1755–1857," PhD diss., Graduate Theological Union, Berkeley, California, 1992, 183–331).

11. Odin to Propagation of the Faith, 6 December 1847, "Odin Letters," CAT.

12. Odin to Rousselon, 4 March 1847, "Odin Letters," CAT.

13. Ibid.

14. Odin to Blanc, 29 August 1848, "Odin Letters," CAT.

15. Odin to Rousselon, 25 June 1848, "Odin Letters," CAT.

16. Bayard, *Lone-Star Vanguard*, 408.

17. Odin to Rousselon, 7 December 1848, "Odin Letters," CAT.

18. Doyon, *Cavalry of Christ*, 15; Bony, *Vie de Mgr. Jean-Marie Odin*, chap. 16, p. 5. For a brief sketch of the Seventh Provincial Council; of Baltimore see Michal J. Roach, "Provincial and Plenary Councils of Baltimore," *Encyclopedia of American Catholic History*, ed. Glazier and Shelley, 1176. Odin to Anstaett, 29 March 1849, "Odin Letters," CAT.

19. Doyon, *Cavalry of Christ*, 16, n.6. In this source Bernard Doyon argues that the extent of Father Telmon's jurisdiction at the time was uncertain. Mgr. Charles Joseph Eugene de Mazenod, founder of the Oblates of Mary Immaculate and Telmon's superior, had sent Telmon to America only a few years earlier. After Telmon's brief stay in Pittsburgh (about a year), Mgr. Mazenod

had ordered him to return to Montreal and stay there. Apparently Telmon had not yet received that communication when he agreed to commit himself and a few other clergy to serve in Bishop Odin's Galveston diocese.

20. Odin to Blanc, 14 September 1849, "Odin Letters," CAT.

21. Odin to Purcell, 30 September 1849, AUND. See also Doyon, *Cavalry of Christ*, 17–19.

22. Odin to Blanc, 6 January 1850, "Odin Letters," CAT. When the Oblates first arrived at Port Isabel near the mouth of the Rio Grande a short distance from Brownsville, Lieutenant Julius Garesche, quartermaster of the garrison, offered them his quarters and helped the missionaries in other ways. Doyon, *Cavalry of Christ*, 19.

23. Odin to Blanc, 9 December 1850, "Odin Letters," CAT; Doyon, *Cavalry of Christ*, 21–31,

24. Odin to Blanc, 9 December 1850, "Odin Letters," CAT. In his letter to Blanc, Odin claimed that he had confirmed more than eleven thousand persons. It must be remembered that no Catholic bishop had been on the scene in that vast region for decades. Thus, many confirmations were needed.

25. Odin to Etienne, 23 December 1850, "Odin Letters," CAT. In this letter to his religious superior Bishop Odin reaffirmed his own fidelity to the Vincentians, but he energetically complained about Father Maller's actions, ones that Father Etienne had approved. Odin voiced his frustration with what he perceived as the Vincentians' habit of closing missions. He was angry about the withdrawal of their men from Texas. Odin had, after all, recruited most of those missionaries personally.

26. George Brown Tindall and David Emory Shi, *America: A Narrative History*, 464; Pool, *Historical Atlas of Texas*, 83. This reference also contains a synopsis of Texas' boundary claims between August 1846 and the promulgation of the Compromise of 1850, 82–83.

27. Odin to Blanc, 19 March 851, "Odin Letters," CAT.

28. Bransom, *Ordinations of U.S. Catholic Bishops*, 22.

29. Odin to Blanc, 30 December 1850, 8 January 1851, "Odin Letters," CAT.

30. Ibid., 10 January 1851.

31. Ibid.

32. Ibid., 23 May 1851, 8 August 1851.

33. Ibid. On the restoration of the Catholic hierarchy in England at that time see Patrick Foley, "British Reaction to the Papal Aggression, October 1850 to August 1851," master's thesis, Santa Clara University, 1969. Cited as appendix A in that thesis is Cardinal Wiseman's letter "From Out of the Flaminian Gate," 78–83.

34. Extensive research on the part of the author has uncovered no reference as to whether or not Jean-Marie Odin's mother was still living at that time.

35. Rev. P. F. Parisot, O.M.I., *The Reminiscences of a Texas Missionary* (San Antonio: Johnson Bros., 1899), 5.

36. Ibid., 5–6; Odin to Propagation of the Faith, Lyon, 28 March 1852, "Odin Letters," CAT.

37. Odin to Propagation of the Faith, Lyon, 28 March 1852, "Odin Letters," CAT; Sister Monica LaFleur, CCVI, "They Ventured to Texas: The European Heritage of Women Religious in the Nineteenth Century," *Catholic Southwest: A Journal of History and Culture* 8 (1997):51, 52.

38. Robert E. Wright, O.M.I., "The Parish of San Agustín, Laredo, 1760–1857," *San Agustín Parish of Laredo: Abstracts of Marriage Book 1, 1790–1857*, ed. Angel Sepúlveda Brown and Gloria Villa Cadena, (San Antonio, 1989), 24–28; Odin to Blanc, 6 January 1853, "Odin Letters," CAT.

39. Wright, "The Parish of San Agustín," 25; Odin to Blanc, 6 January 1853, "Odin Letters," CAT.

40. Odin to Propagation of the Faith, Lyon, 1 July 1853, "Odin Letters," CAT.

41. Ibid., 24 March 1854. The five priests and one subdeacon who died from the fever at Galveston in that fall of 1853 were Fathers Dixon (first name not recorded) on September 4; Matton (first name not recorded) on September 18; Hug (first name not recorded) on September 27;

O'Driscoll (first name not recorded) on September 29; Jean-Marie Baudrand (Oblate superior of the planned college at Galveston) on October 1; and Subdeacon Bajard (first name not recorded) on October 2.

42. Baker, *First Polish Americans,* 25.

43. For just one of many letters or other pieces of correspondence that Odin wrote during the latter 1850s, wherein the Diocese of Galveston's need for financial help was stressed, see Odin to Propagation of the Faith, 4 May 1857, "Odin Letters," CAT.

44. Moore, *Through Fire and Flood,* 100.

45. On the slavery-abolitionist sectional crisis, as well as nativism, see James M. McPherson, *Battle Cry of Freedom: The Civil War Era* (New York: Oxford University Press, 1988), 117–44. For a brief comment on the turbulent character of society in Texas during the 1850s regarding the slavery-abolitionist and nativist tensions, see Moore, *Through Fire and Flood,* 100.

46. *Till Freedom Cried Out: Memories of Texas Slave Life,* eds. T. Lindsay Baker and Julie F. Baker, illustrations Kermit Oliver (College Station: Texas A&M University Press, 1977).

47. "Bill of Sale of Clement and Family," 9 January 1847, CAT. See also Bayard, *Lone-Star Vanguard,* 383; Vincentian Father Louis Derbes in a 25 May 1994 phone conversation to Patrick Foley.

48. Odin to Propagation of the Faith, 14 February 1856, "Odin Letters," CAT.

CHAPTER 15. ADIEU, TEXAS

1. For the date of the calling of the synod see "Galveston, Diocese of: Minutes of the First Synod, June 13, 1858," "Odin Papers," CAT. Regarding the weather in Galveston at that time see David G. McComb, *Galveston, A History* (Austin: University of Texas, Press, 1986), 23.

2. "Galveston, Diocese of, Minutes," "Odin Papers," CAT.

3. Ibid.

4. Odin to Propagation of the Faith, 19 July 1858, "Odin Letters," CAT.

5. Odin to Blanc, 19 November 1858, "Odin Letters," CAT.

6. Odin to Anstaett, 15 October 1858, "Odin Letters," CAT.

7. Odin to Propagation of the Faith, 12 July 1858, "Odin Letters," CAT; Bony, *Vie de Mgr. Jean-Marie Odin,* chap. 17, p. 3.

8. Odin to Blanc, 4 January 1859, 23 May 1859, "Odin Letters," CAT. Bishop Portier had recently established an infirmary in Mobile, which the Sisters of Charity ran. When his final illness set in he retired to that hospital. There he died on May 14, 1859. On this aspect of Portier's death see John Gilmary Shea, *The Hierarchy of the Catholic Church in the United States: Embracing Sketches of All the Archbishops and Bishops from the Establishment of the See of Baltimore to the Present Time* (New York: The Office of Catholic Publications, 1886), 295.

9. Odin to Blanc, 23 May 1859, "Odin Letters," CAT.

10. Bransom, *Ordinations of U.S. Catholic Bishops,* 14. It should be remembered that not only did Bishop Portier assist at the New Orleans consecration of Jean-Marie Odin as bishop and vicar apostolic of Texas in 1842, but back on November 22, 1835, at Saint Louis Cathedral in that same city, Portier had assisted at the consecration of Blanc as bishop of New Orleans. See Bransom, *Ordinations of U.S. Catholic Bishops,* 16. On the Catholic Church in the American South see Miller and Wakelyn, eds., *Catholics in the Old South.* Bishop Odin is identified as a rebuilder of the church in Texas on page 66. Bishop Portier is discussed on pages 23, 64, and 69.

11. Odin to Rousselon, 10 August 1859, "Odin Letters," CAT.

12. For two such examples see Odin to Blanc, 22 November 1859, and Odin to Blanc, 29 December 1859, "Odin Letters," CAT.

13. Bransom, *Ordinations of U.S. Catholic Bishops,* 27; Baudier, *Catholic Church in Louisiana,* 378.

14. Baudier, *Catholic Church in Louisiana,* 378.

15. Odin to Blanc, 13 March 1860, "Odin Letters," CAT.

16. Bransom, *Ordinations of U.S. Catholic Bishops*, 16; Baudier, *Catholic Church in Louisiana*, 411.

17. Kenneally, *Propaganda Fide Archives*, vol. 1: 248, No. 1579; 247, No. 1570; 248, No. 582; 247, No. 1575.

18. Odin to Propagation of the Faith, 1 March and 20 June 1860, "Odin Letters," CAT. This last letter was written on the very day that Archbishop Blanc died in New Orleans.

19. James M. McPherson, *Battle Cry of Freedom: The Civil War Era*, 3–233.

20. Moore, *Through Fire and Flood*, 123.

21. Odin to Rousselon, 28 November, 22 December, 29 December 1860, "Odin Letters," CAT.

22. Ibid., 24 April 1861.

23. Ibid., 7 May 1861; 15 May 1861.

CHAPTER 16. NEW ORLEANS, THE CIVIL WAR AND RECONSTRUCTION, THEN HOME

1. Baudier, *Catholic Church in Louisiana*, 41; Odin to Anstaett, 23 May 1861, "Odin Letters," CAT.

2. "Circular Letter of the Most Reverend Archbishop of New Orleans to the Clergy of His Diocese," 19 May 1861," Catholic University of America Archives and Library (hereafter cited as CUAAL), 5. BV 800. A13.

3. Moore, *Through Fire and Flood*, 124–25; Augustín d'Asti to Jean-Marie Odin, 8 October 1861, VI-2-C, AUND; Asti to Odin, 26 November 1861, VI-2-E, AUND. These are just two of several letters to Odin from Texas after the new archbishop's transfer to New Orleans that were deposited in what was known as the "Vincentians" collection at the AUND.

4. On the Catholic Church and the Negro (using again the historical term for the nineteenth century), see especially Gary B. Mills, "Piety and Prejudice : A Colored Catholic Community in the Antebellum South," in *Catholics in the Old South: Essays on Church and Culture,* ed. Randall M. Miller and Jon L. Wakelyn (Macon: George Mason University Press, 1983), 171–94; James J. Thompson, *The Church, the South and the Future* (Westminster, Md.: Christian Classics, 1988).

5. Jean-Marie Odin," Circular Letter," CUAAL, BI, 61039 no. 15. This circular letter carried no date other than the year 1861.

6. Odin to Archbishop Kenrick, 25 June 1861, Archives of the Archdiocese of Baltimore (hereafter cited as AAB).

7. Jean-Marie Odin, "Pastoral Letter for Lent of 1862," 7, CUAAL.

8. Odin Propagation of the Faith, Lyon, 28 January 1852, 1.

9. Odin to Anstaett, 14 April 1862, "Odin Letters," CAT.

10. Long and Long, *Civil War Day by Day*, 202–203, 1032; Catton, *Grant Moves South*, 277; McPherson, *Battle Cry of Freedom*, 420.

11. Concerning Jean-Marie Odin's views toward slavery, abolitionism, and the church, a few years ago historian Stephen Ochs disagreed with the picture described here. In his article "A Patriot, a Priest, and a Prelate: Black Catholic Activism in Civil War New Orleans" (*U.S. Catholic Historian* 12 [1994]: 49–75), Ochs argued that Archbishop Odin did not favor equality for African Americans. Ochs condemned the legacy of Odin dramatically as a Catholic churchman who failed to treat fairly the African Americans of New Orleans. But in his article Ochs showed no knowledge at all of Odin's pre–New Orleans life relative to his attitudes toward slavery. In fact, Ochs failed to mention any material on Odin prior to the French-born archbishop's arrival in New Orleans. In addition, Ochs failed to comment on Archbishop Odin's efforts to provide education for African Americans in his archdiocese. Thus Ochs misrepresented Jean-Marie Odin and the latter's perceptions about slavery. Such is not surprising inasmuch as Ochs ignored virtually all of the primary sources on Odin from 1822 to 1861. The author of this biography of Jean-Marie Odin sent Mr. Ochs copies of several letters revealing Odin's early encounter and

disagreement with the condition of slaves upon Odin's arrival in New Orleans. Mr. Ochs replied that he was unaware of any of the letters.

12. Odin to Propaganda of the Faith, Lyon, 26 January 1861, "Odin Letters," CAT.

13. Regarding Father Abram Joseph Ryan see Charles E. Nolan, "Ryan, Abram Joseph (1838–1886)," *Encyclopedia of American Catholic History*, ed. Glazier and Shelley, 1224–25; Patrick Foley, "Ryan, Abram Joseph (1838–1886)," *Encyclopedia of the Irish in America*, ed. Glazier, 813–14. On Archbishop Perche see Baudier, *Catholic Church in Louisiana*, 440–59.

14. Moore, *Through Fire and Flood*, 127. See also Bransom, *Ordinations of U.S. Catholic Bishops*, 28.

15. Moore, *Through Fire and Flood*, 127, 129.

16. Baudier, *Catholic Church in Louisiana*, 415.

17. Baudier, *Catholic Church in Louisiana*, 412, 413. The date of August 15 is notable because since November 1, 1950, it has officially been in the Roman Catholic Church the Solemnity of the Assumption. On that date Pope Pius XII defined the dogma of the Assumption. This feast has been celebrated in the eastern world since the sixth century and in Rome since the seventh century. See the *Daily Roman Missal*, ed. Rev. James Socias (Princeton, New Jersey: Scepter Publishers, and Chicago: Midwest Theological Forum, 1993), 1631.

18. Baudier, *Catholic Church in Louisiana*, 413; Gerald M. Capers, *Occupied City: New Orleans under the Federals, 1862–1865* (Kentucky: University of Kentucky Press, 1965), 185. This argument is recorded in Timothy Matovina, "Archbishop Jean-Marie Odin, C.M.: Catholic in America," doctoral research paper, Catholic University of America, 19 April 1990.

19. Odin, "Pastoral Letter to the Faithful of Our Metropolitan See," 19 May 1863, CUAAL. On the date of the censure see also Baudier, *Catholic Church in Louisiana*, 413.

20. Given the lack of thorough resource material on this issue, except for parish records, my coverage of the Father Maistre affair follows the summary found in Baudier, *Catholic Church in Louisiana*, 413, 565. In late 1865 Father Ferec drowned in Lake Pontchartrain. Shortly thereafter, on January 1, 1866, Archbishop Odin named Father Francis Mittelbronn as St. Rose of Lima's new pastor.

21. Matovina, "Archbishop Jean-Marie Odin," 19.

22. Ibid.

23. Long and Long, *Civil War Day by Day*, 306.

24. Baudier, *Catholic Church in Louisiana*, 433.

25. Clarke, *Lives of the Deceased Bishops*, 21.

26. Baudier, *Catholic Church in Louisiana*, 414–15.

27. Ibid., 414; *Morning Star and Catholic Messenger*, 27 September 1868, 4.

28. Ibid., 9 February 1868, 4.

29. Baudier, *Catholic Church in Louisiana*, 415, 420–21.

30. J. Derek Holmes and Bernard W. Bickers, *A Short History of the Catholic Church* (New York: Paulist Press, 1984), 243; Dubuis to Family, 14 December 1869, "Dubuis Letters," CAT.

31. *Morning Star and Catholic Messenger*, 6 March 1870, 4.

32. *Propateur*, "Archbishop Odin's death and Funeral," Katherine Phillipson, Galveston, nd.

33. *Morning Star and Catholic Messenger*, 19 July 1870, 4. For the pastoral letter see Mullen Library, Catholic University of America, BV. 800. A13. V. 5.

34. Will and Probate of Jean-Marie Odin, Second District Court for the Parish of Orleans, 55797, CAT.

Bibliography

ARCHIVES, COLLECTIONS, AND MANUSCRIPTS

Annales de L'Association de la Propaganda de la Foi. Parts 1, 2. De Andreis-Rosati Memorial Archives. Saint Mary of the Barrens Seminary, Perryville, Missouri.

Annales de L'Association de la Propagation de la Foi. Part 3. Lyon: Chez Rusand, Libraire, Imprimeur du roi [publisher]. Paris: a la librairie ecclesiastique de Rusand (1828) 533.

Archives of Georgetown University, Washington, DC.

Archives of the Archdiocese of Baltimore, Maryland.

Archives of the Archdiocese of New Orleans, New Orleans, Louisiana.

Archives of the Archdiocese of St. Louis, St. Louis, Missouri (AASL).

Archives of the Catholic Diocese of Dallas, Dallas, Texas.

Archives of the Catholic Diocese of Fort Worth, Fort Worth, Texas.

Archives of the Catholic Diocese of Galveston-Houston, Houston, Texas.

Archives of the Catholic University of America, Washington, DC.

Archives of the University of Notre Dame, Notre Dame, Indiana (AUND).

Bayard Collection, Box 22, "Seminary History." De Andreis-Rosati Memorial Archives, Saint Mary's of the Barrens Seminary, Perryville, Missouri.

Catholic Archives of San Antonio, Archdiocese of San Antonio Chancery Office, San Antonio, Texas.

Catholic Archives of Texas, Diocese of Austin, Chancery Office, Austin, Texas (CAT).

De Andreis-Rosati Memorial Archives, Saint Mary's of the Barrens Seminary, Perryville, Missouri (DRMA).

Delplace, Elle. "La reception de la constitution Unigentus par la Congregation de la Mission, 1711–1744." PhD diss., Sorbonne, 1990.

Dubuis, Claude Marie, "Claude Marie Dubuis Papers." Catholic Archives of Texas, Chancery Office, Austin, Texas.

Essertel, Yannick, "Lyon et les missions a l'epoque contemporaine, 1815–1962: Prosopographie du personnel missionaire du Diocese de Lyon." PhD diss., Universite Jean-Mouline Lyon III, 1994.

Foley, Charles Patrick. "The Catholic-Liberal Struggle and the Church in Spain: 1834–1876." PhD diss., University of New Mexico, 1983.

———. "British Reaction to the Papal Aggression, October 1850 to August 1851." Master's thesis, Santa Clara University, 1969.

Matovina, Timothy. "Archbishop Jean-Marie Odin, C.M.: Catholic in America." Doctoral research paper, Catholic University of America, 19 April 1990.

National Archives of the United States, Washington, DC.

Odin, Jean-Marie. "Daily Journal." Catholic Archives of Texas, Chancery Office, Austin, Texas.

Odin, Jean-Marie. "Odin Letters." Catholic Archives of Texas, Chancery Office, Austin, Texas.

Timon, John, C.M. "Barrens Memoir." De Andreis-Rosati Memorial Archives. Saint Mary's of the Barrens Seminary, Perryville, Missouri.

Wright, Robert. "Popular and Official Religiosity: A Theological Analysis and a Case Study of Laredo-Nuevo Laredo, 1755–1857." PhD diss., Graduate Theological Union, Berkeley, 1992.

Books and Articles

Abramson, Harold J. *Ethnic Diversity in Catholic America.* New York: John Wiley & Sons, 1973.

Almaráz, Félix D., Jr. *Knight without Armor: Carlos Eduardo Castañeda, 1896–1958.* College Station: Texas A&M University Press, 1999.

———. "The Return of the Franciscans to Texas, 1891–1931." *Catholic Southwest: A Journal of History and Culture* 7 (1996): 91–114.

———. *The San Antonio Missions and Their System of Land Tenure.* Austin: University of Texas Press, 1989.

———. *Tragic Cavalier: Governor Manuel Salcedo of Texas, 1808–1813.* Austin: University of Texas Press, 1971.

———, ed. and comp. *They Came to el Llano Estacado.* An anthology of essays presented at "The Franciscan Presence in the Borderlands of North America," an international symposium conducted at the Bishop DeFalco Retreat and Conference Center, Amarillo, Texas, September 16–18, 2004. San Antonio: University of Texas at San Antonio, 2006.

Ashmore, Harry S. *Arkansas, a Bicentennial History.* New York: Norton, 1978.

Bagen, John J., C.M. *St. Mary's of the Barrens Parish: The Early Days.* Perryville: The Association of the Miraculous Medal, Saint Mary's of the Barrens Seminary, nd.

Baker, T. Lindsay. *The First Polish Americans: Silesian Settlements in Texas.* College Station: Texas A&M University Press, 1979.

Barker, Nancy Nichols, trans. and ed. *The French Legation in Texas.* 2 vols. Austin: Texas State Historical Association, 1973.

Baudier, Roger. *The Catholic Church in Louisiana.* New Orleans: Roger Baudier, 1930. Reprinted in 1972 by Louisiana Association Public Library Section.

Bayard, Ralph, C.M. *Lone-Star Vanguard: The Catholic Re-Occupation of Texas, 1838–1848.* St. Louis: Vincentian Press, 1945.

Beckett, J. C. *The Making of Modern Ireland, 1603–1923: A History of Ireland during Its Three Centuries of English Rule.* New York: Alfred A. Knopf, 1966.

Bertier de Sauvigny, Guillaume de, and David H. Pinkney. *History of France.* Translated by James Frigugliette. Revised and enlarged edition. Arlington Heights, Ill.: Forum Press, 1983.

Biesle, Rudolph Leopold. *The History of German Settlements in Texas, 1831–1861.* San Marcos: German Texan Heritage Society, 1987.

Blumenthal, Henry. *American and French Culture, 1800–1900: Interchanges in Art, Science, Literature and Society.* Baton Rouge: Louisiana State University Press, 1975.

Bokenkotter, Thomas. *A Concise History of the Catholic Church.* Garden City: Doubleday, 1977.

Bony, Abbe. *Vie de Mgr. Jean-Marie Odin, missionaire lazariste, archeveque de la Nouvelle-Orleans.* No publication facts. Located in the Catholic Archives of Texas.

Bransom, Charles N., Jr. *Ordinations of US Catholic Bishops, 1790–1989: A Chronological List.* Washington, DC: United States Catholic Conference, 1990.

Carroll, Warren H. *The Guillotine and the Cross.* Front Royal, Va.: Christendom Press, 2004.

Carven, John W., C.M. "Martyrs for the Faith." *Vincentian Heritage* 8, no. 2 (1987): 101–25.

Castañeda, Carlos Eduardo. *Our Catholic Heritage in Texas, 1519–1838.* Vol. 7. Austin: Von Boeckmann-Jones Company, 1957.

Catton, Bruce. *Grant Moves South.* Boston: Little, Brown, 1960.

Clarke, Richard H. *Lives of the Deceased Bishops of the Catholic Church in the United States.* Vol. 2. New York: P. O'Shea, 1872.

Conrad, Glenn R., ed. *Cross, Crozier, and Crucible: A Volume Celebrating the Bicentennial of a Catholic Diocese in Louisiana.* New Orleans: Archdiocese of New Orleans, in cooperation with the Center for Louisiana Studies, 1993.

Costa, Mildred Masson, trans. *The Letters of Marie Madeleine Hachard, 1727–1728.* New Orleans: Laborde Printing Company, 1974. Originally published in 1727 (1728?).

Coste, Pierre, C.M., ed. *Saint Vincent de Paul Correspondence, Entretienes Documents.* Vol. 12. Paris, 1924.

Cruz, Gilbert R. *Let There Be Towns: Spanish Municipal Origins in the American Southwest, 1619–1819.* College Station: Texas A&M University Press, 1988.

———, ed. *Proceedings of the Second Annual Mission Research Conference.* San Antonio: San Antonio Missions National Historical Park, 1984.

———, ed. *San Antonio Missions National Historical Park: A Commitment to Research.* San Antonio: LEBCO Graphics, 1983.

D'Elia, Donald J., and Patrick Foley, eds. *The Catholic as Historian.* Naples, Fla.: Sapientia Press, 2006.

Dolan, Jay P., ed. *The American Catholic Parish: A History from 1850 to the Present.* 2 vols. New York: Paulist Press, 1987.

Dolan, Jay P., and Gilbert M. Hinojosa. *Mexican Americans and the Catholic Church, 1900–1965.* Notre Dame: University of Notre Dame Press, 1994.

Doyon, Bernard, O.M.I. *The Calvary of Christ on the Rio Grande, 1849–1883.* Milwaukee: Catholic Life Publications, 1956.

Essertel, Yannick. *L'aventure missionaire Lyonnaise, 1815–1962.* Paris: Les Ediciones du Cerf, 2001.

Flannery, John Brendan. *The Irish Texans.* San Antonio: University of Texas Institute of Texan Culture, 1980.

Foley, Patrick. "Missionaries Extraordinaire: The Vincentians from Saint Mary's of the Barrens Seminary." *Vincentian Heritage* 22, no. 1 (2001):1–10.

———. "Builder of the Faith in Nineteenth-Century Texas: A Deeper Look at Bishop Jean-Marie Odin, C.M." *Catholic Southwest: A Journal of History and Culture* 19 (2008): 52–65.

———. "Jean-Marie Odin, C.M., Missionary Bishop Extraordinaire of Texas." *Journal of Texas Catholic History and Culture* 1 (1990): 42–60.

———. "From Linares to Galveston, Texas in the Diocesan Scheme of the Roman Catholic Church to the Mid-Nineteenth Century." *Catholic Southwest: A Journal of History and Culture* 8 (1997): 25–44.

———. "The Sons of St. Vincent from the Mississippi River to the Rio Grande." *Catholic Social Science Review* 1 (1996): 147–55.

Glazier, Michael, ed. *The Encyclopedia of the Irish in America.* Notre Dame: University of Notre Dame Press, 1999.

Glazier, Michael, and Thomas J. Shelley, eds. *The Encyclopedia of American Catholic History.* Collegeville, Minn.: Liturgical Press, 1997.

Habig, Marion, O.F.M. *The Alamo Mission, San Antonio de Valero, 1718–1793.* Chicago: Franciscan Herald Press, 1977.

———. *San Antonio's Mission San José: State and National Historical Site, 1720–1968.* San Antonio: Naylor Company, 1968.

Hannefin, Sister Daniel, D.C. *Daughters of the Church: A Popular History of the Daughters of Charity in the United States, 1809–1987.* Brooklyn: New City Press, 1989.

Hebert, Rachel Bluntzer. *The Forgotten Colony: San Patricio de Hibernia.* Burnet, Tex.: Eakin Press, 1981.

Hegarty, Sister Mary Loyola, C.C.V.I. *Serving with Gladness: The Origin and History of the Congregation of the Sisters of Charity of the Incarnate Word, Houston, Texas.* Houston: Bruce Publishing Company in cooperation with the Sisters of Charity of the Incarnate Word, Houston, Texas, 1967.

Hennesey, James, S.J. *American Catholics: A History of the Roman Catholic Community in the United States.* Foreword by John Tracy Ellis. Oxford: Oxford University Press, 1981.

Hinojosa, Gilberto Miguel. "Enduring Faith Communities: Spanish and Texas Church Historiography." *Journal of Texas Catholic History and Culture* 1 (1990): 20–41.

Holmes, Derek. *The Triumph of the Holy See: A Short History of the Papacy in the Nineteenth Century.* London: Burns and Oates, 1978.

Horgan, Paul. *Lamy of Santa Fe: His Life and Times.* New York: Farrar, Straus and Giroux, 1974.

Jordan, Terry G. *German Seed in Texas Soil: Immigrant Farmers in Nineteenth-Century Texas.* Austin: University of Texas Press, 1985.

LaFleur, Sister Monica M., CCVI. "They Ventured to Texas: The European Heritage of Women Religious in the Nineteenth Century." *Catholic Southwest: A Journal of History and Culture* 8 (1997): 45–64.

Linn, John J. *Reminiscences of Fifty Years in Texas.* Facsimile of the first edition, published in 1883. Austin: State House Press, 1986.

Long, E. B., and Barbara Long. *The Civil War Day by Day: An Almanac, 1861–1865.* Foreword by Bruce Catton. New York: De Capo, 1971.

Melville, Annabelle M. *Louis William DuBourg: Bishop of Louisiana and the Floridas, Bishop of Montalban, and Archbishop of Besancon, 1766–1833*. 2 vols. Chicago: Loyola University Press, 1986.

Miller, Randall M., and Jon L. Wakelyn. *Catholics in the Old South: Essays on Church and Culture*. Macon, Ga.: Mercer University Press, 1983.

Moore, James Talmadge. *Through Fire and Flood: The Catholic Church in Frontier Texas*. College Station: Texas A&M University Press, 1992.

Oberste, William H. *The Restless Friar: Venerable Fray Antonio Margil de Jesús, Missionary to the Americas-Apostle of Texas*. Austin: Von Boeckmann-Jones Company, 1970.

Pool, William C. *A Historical Atlas of Texas*. Maps by Edward Triggs and Lance Wrenn. Austin: Encino Press, 1981.

Poole, Stafford, C.M., and Douglas Slawson, C.M. *Church and Slave in Perry County, Missouri, 1819–1865*. Lewiston, N.Y.: Edwin Mellon Press, 986.

Ramirez, Bishop Ricardo, C.S.B., "The Hispanic Peoples of the United States and the Church from 1865–1985." *U.S. Catholic Historian* 9, nos. 1–2 (winter/spring 1990): 163.

Rieder, Milton P., Jr., and Norma Gaudet Rieder. *New Orleans Ship Lists*. Austin: Texas State Library, 1968.

Robinson, Willard B. *Reflections of Faith: Houses of Worship in the Lone Star State*. Waco, Tex.: Baylor University Press, 1994.

Rybolt, John, C.M. "Vincentian Seminaries in Louisiana." *Vincentian Heritage* 15, no. 2 (1994): 163–90.

Rybolt, John E., C.M., ed. *The American Vincentians: A Popular History of the Congregation of the Mission in the United States, 1815–1987*. Brooklyn: New City Press, 1988.

Sarbaugh, Timothy J., and James P. Walsh, eds. *The Irish in the West*. Manhattan, Kans.: Sunflower University Press, 1993.

Schall, James V., S.J. article "Culture, Multiculturalism, Cultural Wars, and the Universal Culture." *Journal of Texas Catholic History and Culture* 5 (1994): 11–24.

Shea, John Gilmary. *The Hierarchy of the Catholic Church in the United States: Embracing Sketches of All of the Archbishops and Bishops from the Establishment of the See of Baltimore to the Present Time*. New York: Office of Catholic Publications, 1886.

Sibley, Marilyn McAdams. *Lone Star and State Gazettes: Texas Newspapers before the Civil War*. College Station: Texas A&M University Press, 1983.

Teja, Jesús F. de la, ed. *A Revolution Remembered: The Memoirs and Selected Correspondence of Juan N. Seguín*. Austin: State House Press, 1991.

United States Catholic Miscellany 9, no. 49 (5 June 1830): 390.

Weaver, Bobby. *Castro's Colony: Empresario Development in Texas, 1842–1865*. College Station: Texas A&M University Press, 1985.

Williams, Franklin C. *Lone Star Bishops: The Roman Catholic Hierarchy in Texas*. Waco: Texas Press, 1997.

Wright, Robert E., O.M.I. "Local Church Emergence and Mission Decline: The Historiography of the Catholic Church in the Southwest during the Spanish And Mexican Periods." *US Catholic Historian* 9, nos. 1–2 (winter/spring 1990): 27–48.

Index